THE COMEDY OF THE EIGHTEENTH CENTURY

J. AHLUWALIA

ATLANTIC PUBLISHERS & DISTRIBUTORS

Published by
ATLANTIC PUBLISHERS & DISTRIBUTORS
B-2, Vishal Enclave, New Delhi-110027
Phone: 5413460

Sales office
4346/4C, Ansari Road, Darya Ganj,
New Delhi-110002
Phone: 3273880

Typeset at
APD COMPUTER GRAPHICS
B-2, Vishal Enclave, New Delhi-110027

Printed in India at
Mehra Offset Press
New Delhi

To my son

Harpreet Singh Ahluwalia

PREFACE

The present study aims at reviewing critically the comedy of the eighteenth century England with a special reference to the playwrights who followed Jeremy Collier's crusadr against the immoraility of the seventeenth century comedy. With the changing ethos the eighteenth century playwrights, viz. Colley Cibber, John Vanbrugh, George Farquhar, Richard Steele etc., added a moral dimension to the comedy of the previous era. Keeping their eye on "Instruction" as the end of comedy the playwrights inducted exemplary characters, overt moralizings and emotionally poignant sentimentalised scenes drawing on pity and the theory of "exquisite joy" after Terence's tradition.

The major portion of the book is the thesis presented for the award of the Ph.D. degree and a few more chapters on some vital issues have been added to it. The present study is divided into three sections comprising the perspective, the playwrights and the major problems and issues. It is hoped that the study will help the students and scholars of eighteenth century drama in having a better understanding of the developments that changed the course of english comedy.

I am thankful to Dr. Zafar Zaki, the Chairman of English Dept., Aligarh Muslim University for his supervision and valuable guidance. I also wish to express my gratitude to Mr. R.A. Naqvi, Mr. J.S. Chaddha and my friends for their assistance at every step. I express my gratitude to my husband and children who (with their untiring patience and cheerfulness) saw the book through.

J. Ahluwalia

CONTENTS

SECTION I

THE PERSPECTIVE

1
Social and Political Background

Before considering the nature of English Comedy in the late seventeenth and early eighteenth centuries it is worthwhile to have a look at the political, social, economic, cultural and other aspects of life in England during this period and their impact on the theatre.

In keeping with England's age-old socio-political set-up, the institution of a hereditary monarch, which was suspended during the Commonwealth period from 1649 to 1660, was restored by the Convention Parliament which crowned Charles II as the King of England on May 29, 1660. Charles II, a victim of puritan excesses, returned from the exile and immediately a reaction set in against everything associated with Puritanism, *viz.*, faith in God and religion, sobriety in dress as well as in speech and manners and commitment to virtue and truth. People disbelieved and questioned the Puritan faith in this life as a preparatory ground for the life to come. The king and his Court, the 'sons of Belials' as they were called,[1] led a most dissipated life of libertines and moved in the orbit or wine, women and wit. Charles II publicly acknoweledged and rewarded his mistresses and his illegitimate offsprings. So did most of his courtiers and court wits, like the Earl of Rochester, the Duke of Buckingham and Sir Charles Sedley. Hume says that in the culture of the fashionable leisure class society "a little gaming and a bastard or two were nothing which could not be expected of a high-spirited young gentleman."[2] They set an example of corruption, as Dryden avers in the epilogue to Vanbrugh's Pilgrim (1700):

> But sure, a banish't Court, with lewdness fraught,
> The seeds of open Vice returning brought,
> Thus lodg'd (as Vice by great Example thrives)
> It first debauch'd the Daughters and the Wives.
> London, a fruitful soil, yet never bore
> So plentiful a Crop of Horns before.[3]

They did not attach any sanctity to marriage, had a cynical attitude towards love and indulged in intrigues and assignations. The drama of the period, after the reopening of the theatres in 1660, reflected this dissipated life.

Charles II and his courtiers, besides setting examples before the playwrights and providing material for comedies, evinced a keen interest in the theatre. The King along with Thomas Killigrew and Sir William D'Avenant, companions of his exile, had cultivated interest in Spanish dramatists during his stay in the Netherlands. Once back home, he suggested plots to the playwrights. To Samuael Tuke he gave the idea of the plot for *The Adventures of Five Hours* (1663) and to John Crowne for *Sir Courtly Nice* (1665). The King brought with him a taste for French language, literature and, especially, drama. D'Avenant, Killigrew, Etherege and Wycherley transplanted Molière, Corneille, etc., on to the English soil, treating the former as a public storehouse of plots, incidents and characters. The court wits admired French wit, its clarity, refinement, polish, etc., and tried to copy it.

Patents were given to Thomas Killigrew and Sir William D'Avenant who besides being court wits were also playwrights of some note. The King was the patron of the two theatre groups, the King's Company and the Duke's Company. The Chief concern of the dramatists of the period was to write plays to please the King, and consequently, gave full vent to their own predilection for licentiousness. This tendency is referred to by Dryden in the epilogue to *The Pilgrim:*

> The poets, who must live by Courts or starve,
> Were proud, so good a Government to serve,
> And mixing with Buffoons and Pimps profain,
> Tainted the stage, for some small snip of Gain.[4]

Charles II's licentious coterie formed the audience. It comprised the King himself, the royal family, court wits, aristocracy, fops, critics and women of fashion. The citizens and traders who believed in puritan values and did not conform to the cult of the "merry monarch" shunned the Court and the Westminster as well as the playhouses. Thus it became a class drama written by the courtiers for the courtiers and of the courtiers.

A landmark of Charles II's regime was the employment of the women for female roles. Mrs. Knepp and Elizabeth Farley were the first women to act and sing on the public stage. Nell Gwyn, who appeared in breeches in *The Secret Love* (1667), with her talent and beauty made the playwrights create the stock character of the gay heroine of Restoration comedies. In Killigrew's *The Parson's Wedding* (staged in 1664), a "bawdy loose play"[5] full of flagrant indenceny, all the roles were played by women. Actresses brought a new lustre to the theatre, for many a gallant came to see them rather than the plays in which they were acting and the playwrights strove hard to tailor their plots to fit these women in their plays.

The influence of the Court on the threatre decreased with the lessening of the King's power over the Parliament which grudged his revenues and disapproved of his religious policy. The Parliament in 1660 did not give absolute power to the monarch and sanctioned revenues which were not sufficient to provide for the needs of the State and the King's private expenditure. Lack of money and fear of internal sedition compelled Charles II to enter into an economic alliance with Louis XIV. Secret treaties to this effect annoyed the Parliament which disliked dominance of France over England. Besides, Charles II's religious policy created unrest among the protestants. He was a Roman Catholic at heart but he never owned it. A rumour regarding the supposed Popish Plot in 1678 started by Titus Oates, created apprehension in the minds of the people that the Pope wanted the assassination of King Charles to re-establish the authority of Rome in England. This rumour aroused a great amount of heat which was followed by murders of several Catholics. The House of Commons impeached the Catholic peers and excluded them from the Parliament. Charles II dissolved the Parliament in 1679 and announced the nomination of his Catholic brother James as his successor. The fear of Roman Catholicism turned into dismay when after the death of Charles II in 1685, James II ascended the throne and proclaiming his Catholic faith, divorced himself from the Church of England. He antagonised the Parliament and the Protestants by controlling the press and permitting only the publication of Catholic literature. From 1685 to 1688 he fought a religious battle through his courtiers and paid writers including the chief verse satirist, Dryden, who wrote *Hind and the Panther* (1686) to defend the Church of Rome. In 1685 James II replaced Protestant ministers with Catholics and in two Declarations of Indulgence in 1687 and 1688 not only gave freedom of worship to Dissenters and Catholics but also suspended the laws debarring them from civil and military posts. The King's religious policy in favour of the Roman Church created wide discontentment which reached its climax when a son was born to him on June 10, 1688. It made the Parliament pass the Exclusion Bill which Shaftesbury had been introducing from time to time since 1681.

With the death of Charles II, Comedy got a set-back and lost its centrifugal force, *i.e.* the King and his coterie, for James II, concerned more with religion and politics, had not time for art or literature, especially theatre. The stage felt the need of seeking patronage from other quarters and this it got in the corridors of the Westminster.

The Parliament's invitation to Prince William of Orange, a protestant, and Mary, the eldest daughter of James II, to rule over England jointly brought about what is popularly known as the Glorious Revolution. It was a very significant development as it replaced absolute monarchy with limited monarchy, vesting sovereignty in the hands of the Parliament. The new monarch owed his crown to an Act of Parliament, which not only controlled the revenues but also made it impossible for him to dispense with it or resort to despotism. The Bill of Rights passed in 1689 provided that no Roman Catholic could ascend the throne of England, that no standing army was to be maintained in the time of peace, and that no fines or taxes could be levied without the consent of the Parliament. The Mutiny Act of 1689 controlled the armed forces and, thus, ensured that the Parliament msut meet once a year. It fixed the King's revenues and separated his private expenditure from the state expenditure. Thus the Glorious Revolution of 1688 saw the establishment of a limited monarchy and a parliamentary consitution to safeguard the religion and the liberties of the nation. It was this Parliament the playwrights turned to for protection and patronage.

The House of Commons, the backbone of the Parliament, included people from various walks of life, *viz*., judges, lawyers, men from civil services as well as generals, city merchants and representatives of the landed gentry, scientists and writers. Nine-tenths of the elected members belonged to the landed aristocracy for most of the parliamentary boroughs were under its control, including the squires and the knights who represented these interests in the Parliament. Shaftesbury came of this class as did the fictional Sir Roger de Coverley of the *Spectator*. After 1688, comedy which had hitherto been ridiculing the squirarchy and merchant class started showing great respect to them. The change in the attitude of the playwrights towards the landed gentry and the affluent merchant class, their values and sensibilities, can be ascribed to the new political set up, chiefly due to the presence of these classes in the now all-powerful Parliament.

Changes in the political and social life of the country seem to have been hastened by the new ideas coming from the political and moral thinkers of the century. The Royal Society which was conceived somewhere in 1640 but was chartered only in 1662 had launched a new era of thinking. Its members, representing various walks of life and various disciplines – Robert Boyle, a distinguished Chemist; Isaac Newton, a famous Physicist: Duke of Buckingham, the politician; Borrow, the Divine; Evelyn, the Country gentleman; Dryden, the Court Wit; Pepys, the diarist and John Gaunt, the tradesman – all contributed to the creation of a new intellectual climate. Their deliberations and findings shattered the medieval thought. Newton's law of gravitation and Boyle's theory of molecules revolutionised not only the concept of the physical nature of the earth but also influenced religious thinking. Mechanical philosophy which maintains that all matter is made of particles which interact while in motion and result in various natural phenomena was the core of the new scientific outlook. To the scientists of the age all nature was a great machine, an engine working in space and time. The scientific study of astronomy changed the age old Biblical concept of the Universe, with its theory of space and several solar systems and the earth being one of the satellites of the Sun. The earth was no more considered a place created by God to punish Adam and Eve and their progeny, a symbol of man's original sin. Man was no more a branded perpetual sinner but a being at the apex of the life on the earth. There was a clear shift from the other world to "this worldliness". Since the wonders of nature instilled in man reverence for it, the scientific study of Nature and man proved an adjunct to theology for it maintained that science and faith are reconcilable. To the scientists, there was God, not the God of the Gentiles, but the supreme creator, the First Cause, who designed and moved this world machine. Scientific knowledge accepted deism, *viz.*, the natural religión which was demonstrable and was based on reason. The scientific knowledge of the space, the earth and man had a leavening influence on contemporary thought and prepared the way for the eighteenth century ideals of rationalism and humanism.

Scientific thinking had its impact on philosophers who further influenced morality and society. Thomas Hobbes (1588-1679) stands out for advancing a new philosophy. He joined hands with the scientists in demolishing the age old dogmas and beliefs. His masterpiece, *The Leviathan* (1651), based on scientific principles of mechanical materialism, carries the suggestion that the universe is corporeal and is made up of matter. Both nature and human nature are nothing but systems of cause and effect. Man uses the laws of nature for his own advantage. The materialist Hobbes did not believe in soul and the death of body, according to him, was the death of man. Man had no links with heaven or hell. To man the only thing that mattered was this life and self-preservation. Heaven or hell were nothing but states of joy and sorrow on this earth. Hobbes' views on man and human psychology led him to propound his political theory. Hobbes considers man as a tabula rasa, who learns from his environment, and is, in the state of nature, a warring animal fighting for his survival. Men's fear of death and struggle for self-preservation make them enter into a social contract which gives absolute power to the sovereign, whom they call the "mortal God". The sovereign demands complete obedience. Hobbes's political theory was revolutionary so far as it stressed utilitarianism and individualism *i.e.* society created for individual self-interest, and his rejection of the theory of the Divine Right of kings was found in accordance with the new scientific thought. But Hobbes's presentation of the king as absolute ruler over and above the law and authorised to confiscate individual liberty in the name of peaceableness, annoyed the dissenters. Hobbes' dismissal of the scriptures and the Revelation and the negating of Spiritualism offended the clergy whereas his downright materialism and a negative picture of man's nature encouraged pessimism, as now in the absence of a firm faith man had nothing to anchor on. Consequently, his views promoted scepticism, a marked feature of the reign of Charles II, and earned him the title of an atheist, compelling him to flee from England. The positive influence of his theory was not fully developed before the nineteenth century. Nevertheless, his disapproval of covetousness and advocacy of the role of reason in the life of an individual and his consideration of "thrift" and "virtue", rather than birth, as the characteristic of true "nobility"[6] did please the people to some extent.

Another group of thinkers who tried to modify the seventeenth century thought, especially Hobbesian philosophy, was that of the Cambridge Platonists. This group of moralists, divines and philosophers was deeply religious but hostile to fanaticism and enthusiasm of the Puritans. They drew from Plato faith in Reason and goodness of Man. They tried to rationalise religion by combining it with philosophy and reconstructing old beliefs in the light of new knowledge. As a defence against Hobbesian atheism, they asserted that God always ordains what is good and to be a good Christian one should share in God's rationality. To them God's existence was demonstrable from the order of Nature and the moral sense. They appealed to Christian values of sobriety, modesty, gentlessness, humility, obedience to God and charity to men. To them conduct was more important than creed and the purpose of religion was to produce men of God-like temper. The Cambridge Platonists exercised some influence on the elite of Charles II's reign, especially the Earl of Shaftesbury, and strove to restore faith in man, religion and reason.

The last decades of the seventeenth century witnessed another great thinker who influenced the society and literature of the time. John Locke (1632-1704), a member of the Royal Society, expressed his views on political theory in *Two Treatises on Government,* written about 1681 in answer to Robert Filmer's *Patriarcha* which justified the divine right of the kings. Locke, in *The Second Treatise on Government*, expressed his belief that the Government was the product of a social contract between the commonwealth, formed after the "Original Compact" between the people and the government which was conceived as an agency meant for protecting life, liberty and estate of the people. He asserted that the government is responsible to the people it governs for it is the society which places sovereignty in the hands of the monarch or Parliament. Locke maintained that whenever the sovereign puts himself into a state of war with his people, rebellion is justified and the people have full right to overthrow such an unjust monarch. Locke, thus, defended the moral right of the people to resist tyranny. Locke's political theory proved a challenge to the divine right theory for he advocated the idea of a constitutional monarcy in which absolute power was vested in the Parliament which represented the people. His ideas were in accord with the whig liberalism of the eighteenth century and the Glorious Revolution of 1688 was based on his political theory. His disapproval of the exercise of restrictive authority made its impact on family relations as well since the weakening of the authority of the sovereign also weakened the parental authority. Locke defended the right of the individual even in the family. In his *Two Treatises*, Locke advocated the independence of the grown up sons and daughters and their defiance of parental authority if it is unjustly applied. He even pleaded for the rights of the domestic servants. Locke's views on the nature of man, religion and earth are expressed in his *Essays Concerning Human Understanding* (1686), *Letters Concerning Toleration* (1689-92), *Some Thoughts Concerning Education* (1693) and in *The Reasonableness of Christianity* (1695). His philosophy probes into traditional issues, *viz.*, the nature of self, the world, God, knowledge, and etc. He averred that man is a virtuous and rational being, the supreme creation in the universe and that between God and man, there is an inscrutable and unknowable spiritual world. To him man is endowed with good sense, and with virtues like charity, generosity, devotion, tolerance and piety. He believed that everyone has an immortal soul the fate of which is decided by man's faith and conduct in this world and that Reason could lead him to God. In his view property is an essential attribute of man. He is capable of self-discipline and thus can emerge as a virtuous and free-spirited individual. Faith and reason are reconcilable to him. A product of puritan upbringing, Locke proclaimed the reasonableness of Christianity and accepted the scriptures. Nevertheless, he was against the 'enthusiasm' of the Puritans. His repeated reference to Christian values, his spirit of moderation, his faith in man's good sense and quest for God in Nature inspired optimism and faith in man., To him the proper study of mankind was man whose conduct could lead him to happiness. This sunnier view of man and his rights reverberated throughout the coming centuries and, as Sabine says, Locke became the ideal spokesman of the middle class which exercised a great influence throughout the eighteenth century.[7]

Locke's views were further propounded by his friend and pupil, the third Earl of Shaftesbury (1671-1713). Like Locke he believed in the "good nature" of man and considered him as a beneficent social being who can achieve happiness through faith, justice, honesty and virtue. Shaftesbury advocated Beauty and Truth, as he was of the view that "the taste of Beauty, and the Relish of what is decent, just and amiable, perfects the character of the gentlemen".[8] His *Characteristics of Men, Manners, Opinions and Times*, published in 1711, expresses his conviction that to be moral means to be natural and to be natural means to secure a right application of affections. He recommended that one should follow nature, reason, decorum and order. According to his theory of natural philosophy, man should maintain a balance between his "natural affections" and "self affections". Man's natural affections, *viz.* love, gratitude, generosity, pity and etc. are congenial to the public good and are compatible with his self affections *viz.*, love of self, life, luxury, ambition and etc. which are conducive to one's private good. They lead man to individual and social happiness, while man's "unnatural affections" *viz.* inhumanity, misanthropy, tyranny and etc. lead him to misery. Shaftersbury's moral man is natural, tolerant and social. His moral philosophy thus further infused optimism and cheerfulness in the people of his time. His theory influenced the practical moralists like Steele and Addison who started *The Spectator* to moralise wit and reform men and manners of their time.

These political and moral philosophers and scientists secularised thinking, replacing the idea of divine Godhead with the First Cause, and of divine powers with the temporal powers which were further transferred to individuals. Thus, individual became more important than society which was created for him and man was the focus of all creation. The theocratic view of life gave way to the homocentric one. The scale of duties also changed with philosophical thinking. The individual assumed prime importance. By the approach of the eighteenth century man was no longer being considered as an egoistic warring creature of Hobbes but as a social and reasonable being with peaceableness and tolerance as his chief attributes.

Another aspect of social change was that after the Revolution of 1688 'property', especially land, became the major source of economic and political power. Landed aristocracy dominated agriculture, trade and commerce and society as well as Parliament. Land attracted all. People from different classes vied for it and tried to buy new estates or to extend the existing ones in the country. Country people had suffered because of the land taxes levied during the Dutch wars of 1665-1667 and 1672-1674. Before 1688 the kings arbitrarily increased land taxes to finance the wars which affected the land owners. The small squires who were most adversely hit by these enhanced taxes were compelled to sell off their lands either to the big squires or to the rich merchants. Besides, scientific knowledge and scientific experiments in rotation of crops, better methods of cultivation, and the use of scientific tools made it necessary for the agriculturists to have more money to invest and to cultivate large enclosed farmlands instead of small strips of open fields. The big squires started buying up the lands of the smaller ones since only the big land owners could survive under the altered conditions.

Land attracted traders and merchants too. Traders, dealing in the country produce, especially, corn which became surplus between 1660 and 1689, started exporting it and thus raised their position as well as that of the growers. Moreover, the sons of the dissenters who had been forced by the Five Mile Act during Charles II's reign to keep away from the Court and Westminster had taken up trade. This abolished the social barrier between the landed gentry and the trading class and mobility between the two became the marked feature of the age. Younger sons of the gentry also helped in this social mobility. Compelled by the law of primogeniture, frequently referred to in comedies of the period, the younger sons sometimes chose trade and often got richer than their elder brothers. They bridged the gap between these two classes. The establishment of the Bank of England in 1694 raised the status of the financiers and traders and helped them in expanding business. This development also finds reference in the contemporary literature. Both Sir Andrew Freeport (*The Spectator*, No. 549) and Mr. Charwell (*Guardian* No. 9) leave the town to estbalish flourishing estates in undeveloped countryside. Sealand, a merchant in Steele's *The Conscious Lovers*, talks about the prestige of his class when he says:

> We Merchants are a Species of Gentry, that have grown into the World this last Century, and are as honourable and almost useful, as you landed Folks.[9]

Sir Andrew Freeport presents the case of the merchant class buying land in the country when he says in *The Spectator*, No. 174:

> Certainly he deserves the Estate a great deal better who has got it by his industry than he who has lost it by his negligence.

This change of attitude towards the merchant class is evidenced in the comedies written after the Glorious Revolution. The 'citizens' were ridiculed during the reign of Charles II but within a short period, the affluent merchants earned so much respectibility that the gentry welcomed marriage proposals from them and the merchant class too realised that marriage with land and title was the best social investment. It was the best way to 'gentilise' themselves. The merchant class had puritanical tendencies and faith in Christian values, believing in thrift, sobriety, honesty, etc. and they also set the examples of morality. Accordingly, the comedies of the period present them as virtuous and respectable members of the society.

The royalty also helped in creating a moral climate in the country. Religious and moral activity marked the reign of King William and Queen Mary who themselves were examples of moral rectitude. Literature and the stage seldom attracted King William, but his wife, Queen Mary was fond of plays which were free of wanton indecency. The portraits of women of Queen Mary's Court showing them modestly and more decorously dressed than those of the Court of Charles II reflect the Queen's taste. Because of the examples of virtue and piety provided by the royal couple, the White Hall was no longer the haunt of pleasure and seekers of profligacy. The King discouraged vice and issued a proclamation (January 21, 1691) against vicious, debauched and profane persons.[10] When Queen Anne, Queen Mary's sister, ascended the throne in 1702, she set a still more severe example of piety and virtue. She took stringent measures against dissipation by issuing a proclamation (March 26, 1702) discouraging debauchery "particularly in such (people) as are employed near our Royal Person". She also declared her intention to "distinguish persons of piety and virtue" by showing them royal favour.[11]

But it was not the royalty alone that assisted in bringing about this moral climate. Religious societies born in the last decades of the seventeenth century consisted of groups of serious youngmen who, under the guidance of clergymen, had started creating religious and moral awakening among the people. They tried to check vice and impertinence by enforcing laws against such offences as drunkenness, swearing, whoring and wenching. They wrote and distributed religious literature. Another body that assisted them was the Society for Promoting Christian Knowledge founded in 1698. It started charity schools which were financed by wealthy founders, small shopkeepers and artisans. Besides educating the poor in the three R's, the Society taught moral discipline and the principles of the Church of England. In 1707 Swift published *A Project for the Advancement of Religion and the Reformation of Manners*, in one passage of which he referred to the contemporary stage and appealed to the government to take stringent measures to curb its activities.

Religious and moral reform led to legal reforms. Matrimony which had lost its sanctity during the Restoration now regained some of its solemnity with people's cry for decency and virtue. Adultery and cuckolding were once again decried. The institution of matrimony was taken as something not to be trifled with. Even though the Civil Marriage Act passed in 1653 had empowered the temporal courts to grant divorces, they had to be ratified by the Parliament. The practice, however, was so rare that only six divorces were granted during Queen Anne's twelve years of reign. This made the possibility of getting a divorce decree extremely difficult. This shows that matrimony was no longer being taken lightly. Nevertheless, matrimony, with contractual model had become an economic enterprise. Marriage offers were weighed and arranged by the guardians of the boys to extend the estates though mercenary marriages were denounced in theory. The notion of matrimony as a voluntary contract gave equality to women and inspired them to question the prevalent double standards prescribing norms of behaviour for women different from those of men. Still women were not considered equal to men in matters of property. Even Hobbes and Locke, the champions of individual liberty, had bowed to male supremacy. The comedy of the Restoration days reflected sceptical attitude towards matrimony by presenting fornication and adultery as consequences of incompatible matches. With the doctrine of compatibility of men and women, matrimony assumed dignity. As Susan Staves maintains, matrimony gets regulated under the influence of practical morality and puritanical tendencies of the middle classes.[12] Comedy after 1688 reflects the temperament of the period in this respect as well as by depicting the blessings of marital fidelity.

The people of England had witnessed an excess of prudery under puritanism and had come to hate it. They had seen the dissipations of the Merry Monarch's reign and were in turn disgusted by it. They saw the bourgeois morality with its practical economic and social and its Christian spirit and they embraced it. They attended the churches but did not become fanatics. They were also devoted to their vocations as they were devoted to their religion. They emphasised decorum, respect for the institution of marriage and considered women as virtuous and esteemable companions. On the whole, it was an age which was seeking a balance between the old and the new, the spiritual and the material, the society and the individual and, also, between lofty ideals and the demands of practical life.

NOTES

1. J.H. Wilson, *A Preface to Restoration Drama* (Massachusetts, 1968), p. 24.
2. R.D. Hume, "The Myth of the Rake in Restoration Comedy," *Studies in Literary Imagination,* 10 (1977), p. 40.
3. M. Summers, ed., *The Dramatic Works of John Dryden* (London, 1931), VI, p. 488.
4. Dryden, *op. cit.*, Vol. VI, p. 488.
5. Robert D. Hume, *The Development of English Drama in the late Seventeenth Century* (Oxford, 1976), p. 244.
6. J.E. Spingarn (ed.), *Critical Essays of the Seventeenth Century* (Ithaca, 1957), Vol. I, p. 31.
7. G.H. Sabine, *A History of Political Theory*, Indian rpt. (Calcutta, 1968), p. 540.
8. R.W. Harris, *England in the Eighteenth Century* (Delhi, 1978), p. 94.
9. *Richard Steele, Plays,* ed., S.S. Kenny (Oxford, 1971), p. 359.
10. J.W. Krutch, *Comedy and Conscience after the Restoration* (New York, 1967), p.166.
11. *Ibid.*, p. 166.
12. Susan Staves, *The Players' Scepters: Fiction of Authority in the Restoration* (Nebraska, 1979), p. 116 and p. 189.

2

English Comedy from 1660 to 1700

Comedy which had met with a set-back during the Commonwealth period got exceptional encouragement in 1660 when Charles II, soon after his restoration, granted patents to Sir William D'Avenant and Thomas Killigrew and allowed them to adapt and alter the existing plays or write new ones. This opened new vistas for the dramatists. The presence of comedians like Hart, Mohun, Betterton and Kynaston along with actresses of fame like Mrs. Knepp, Mrs. Grey, Elizabeth Farley, Mrs. Hughes and Nell Gwyn inspired the dramatists to tailor their plots according to their talents. The dramatists borrowed from all the possible sources ranging from Shakespeare and Johnson to Molière and Corneille. They attempted writing original comedies but had no scruples in taking plots, characters and situations from these sources. Their comedies present gay couples, battles in repartee, sex antagonism, amorous intrigues and satire on corrupt priests, the country squires and on the affectations of the town. The Restorastion playwrights added to the sexual licence prevalent in the contemporary fashionable London and created gay heroines after the brilliant Court ladies and royal mistresses. Killigrew and D'Avenant inducted Spanish comic elements filtered through France, *viz.*, highly complicated intrigues, character types – the choleric and strict fathers, high spirited young gallants, adventurous women in veils, heroines objecting to arranged marriages, stupid valets – mistakes of identity, nocturnal sword play in parks and gardens, love affairs of servants as foils to those of their masters and etc. Many of the Restoration playwrights utilised these ingredients to provide entertainment to their audiences. Dryden, Shadewell, Etherege, Wycherley and Congreve stand out amongst those who served the Restoration comic muse.

John Dryden (1631-1700) is one of the foremost playwrights

of the post-Restoration England. In his comedies he captures the spirit of libertinism pervading the contemporary court life and juxtaposes it with heroic plots based on love and honour. The plot patterns are the amours of the cheerfully promiscuous gay couples who have cynical attitude towards love, marriage and life. The witty gay couples include Loveby and Constance (*The Wild Gallant*, 1663), Celadon and Florimel (*The Secret Love*, 1667)[1] Warner and Millisent (*Sir Martin Mar-all*, 1667), Wildblood and Jacinta and Bellamy and Theodosia (*An Evening's Love*, 1668), Rhodophil and Doralice (*Marriage a-la-Mode*, 1671) and Lorenzo and Elvira (*The Spanish Friar*, 1680). Most of these rakes swear, indulge in whoring and love intrigues and oppose marriage of convenience. Loveby is suspected to be carrying on an affair with his landlord's wife and has 'three wenches more', Celadon is a perfect rake while Wildblood is a profligate prodigal, Rhodophil has an intrigue with the betrothed of Palamede, while Palamede, in his turn, has an affair with Rodophil's wife. Lorenzo leaves no stone unturned to get sexual satisfaction and Woodall is a vulgar disagreeable rake having affairs with whores, as well as with married and innocent women. Dryden avers in the Preface to *An Evening's Love* that these rakes reclaim themselves first from vice "when they resolve to marry; for then enjoying what they desire in one, they cease to pursue the love of many"[2] but this reclamation does not transform them into virtuous beings. However, Dryden was never tired of defending them as he believed that their "faults and vices, which comedy laughs at are but the sallies of youth and the frailties of human nature...such as may be forgiven".[3] Dryden's heroines possess wit, beauty and fortune, have wit-battles with their lovers, use disguise and other methods to test the sincerity of their lovers and finally they bow to matrimony with certain clearly stated provisos. They too revolt against marriage of convenience and hoodwink their cantankerous guardians but are more or less decent and polished in speech. Constance (*Wild Gallant*) gulls her foolish father, Lord Nonsuch; and Millisent (*Sir Martin Marall*) has a clandestine marriage with Warner, a witty prodigal working as her servant. Doralice (*Marriage a-la-Mode*), even after her marriage, questions the sanctity of the marriage vows and has assignations with her husband's friend, Palamede. His virtuous women include Lucretia (*The Assignation*) who frustrates the lustful designs of her lover's father, Mrs. Pleasance (*Limberham*) who reclaims Woodall and Florimal (*Secret Love*) who succeeds in curing the rake of his libertinism. Besides the gay couples indulging in love game and witty repartees there are the platonic lovers of the heroic plots. The queen (*The Secret Love)* never voices her love as she deems it to be below her dignity and Palmyra and Leonidas suffer and sigh but never trifle with their love.

Dryden has blended the love-intrigue comedy of Beaumont and Fletcher with that of Johnson by portraying satiric characters as "mechanic" humours. Lord Nonsuch (*The Wild Gallant*) is an embodiment of foolishness and gullibility, Sir Moody (*Sir Martin Mar-all*) of absurd downrightness, Don Alonzo, Jacinta's father (*An Evening's Love)*, of loquacity and Woodall's father, Aldo (*Limberham*) of superannuated lechery. Dryden provides his 'fools' complementary pertners. For example, the timid idiot, Sir Timorous (*The Wild Gallant*), is duped into marrying a fortune-hunting woman and Sir Martin (*Sir Martin Mar-all*) an extravagant self-conceited blundering fool, is tricked into marrying the heroine's maid. The band of fools also includes jealous husbands. Miselry, cowardly Gomez (*The Spanish Friar*) who is beaten and almost cuckolded is one of them. Brainsick and Limberham (*Limberham*) fare worse than him as they do get themselves cuckolded. Dryden mocks social climbers and the fops too; Melantha (*Marriage a-la-Mode*) is one such character given to affected frenchifed discourse and so is Aurelia (*An Evening's Love*). The witty servants have love intrigues of their own which parallel those of their masters. Though marriage vows are taken sceptically, as in *Marriage a-la-Mode*, marital fidelity is ultimately found to be the best solution to man's sexual problems. Marital incompatibility is presented in *The Spanish Friar* and *Limberham* as the cause that leads the couples to the very threshold of adultery. *The Wild Gallant* has lewdness in the tailor's bad jokes, *An Evening's Love* and its prologue abound so much in sexual promiscuity, *double entendre* and lascivious dialogue that Pepys could not help branding it as "very smutty".[4] Propriety and decorum are violated in *The Wild Gallant* too in a farcial situation where Constance pretends to be pregnant with the help of a pillow and makes Lord Nonsuch believe that he and his servants have also been impregnated by the devil. In *Sir Martin Mar-all*, Mrs. Christian, the feigned innocene, is instructed by her aunt to sell her body to a lord and is ultimately palmed off to a fool. *Limberham* is the most indencent play of Dryden in its dialogue as well as action.[5] In a grossly vulgar situation Woodall is seen with three amorous old women, two under his bed and the third one, the hypocritical puritan, Mrs. Saintly, on his bed, urging him to make love to her. In another situation one of these women is seduced by the hero's servant. Wildblood and Bellamy (*An Evening's Love)* accost and court the girls in a chapel and the girls too visit the chapel not for praying but for ogling. Dominic, an old and hypocritical greedy friar (*The Spanish Friar)*, is an agent of incest. He deliberately plans cuckolding and murder. Though Dryden for the best part of his dramatic career maintained that his comedies served the cause of virtue, there were certain occasions when he felt otherwise. One such instance is found in the preface to *An Evening's Love* where talking of the immorality in the play he says:

> ...but I confess I have given too much to the people in it and am ashamed for them as well as for myself, that I have pleased them at so cheap a rate.[6]

Dryden's 'Mac Flecknoe' and self-claimed successor of Jonson, Thomas Shadwell (1642-1692) treats, in his comedies, themes of fortune hunting and marital incompatibility. His first comedy, *The Sullen Lovers* (1668) has two pairs of lovers, the sombre couple, Stanford and Emilia and the gay one, Lovel and Carolina. The other couples are Raymund and Theodosia (*The Humourists,* 1670), witty Bevil and Caroline, Raines and Lucia (*Epsom Wells*, 1672), Bruce and Miranda, Longvil and Clarinda (*The Virtuoso*, 1676), Bellamour and Isabella, Carlos and Theodosia (*A True Widow*, 1678) and Bellamy and Gertrude (*The Bury Fair*, 1689). The lovers are frequently made to face and outwit difficult guardians. They are not libertine rakes like those of Dryden. Belfond Junior (*The Squire of Alsatia*, 1688) is the only hero in the plays of Shadwell who has had a licentious past with a cast-off mistress and who has seduced and deserted the innocent daughter of an attorney. But he too is reformed by his sincere love for Isabella. In *Bury Fair* a duel takes place between the hero and his friend who is also his rival in love. Bruce and Longvil (*The Virtuoso*) exchange their beloved like men of sense when they learn where the women's affections are placed. Caroline and Lucia

(Epsom Wells) and Miranda and Clarinda (*The Virtuoso*) are as gay and wild as their other Restoration counterparts but the rest of Shadwell's heroines are somewhat sober and governed by sense. Most of them emerge as 'difficult' heroines and accept the lovers only on certain hard conditions. Stanford and Emilia (*The Sullen Lovers*) behave sensibly and agree that "if either grows a fopp the other shall have liberty to part".[7] The heroines of *Epsom Wells* receive their lovers on probation as 'servants' and the rake Belfond Junior is accepted only when he is reformed. *The Virtuoso* (1676) abounds in men and women of easy virtue and they are put into ridiculous situations so that they are thoroughly exposed. Sir Nicholas Gimcrack, the virtuoso, is a scientist whose knowledge is not functional so he fails badly in life. He is mercilessly ridiculed for his excessive enthusiasm for silly experiments.[8] Sir Formal Trifle is another humorous character who prides himself on his supposed skill in oratory, creates enemies, and is beaten up. Snarl is an old man who, while sharply criticising the younger generation for its novel manners, makes a fool of himself by pursuing young women. The title of another play of Shadwell, *A True Widow* is an ironic reference to Lady Cheatly, who, as her name suggests, is an expert in fraud, but is finally exposed and punished. *Epsom Wells* ridicules jealous husbands in the persons of Bisket, a confitmaker, and Fribble, a drinking and brawling haberdasher, who both are cuckolded, and a Country Justice, Clodpate, who runs after witty women of town but is married to a jilting maid to be released from whom he has to part with a large amount of money. *Bury Fair* has ridiculous characters like Oldwit, the strict orthodox father, Sir Humphrey Noddy, a lover of puns and jokes, an affected French Count who is proud of his French manners, courts a lady of quality and receives a good amount of cudgelling. Shadwell's comedies are replete with immoral dialogues and sexual wit, assignations, switching of letters, disguises, impersonations, as well as duels. Besides these stock comic devices, Shadwell has also created grossly vulgar and farcical situations to provide cheap entertainment. Gimcrack's uncle, Snarl, is put into a woodhole with his mistress, Figgup and is later visited by Lady Gimcrack and Hazard. The sexual irregularity of these two couples is exposed by Sir Nicholas Gimcrack and his mistress Flirt who also come to the woodhole with similar intentions. Their exposures of each other lead to accusations, and counter-accusations. Besides, Flirt and Lady Figgup, women of depraved characters, Lady Gimcrack is a woman with adulterous inclinations, having illicit relations with Hazard. *Epsom Wells* presents two husbands one of whom beats his wife and the other is beaten by his at the instance of the other. In a farcical scene, Bisket and Fribble vie with each other in elaborating upon the physical charms of their wives before their friends, Kick and Cuff. *Epsom Wells*, in spite of its immoral dialogue, characters and situations is a satire on marriages of convenience which so often lead to adultery.

Shadwell's *The Squire of Alsatia* presents a zealous reformer in Sir Edward Belfond who stands for lenient upbringing of young wards as opposed to the old strict discipline. It describes a rake's follies as frailties of youth which are renounced before he bows to matrimony. Nevertheless, Belfond Junior is a rake with some scruples. He helps his elder brother and he is respectful to his elders. The only blot on his character is his illicit affair with an innocent girl. He, like other gay heroes of Shadwell, is not like the swearing, drinking, whoring ruffians denounced by Shadwell in the preface to *The Sullen Lovers*. Nor are Shadwell's heroines "impudent, ill bred tomrigs".[9] Morality is taken care of when matrimony is treated with due respect, vice and follies are punished and the principal characters are shown as people of 'wit and sense'. The rakes too, after being repulsed by the heroines, revert to the path of virtue, and are accepted on probation. These traits are in keeping with Shadwell's didactic outlook pronounced in the Prologue to *The Squire of Alsatia:*

> He to correct and inform did write
> If poets aim at naught but to delight.
> Fiddlers have to the Bays an equal right.[10]

Another important Restoration playwright, Sir George Etherege (1634?-1691?), was directly influenced by French literature and manners. He led a most licentious life and accordingly his comedies present the picture of a society profligate in its manners and sceptic in respect of the established norms of religion, love, matrimony, etc. But at the same time, Spanish influence, received through France, can also be seen in his plays, especially in the heroic plots dealing with platonic love which is serious and self annihilating;

and the duels that are fought for a lady. Honour is the dominant element in such plots. The moral and pathetic tone of the main plot is often juxtaposed with the sexual immorality of the comic sub-plot. It presents fops, fools and women who have adulterous inclinations. The amorous women are either seduced by the hero or are on the verge of adultery. However, morality is superficially taken care of when these women are shown as admitting that adultery offers no solution to an unhappy marriage. Likewise, in the love-game plots libertines are finally made to yield to matrimony. However, overt immorality in action can be seen here and there, for example, when Dorimant (*The Man of Mode*) is seen coming out of his room after spending the night with Belinda. In *She Wou'd if She Cou'd* Mrs. Cockwood's relations with the hero can be regarded as innocent freedoms enjoyed by a woman in a sexually liberated society. The dialogue of all the three comedies of Etherege is replete with smut, witty promiscuity and *double entendre*. Etherege's heroes have their affection fixed at one place, *i.e.*, a virtuous woman of wit and fortune who succeeds in reclaiming them. Sir Frederick Frollick has no love intrigue in the play other than with a widow, but he has a forsaken mistress. Dorimant is a most dissipated rake who swears, curses and womanizes without any scruples. Mrs. Loveit is Dorimant's ex-mistress, and she is used by him as his agent to further his love for Harriet. In Belinda Etherege has created a woman of weak will and strong passions. But Courtall and Freeman (*She Wou'd if She Cou'd*) do not have even a shade of libertinism in their characters. They are rather romantic lovers in pursuit of beauty, wit and fortune, taking part in intrigues only to gain access to their beloveds. They pursue their love till they are accepted. The heroines in Etherege's comedies are women of wit and gaiety but 'difficult', for they do not surrender to the rakes' advances till they are fully reformed. Gatty and Ariana with their innocent freedoms and wit-battles (*She Wou'd if She Cou'd*), the widow with her honour and virtue and platonic lovers (*The Comical Revenge*) and Harriet and Emelia (*The Man of Mode*) are virtuous women who treat love and marriage soberly and seriously. The widow accepts Sir Frederick with a proviso that he would have no control over her wealth, Gatty and Ariana accept the romantic lovers on one month's constant service to them and Harriet makes Dorimant agree to retire to the country after their marriage. The fools in Etherege's comedies include Dufoy, a low comedy character who apes the manners of his superiors and is ridiculed for his frenchified pronunciation and pox. He pretends love for a maid who locks him up in a tub when she discovers his perfidy. Then there are 'humour' characters, Sir Joslin Jolly and Sir Oliver Cockwood (*She Wou'd if She Cou'd*), the former a man with wenching propensities and the latter a cowardly husband with superficial fondness for his wife. Sir Oliver Cockwood is a stock comic character constantly haunted by the fear of being cuckolded. In *The Man of Mode* Etherege has combined the fool with the fop in the immortal character of Sir Fopling Flutter, a descendent of Molière's Mascarille of *Les Précieuses Ridicules* and created him both "to please and to instruct".[11] Usurers and traders are satirised in Wheadle and Palmer, for their lustful designs and avarice. These lascivious rascals are eventually fobbed off to women with no fortune and no character. On a superficial study Etherege seems to have rewarded the most dissipated rakes with virtuous heroines but a deeper look into his comedies reveals that youthful flirtations of these rakes, who are his heroes, are directed only towards depraved or amorous elederly women. Moreover, the rakes' 'inevitable reformation is a moral gesture. There is seldom any trace of profanity in his plays and the principal characters are hardly seen drinking or gaming. Etherege's ridicule is clearly directed towards the contemporary vices and follies of the fashionable men and women of London. Sexual wit is veiled and immoral conduct, of which there is a great deal in his plays, is either punished or reformed.

Like Etherege, William Wycherley (1640-1715) was also a philanderer. He depicts the Restoration ethos with its most degraded facet.[12] His comedies, *Love in a Wood*, (1660), *The Gentleman Dancing Master* (1666), *The Country Wife* (1675) and *The Plain Dealer* (1676) treat the theme of sex relationship in a shockingly frank manner. The sexually immoral society depicted in these comedies is populated by depraved characters; jealous husbands, puritan citizens, and pretentious people. *Love in a Wood* has several humour characters including social types. For example, Sir Simon Addleplot, who has wenching propensities and is duped into marrying a woman with no fortune; Alderman Gripe, a covetous old puritan usurer who is tricked into marrying his own mistress and Dapperwit, a witling who marries a supposedly rich girl who foists her unborn illegitimate child upon him. To this group of depraved characters belongs Horner, a most perfect rake and cuckolder in *The Country Wife*. He feigns impotence to further his immoral designs upon the women of quality who, though depraved, are eager to maintain a facade of virtue and honour. There is a jealous husband, Pinchwife, who treats his wife as a piece of property and is always haunted by the fear of cuckoldom. He is contrasted with Sir Jasper Fidget, a complacent husband who virtually throws his wife into Horner's arms. Even when cuckolded, true to their type, the husbands dissemble and find it convenient to consider their wives virtuous. Wycherley's fools include the whimsical strict father, Sir James Formal (*The Gentleman Dancing Master*), an eecentric English merchant who assumes the Spanish name Don Diego and apes Spanish manners. There is also Monsieur de Paris, a vain coxcomb affecting French language and fashions who unwittingly helps his rival in marrying the young lady he himself was courting. Another comic character in this set is Mrs. Caution, an impertinent old aunt whose lewd suggestions are contrary to her apparent prudery. Besides these satiric characters, Wycherley has also created villains and cheats. Vernish and Olivia (*The Plain Dealer*) conspire to cheat the hero, Manly, of his money and love. Olivia turns unfaithful to Manly and marries the villain but they are exposed and punished. Manly in some respects is ultimately like Horner, whose downright plain dealing degenerates into bed-trick to expose and punish Olivia. But Wycherley who had not spared Horner does not spare Manly either. Horner is singled out as being fit only for the company of the dancers and Manly is put to shame and repentance when he finds that the woman he has been trying to seduce is his faithful follower Fidelia. Among the women satirised and ridiculed by Wycherley are those who have pretence of honour "though it may be a counterfeit" jewel (V, iv). Lady Flippant (*Love in a Wood*) is extra-ordinarily keen on having a husband while she outwardly denounces matrimony. She manages to make Sir Simon Addleplot seduce her. Flirt and Flounce (*The Gentleman Dancing Master*) are two whores who punish Monsieur de Paris by getting separate maintenance from him. Wycherley satirises the litigious widow in Mrs. Blackacre in *The Plain Dealer*. She is gulled by her own son and Freeman, a wit. Wycherley also portrays virtuous Platonic lovers in Christina and Valentine (*Love in a Wood*). Harcourt and Alithea (*The Country Wife*) who uphold positive norms of behaviour, and Fidelia (*The Plain Dealer*) who disguises and follows Manly and saves him from moral downfall by taking Olivia's place belong to the same class of characters. Eliza, Olivia's cousin, is another virtuous woman, who serves as a censor to Olivia. Hippolita, though revolting against marriage-de-convenience and bubbling with teenage impulses, is basically a virtuous young lady. She refuses to elope with the gay hero and seeks love and security in wedlock. Nevertheless, there is too much of *double entendre*, lascivious dialogue and lewd situations in his comedies. *Love in a Wood* is all confusion in St. James Park at night, *The Gentleman Dancing Master* shows the lovers dancing while the girl's father and aunt make lewd commentary, *The Country Wife* is full of lewd scenes and sexual innuendoes, and *The Plain Dealer* presents a morally shocking bed-room scene. These obscene plays with an unmistakable satiric intent, poetic justice, absence of profanity and blasphemy are justly called immoral-moral comedies.

Congreve, in his comedies, *The Old Bachelor* (1693), *The Double Dealer* (1693), *Love for Love* (1695) and *The Way of the World* (1700) follows Etherege in depicting the life of the contemporary high society with carefree abandon. His comedies depict love intrigues of the rakes who pursue women of wit, beauty and fortune. Bellmour and Vainlove (*The Old Bachelor*), Mellefont (*The Double Dealer)*, Valentine (*Love for Love*) and Mirabel (*The Way of the World*) are the gay fashionable youngmen who give up, or are on the point of giving up, their loose ways of life on finding women truly worthy of their love. Vainlove has a cast-off mistress in Silvia but is an honest lover of Araminta. Bellmour, a champion of libertinism who considers sexual licence as his prerogative and pleasure his occupation, seduces Laetitia Fondlewife and is more or less of the same cast as his friend Vainlove, with the difference that he is yet to find his Araminta. Mellefont is an honest and serious lover seeking the hand of Cynthia. Whereas Valentine is a prodigal rake who has bastards to support but, once in love with Angelica, has pledged to be virtuous. His shady past has disappointed his father and compels Angelica to put him to severe trial. Mirabel of *The Way of the World* has an affinity with Etherege's Dorimant in the sense that he too is a libertine who gives up his licentious ways and pursues an honest lady, Millamant. He has had illicit relations with Mrs. Fainall and has antagonised Marwood by rejecting her advances. He feigns love to Millamant's amorous guardian-aunt in order to gain access to his beloved. The heroines of Congreve's comedies are witty and virtuous women, not madcap gay women. Belinda in *The Old Bachelor* has her wit-battles and love chases but she never steps out of the bounds of virtue and, likewise, Araminta too is a lady of character who is always on guard in respect of her conduct and reputation. In *The Double Dealer* Cynthia, though in the midst of treacherous people, is steady and constant in her love for Mellefont. Millament enjoys the company of fops and plays the coquette too, but she is sincerely in love with Mirabell. Her fears, "if Mirabell should not make a good husband, I am a lost thing" (IV, i) echo Cynthia's apprehension and hesitation toward matrimony expressed in scene I Act II of *The Double Dealer*, " 'tis an odd game we're going to play at; what think you of drawing stakes, and giving over in time?". Congreve ridicules fops and fools, punishes bad characters and makes fun of the abnormal ones. Heartwell's unjust diatribes against young people's amours in *The Old Bachelor* make him a butt for ridicule when he is duped into the silly situation of marrying a whore. Congreve satirises the stock character of the old jealous husband in Fondlewife who is a city merchant and a hypocritical puritan. He is cheated and cuckolded by Bellmour, but like his tribe, prefers to believe that his wife is innocent. Sir Joseph Wittol, a complete fool and false wit and his cowardly and foolish escort, Captain Bluffe, both equally vain of their amours, are also duped into marrying unchaste women. Sir Paul Plyant (*The Double Dealer)* is an uxorious foolish old knight who virtually pushes his wife into adultery and thus makes himself a cuckold. Lord Touchwood (*The Double Dealer*) is another old foolish husband who is bullied by his wife and keeps his cool in spite of her adulterous conduct. Lady Plyant, a wife who is insolent to her husband, is always ready to have other lovers. She allows herself to be seduced by Careless in her own house. Lady Froth (*The Double Dealer*) also belongs to the class of unfaithful wives. A great coquette and pretender to poetry, wit and learning, she sacrifices her honour to Brisk, a coxcomb. Sir Sampson Legend (*Love for Love*) is yet another ridiculous character. He is presented as a foolish strict father who wants to disinherit his eldest son, a gay but lovable youngman, in favour of a foolish son. He also tires to marry his elder son's beloved. Foresight, of the same play, is a typical foolish old man, who has married a young wife. He is a believer in superstitions and astrology. His ridiculous passion for astrology makes him blind to the behaviour of his wife who has found a lover for herself in Scandal, a half-wit. Tattle, always after satisfying his lust, flirts with every woman that he gets acquainted with and is duped into marrying a depraved woman, Mrs. Frail. *The Way of the World* satirises amorous old women in Lady Wishfort. She is not only a woman of affectations and amorous inclinations, but is also a strict guardian. She has her designs upon the hero and is more than eager to marry a supposed knight who is actually a servant of Mirabel in disguise. Mrs. Fainall has been Mirabel's mistress but has married Fainall to foist her unborn child on him. Fainall, in his turn, has married her only for her fortune which he fails to get. Mrs. Marwood, Fainall's mistress is a jealous and vindictive woman who vainly tries to create problems for Mirabel for having rejected her advances. Maskwell in *The Double Dealer* is the incarnation of treachery, villainy and lust. He conspires against Lady Touchwood as well as against Mellefont in order to defame them and win the hand of Cynthia. Lady Touchwood wishes to be revenged upon Mellefont for rejecting her amorous advances. Maskwell fails in his evil designs and Lady Touchwood repents when she is exposed before her husband.

Congreve's comedies contain a good many *double entendres*, lascivious dialogue, and immoral situations and gestures. The near seduction scene in Fondlewife's house, Sir Sampson Legend's eagerness to marry his son's beloved, Tattle's use of lewd language while teaching Prue seductive manners, Mrs. Foresight and Mrs. Frail's comic exposures of each other's depravity, Lady Touchwood's surprising of Mellefont with her lascivious gestures are evidences of the immoral cast of Congreve's characters. Bellmour's disguising as a parson and using a book of romance as the Bible to seduce Laetitia Fondlewife is a profanation of the priest's calling. Bellmour also disguises as a parson to perform the mock marriage of Heartwell and Silvia. *The Double Dealer* too satirises the clergy through a mercenary corrupt priest, Saygrace, who can do or undo anything for money. The notable features of Congreve's comedies are their polished wit and brilliant dialogue. His heroes really love the virtuous women whose supremacy over other female characters is never in doubt. Rakes of yester-years, they (the heroes) are in the process of being reformed into serious and sincere lovers. Like the heroines, they too outshine the members of their own sex in wit, intelligence and other noble qualities and attainments. In each one of his comedies poetic justice is disbursed and cynical attitude toward matrimony is toned down.

A close look into the comedies of some of the major playwrights of the period reveals that the Restoration comedy was not alien to the English audiences but was rather a continuation of the pre-civil war comic traditions. It follows satirical strokes of humour after Jonson, and of manners after Beaumont, Fletcher and Shirley, etc. It presents assignations, love intrigues and extra-marital sexual experiences, mostly for men and sometimes for women too in a licentious society in a manner resembling Middleton, Dekker, Beaumont and Fletcher.[13] The young heroes are presented as rakes, witty and cynical about love, sex and matrimony. There are rich witty young girls who succeed in making the rakes give up their immoral pursuits for the sake of matrimony. Though these libertines are depicted favourably and rich heiresses are provided for them, they have to reform themselves before being accepted by their beloveds. Free and smutty dialogue abounding in *double entendre* and innuendoes[14] and lewd lascivious situations are frequently present in these comedies. The dialogues have a good deal of cursing and swearing too. But all these elements are the continuation and elaborations of the earlier traditions and are designed to meet the demands of the contemporary audiences.[15] The immorality of the Restoration comedy; its rake heroes and gay heroines, adulterous couples, lewd situations, smutty lascivious dialogue and cynical approach to matrimony and love, etc., were the common features of comedy before the closure of the theatres. The Restoration Comedy did neither invent them nor import them. It brought them into focus and presented a close up of these elements which coincidentally were the basis of the code of conduct of King Charles II and his coterie. Charles II patronised this type of comedy for full twentyfive years and throughout this period the Restoration Comedy with its overt immoral characters, situations and witty dialogue ruled and monopolised the theatre.

Restoration dramatists were not totally bereft of social concern and seriousness of purpose as is generally assumed. Time and again we find both Dryden and Etherege questioning the prevalent marriage-de-convenience and double standards of conduct. Wycherley frequently satirises the vices and follies of the corrupt society and presents positive norms of behaviour. Shadwell also pictures the same society but virtue in his comedies reclaims the errant characters. Congreve was a dramatist of a different cast. Though still depicting the vicious features of the contemporary society, he strove to make love and marriage a serious business.

NOTES

1. Celadon is a direct successor to Mirabel, the rake in Fletcher's *The Wild Goose Chase* (1621), who treats love as a game and views matrimony sceptically.
2. Dryden, *The Dramatic Works*, Vol. II, p. 246.
3. *Ibid*. Such arrangements were frequently put forth at the time of the publication of a play, in prefatory notes or in dedications. They hardly carried any conviction.
4. F.H. Moore, *The Nobler Pleasure: Dryden's Comedy in Theory and Practice* (Chapel Hill, 1963), p. 80.
5. Dryden once again claimed in its preface that the play was a satire against the sin of keeping.
6. *Works*, Vol. II, p.242. Dryden's self-admonishing should not be taken as a candid expression of the playwright, for, it, like his religious beliefs, seems to be an opportunistic move.
7. *The Complete Works of Shadwell*, ed. M. Summers (London, 1927), Vol. I, p. 83.
8. The play anticipates Swift and Pope's biting satire on the members of the Royal Society.
9. Works, I, p. 11.
10. *Ibid*. IV, p. 204.
11. J.H. Wilson, *The Court Wits*, p. 164.
12. Hume, *op. cit.*, p. 103.
13. For such situations see Middleton's *The Phoenix*, Dekker's *The Honest Whore* and Fletcher's *The Custom of the Country*, and *The Tamer Tam'd*.
14. Fletcher's *The Tamer Tam'd* (1611) was suppressed in 1633 upon complaints of foul and offensive matters contained therein and the actors' text was cleansed of the "Oaths and prophaneness" (*Politics, Religion and Literature in Seventeenth Century*, William Lament and Sybil Old Field, London, 1975), p. 32.
15. Jonson's *The Bartholomew Fair* (1614) is full of gross and indecent dialogue and the characters are given to drinking, boasting and swearing.

3

The Restoration Comedy and Its Critics

The theatre in England has been the target of attack from various quarters since almost its inception, especially from the Church, civic authorities and pamphleteers. It was in the Church that the drama originated and it was the Church which denounced the theatre through sermons delivered by zealous puritan priests. The most forceful sermon against actors was given by John Stockwood, the divine at St. Paul's Cross in 1578. The civic authorities joined hands with the Church. The Lord Mayor in the mid-sixteenth century seems to have held actors responsible for disturbance and administrative problems during theatrical performances. In fact, no theatre was allowed to be built in the London city proper. They were all situated on the other side of the Thames. Actors were looked down upon as parasites living on the society. In 1559 the Lord Mayor succeeded in getting the power to censure the theatre and in 1597 he got Sunday performances banned.[1] He would have abolished the theatre altogether had his efforts not been thwarted by the intervention of the Court giving royal patents to the Master of Revels in 1559 to stage plays. The efforts of the clergy and the civic authorities were reinforced by the puritan pampheleteers. The most important pamphlet against the theatre was written by Phillip Stubbs, a puritan social reformer, who in *The Anatomie of Abuses* (1583) includes a chapter on the wickedness of stage plays and interludes. He ascribes the immorality of the plays to their origin in the Devil and Vice in the miracles and the moralities. He maintains that "to worship devils and betray Christ" can seldom be a blessing to a society. When Queen Henrietta Maria invited French actresses in 1628 to perform at Blackfriars, Prynne, a puritan enthusiast denounced them as 'notorious whores' in his *Histriomastix*. A glimpse into these attacks on the theatre reveals that the puritans aimed at abolishing it by condemning the actors' profession itself. Seldom did they attack any playwright for such faults before the Restoration.

As soon as the theatres reopened after 1660, the puritans availed themselves of the opportunity to attack it. Richard Flecknoe, a divine, in *A Short Discourse of the English Stage* (1664) referred to artistic flaws in Shakespeare, Jonson, Beaumont and Fletcher. He found Fletcher's plays replete with obscenity[2] and averred that the theatre should be a school setting examples of good language and behaviour. The end of comedy to him was to render folly ridiculous, vice odious and virtue and nobleness amiable. He appears to be the first moral critic of theatre after the Restoration. He set the ball rolling. Soon sporadic attacks followed from various quarters till a massive assault was made on the theatre, particularly on its immoral comedies.[3]

John Evelyn (1620-1706), the diarist, complained against the stage in a letter saying:

> Plays are now with us become a licentious excess, and a vice, and need severe censors that should look as well to their morality, as to their lines and numbers.[4]

Gilbert Burnet (1643-1715) in *History of My Own Times*, published posthumously in 1723, called the plays "the greatest debauchers of the nation"[5] while Samuel Wesley maintained that "our infamous theatres seem to have done more mischief than Hobbes himself to the faith and morals of the nation".[4] Besides these protests from various quarters, the poets and playwrights too appear to have felt the pulse of the society. Shadwell, a man outside the orbit of the Small wits – in the preface to *The Sullen Lovers* (1668) denounced contemporary comedies as "an indecent way of writing" and protested against the debauched witty couple with "a Swearing, Drinking, Whoring Ruffian for a Lover", and "an impudent Tomrig" for mistress, who talked of nothing but "bawdy and profaneness."[7] Wycherley too felt the ladies' dissatisfaction with *The Country Wife*, especially with its china scene, as is evidenced from his dedication to *The Plain Dealer* (1676) which says that the former play had "lost its reputation with the ladies of stricter lives in the play house."[8] The prologue to Edward Ravenscroft's *Dame Dobson* (1684) shows how some ladies protested in the theatre itself when his *London Cuckolds* (1681) was staged. "They made visits with design to cry it down".[9] Robert Gould in *The Play House, A Satire* (1689) points at the faults of the plays thus:

> In short, our plays are now so loosely writ;
> They've neither manners, modesty, or wit.
> How can these things to our instruction lead
> Which are unchaste to see, a crime to read?[10]

James Wright, in *The Country Conversations* (1694), echoes Shadwell when he arraigns the libertine characters addicted to drinking and whoring.[11] Sir Richard Blackmore, in the preface to *Prince Arthur* (1695), considers "Instruction of Our Minds and Regulation of Our Manners" as the end of poetry.[12] He avers that the business of Comedy is "to render Vice ridiculous and to expose it to Public Derision and Contempt."[13] He accuses the stage poets of "runining the End of their Art" and bringing "Vice and Corruption of Manners into Esteem and Reputation" by portraying the "fine gentleman" as "a derider of Religion," an idler dissolved in luxury, abandoned to his pleasures and extravagance, and a debaucher of women.[14] A similar fault is found with the portraits of women who are presented as disobedient, immodest and profane in their speeches and so expert in intrigues and assignations that they marry the debauched heroes without the consent of their parents. Blackmore refers to the abuse of the churchmen by the stage poets who not only ridicule the character and profession of the clergy by presenting them as pimps, blockheads and hypocrites but also bring the very order into contempt.[15] Besides the absue of the clergy, he finds that in the plays the citizens' wives are encouraged to infidelity and the citizens themselves are presented as the most contemptible creatures who deserve to be cuckolded by the fine gentlemen. Thus Richard Blackmore launches a moral criticism of the contemporary dramatists but, strangely enough, without giving any specific example from their plays. Profanity in plays is also objected to by the anonymous writer of *A Reflection on Our Modern Poesie* (1695) in the following words:

> See, now the poet's bold in mischief grown,
> And turns to ridicule the sacred gown.[16]

However, the most scathing and systematic attack on the stage came from Jeremy Collier (1650-1726) in his pamphlet *A Short*

View of Immorality and Profaneness of the English Stage (1698) which was published at a moment when dissatisfaction with the English stage was at its height. Collier had been outlawed for absolving and blessing two conspirators connected with the assassination plot against King William and was condemned by the Whig politicians as well as by the bishop of his church. In order "to divert attention from his own offences to some other victim of popular indignation",[17] Collier chose a convenient target and plunged into the battle against the theatre. Within a short time he got his reward. William III pardoned him, the bishops thanked him and a large section of the people applauded him.

His work, containing six chapters, deals with the immodesty of the theatre of his time, its encouragement of immorality and its absue of the clergy. The final chapter recounts general denunciatory pronouncements against the theatre from the classical times. His thorough acquaintance with the contemporary plays helped him in exposing the immorality and lewdness of the Restoration Comedy. He holds "the stage poets responsible for debauching the Age" and taking "Virtue and Regularity for great enemies".[18] He attacks "Mr. Dryden, and his Fraternity", for having "debauched the Town and Poyson [sic] their pleasures to an unusual Degree".[19]

The opening sentence of his pamphlet – "The business of plays is to recommend virtue, and discountenance vice..." (p. 1) – has been inscribed on the banner of the supporters of art for morality's sake since the ancient times. Collier attacks the stage poets on the ground that the fundamental purpose of literature is to teach morality *i.e.* to instruct by example. Besides citing Horace, Aristotle, Rapin, etc. he quotes Jonson to stress that it is the duty of a comic poet to imitate justice and to instruct. He attacks Dryden for believing that the chief end of comedy is "divertisement and delight"[20] contending that "to make *Delight* the main business of *Comedy* is an unreasonable and dangerous principle" for it "opens the way to all licentiousness and confounds the distinction between Mirth and Madness." (p. 161)

Collier further attacks the Restoration dramatists for violating the principle of poetic justice. Accusing them, especially Dryden and Vanbrugh, for making debauched persons their protagonists, he says that they "generally make them rich and happy, and reward them with their own Desire" (p. 148) *i.e.* with the ladies of birth and fortune. Talking of vice and virtue he argues: "When vice is varnished over the pleasure, and comes in the Shape of Convenience, the case grows somewhat dangerous; for then the Fancy may be gain'd and the Guards corrupted, and Reason suborn'd against itself". He asks "To what purpose is Vice thus prefer'd, thus ornamented and caress'd, unless for Imitation?" (p. 141)

Collier cities instances of immorality and profaneness from the comedies of the Restoration playwrights. He accuses them of stooping so low as to picture the immoral and foul characters and their lives instead of presenting examples of good moral behaviour. He says that debauchery is depicted on the stage among the "fine gentlemen" who are a mixture of smut and profanity. Wildblood, Bellmour, Dorimant and Young Fashion are mentioned as instances of "whoring, swearing, smutty atheistical" men, who burlesque the Bible, swear upon all occasions, talk smut to ladies, speak ill of their friends behind their backs and betray their interests (pp. 255-56). Another fault that Collier finds in the comedies is that such libertines are presented as heroes and are unduly rewarded. Dryden's 'fine gentlemen', Wildblood and Bellamy, are debauchees who ridicule marriage and treat women with no regard and are allowed "to take leave (of the audience) without the least appearance of Reformation" (p. 152). He attacks Wycherley for making Horner a principal character and for showing Harcourt as being false to his friend, Sparkish, who uses him kindly. He refers to Freeman (*The Plain Dealer*) who talks coarsely, cheats a widow, debauches her son and makes him undutiful. According to Collier, lewdness and immorality are present in Congreve's characters as well; in Bellmour (*The Old Bachelor*), in Mellefont (*The Double Dealer*) who asks Careless to debauch Lady Plyant in order to meet Cynthia, and in Valentine (*Love for Love*) who is a "compound of vice, a prodigal debauchee, unnaturally profance, obscene, saucy and undutiful" (p. 143). The same fault is found in Vanbrugh; Young Fashion (*The Relapse*) is censured as a prodigal rake who is given by the playwright a "second fortune, only for debauching away his first" (p. 277). Fault is also found with Constant (*The Provok'd Wife*) who swears at length, solicites Lady Brute, boastfully talks of his lewdness and prefers debauchery to marriage. He calls matrimony "a corrupted soil, Ill Nature,

Avarice, Sloth....are all its products" and is deplored for treating whoring as "a brave and generous agent" (p. 143). The heroines too, the fine ladies of these comedies, Collier finds, tailored on the same pattern, for they appear rude to elders, profane and smutty in speech and lewd in conduct. They are depicted as dishonourable ladies. Bawds and whores populate these comedies and the heroines lack in modesty. He cites the instances of Lady Fidget, Widow Blackacre, Olivia, Jacinta, Elvira, Lady Plyant etc. Ladies in *The Country Wife*, especially Lady Fidget and Margery Pinchwife, are shockingly immoral. Laetitia Fondlewife (*The Old Bachelor*) is adulterous, and almost all other ladies in this play are "foul and nauseous". *The Double Dealer* presents three ladies out of four as regular whores. Angelica, the heroine in *Love for Love*, is immodest and talks saucity to her uncle, whereas Prue is coarse and immodest and silly. Collier lashes out at Jacinta's impudence, smutty speeches and lewd conduct in *An Evening's Love*. Hoyden in Vanbrugh's *The Relapse* appears silly and coarse. She does not seem to fit the description of a great heiress. Berinthia helps Worthy to corrupt the virtuous heroine, Amanda, and herself indulges in debauchery. She abuses her whole sex and defines the "Faculties of women as hypocrisy, invention, deceit, flattery, mischief and lying" (p. 173). Collier cites Rymer and attacks Vanbrugh for violating the rules of decorum. He avers that "An impudent woman is fit only to be kicked and expos'd in Comedy" (p. 220). Belinda in *The Provok'd Wife* confesses to Lady Brute her inclination for a gallant (p. 146) and the latter, in order to reform her husband, encourages her lover, Constant, to cuckold her husband. Collier refers to Terence who has regard for women and their modesty, and says that even depraved women of Terence are better behaved than the women of quality in the comedy of his time. Collier cites examples from Plautus to show that he gave no such liberties to women except to the slaves and low persons (p. 15).

Another fault that Collier finds in the comedies of his time is the distorted representation of the people of quality who are not given their due regard. "What necessity", he demands, "is there to kick the Coronets about the stage, and to make a Man a Lord only in order to make him a Coxcomb?" (pp. 175-76). Lord Froth in *The Double Dealer* is called a coxcomb, and the true characters of Lord Plausible in *The Plain Dealer* and of Lord Foplington in *The Relapse* are revealed in their names. Questioning the propriety of the jests upon titles, he asks, "Can't they lash the Vice without pointing upon Quality?" (p. 17). He asserts that one must represent characters by types; and the type of a Lord is not a fool but truly a nobleman. He objects to the language that the nobles like Sir Tunbelly, Manly, and etc., are made to speak. Sir Tunbelly's speech and conduct do not become a justice. He thinks that the playwrights overlook honour and custom when they make a lord a fool (p. 176).

Besides having lewd and debauched characters, Collier finds the plays replete with smuttiness of expression. Smut is spoken by most of these characters without any regard for their age, sex and status or for other characters. Thus he finds these characters opposite of the norms that are expected of poetry and ceremony. He believes that nothing should be put into the mouths of persons which disagrees with any of these circumstances. "It is not enough", he says; "to say a witty thing, unless it be spoken by a likely person upon a proper occasion" (pp. 165). This impropriety of manners is found in witty repartee, railing and in similitudes pivoting on sex. Smut is often expressed in *double entendre*, and sometimes smutty songs too are there. Referring to such a song in *Love for Love* Collier says, "Music doubles the force of mischief" (p. 24). In his view, Queen Leonora in *The Spanish Friar* talks of her love in an unbecoming manner, and its men and women of quality speak smut amongst themselves without any restraint. Besides, the prologues and epilogues of the plays, where the author directly speaks to the audience, appear equally objectionable to Collier as there too he finds a good deal of obscenity. In support of this he refers to the prologues of *The Country Wife* and *The Old Bachelor* which have much of sexual promiscuity and to the preface to *An Evening's Love* which defends the profligacy of its hero (p. 147). Much more shocking for Collier was the fact that these prologues and epilogues were often spoken by young girls; for example, the lasciviously witty prologue to *The Relapse* which was spoken by a young girl, Miss Cross. Collier even considered the prologue to *An Evening's Love* unprintable on account of its overt obscenity.

Another grave charge levelled by Collier against Restoration Comic writers is that of profaneness. He ironically says that cursing and swearing are the valuable qualities of their libertine heroes who swear and do so on all occasions for business as well as for exercise. Their speechers are full of 'Hell', 'devils', 'diseases', 'plagues', etc. Collier thinks that swearing and cursing inflame guilt and are ungentlemanly and unchristian especially before the ladies in the audience as well as on the stage. Collier finds the plays profane for their abuse of such grave things as religion and holy scriptures (p. 60). Wildblood, the hero of *An Evening's Love*, sports with the scriptural figures and explains the devil's sneezing as caused by being out of the fire. Jacinta swears by Mahomat, makes a jest upon Hell and chides her cousin Theodosia for praying in the church in her company. Heaven, Paradise, godliness are demeaned in ordinary conversation and obscene thoughts are expressed in scriptural phrases (p. 78). Collier also refers to Bellmour's jests upon Heaven in Congreve's *The Old Bachelor* and also to the use of a priest's disguise to solicit Laetitia Fondlewife who, in her turn, is equally profane in her apology to her husband. Fondlewife, though a puritan, is shown abusing the text of the scriptures. Giving further example, Collier mentions *The Double Dealer* where Lady Plyant swears by Jesus before uttering a smutty expression and Lady Froth burlesques the holy text and calls Jehu a hackney coachman. *Love for Love* is charged with a similar fault; Scandal equates adultery with martyrdom when he tells Mrs. Foresight that he will die a martyr rather than disclaim his passion. Foresight and Angelica play with the names of Soloman and Samson (p. 80). Sir Paul Plyant, besides, ridicules Providence and Cynthia jests upon the holy text to mock matrimony. Collier finds Vanbrugh's comedies also replete with profaneness. Razer, a railleur in *The Provok'd Wife* talks in scriptural phrases to deliver an obscene thought and calls Lady Fanciful "the woman that tempted" him. Lord Foplington of *The Relapse* considers "Sunday a vile day" and Young Fashion defies conscience. Worthy applies words from the holy text for cuckolding and Amanda does not hesitate to abuse herself and the scriptures too when she says, "What slippery stuff men are composed of? And it was the woman's Rib, that they were form'd of". Berinthia too is equally lewd and profane.

Another sort of profanity that Collier finds is the abuse of the clergy. He argues that railing at the clergy is a certain sign of depravity (p. 10). Instances are cited where the priests are made to act as pimps, to counterfeit and to swear and where their profession is railed at as much as their dress. Their holy garb is often described as a cloak most suitable for covering carnal knavery, greed and lust. To disguise as a priest, for the purpose of jesting or gulling, Collier considers both gross and clumsy. He cites examples from Homer and Virgil, the great masters of propriety, to show that they never mention priests without some marks of respect (p. 114). He attributes this fault of the 'contemporary playwrights' to their inclination to nonsense and dullness (p. 109). Singling out Dryden's *The Spanish Friar,* he refers to Friar Dominic, who acts as a pimp for Lorenzo. Lorenzo shows contempt for the Friar when he says, "He (Dominic) preaches against sin. Why? Because he gets by it" (p. 23) and that his job it is "to be impudent and swear devoutly" (p. 37). The Friar is treated with disrespect and on one occasion is unceremoniously pushed off the stage. Thus Collier makes his point that Dryden rails at the very profession of a clergyman. Wycherley's Horner ridicules the churchman when he calls him the greatest atheist and gives Harcourt the robe of a Divine (p. 3). Maskwell (*The Double Dealer*) ridiculous the clerical profession when he talks about Saygrace, the corrupt priest, thus: "There must be a levite in the case, for without one of them have a finger in't no plot, public or private, can expect to prosper" (p. 71). As a matter of fact, Saygrace is always ready to play with sermons for money. "I would break off in the middle of sermon, to do you pleasure", he assures Maskwell. Vanbrugh too is attacked by Collier for ridiculing the clergy. John Brute (*The Provok'd Wife*) not only puts on the garment of a clergyman, but drinks, swears and is rowdy. Bull, the Chaplain in *The Relapse, blesses* Young Fashion and Hoydon in a smutty and profane language (p. 71), advocates bigamy, ridicules the church and conscience. He is lewd and is given to wine and whores and allows himself to be treated with contempt by other characters. Thus Collier maintains that the comedies of his time are profane as well as immoral.

Attacks on the theatre had both perceptible and imperceptible impact on it. Actors and playwrights could hardly escape being affected by such a vigorous campaign. On May 12, 1698 Congreve and D'Urfey were brought before the Middlesex Magistrate for writing immoral comedies like *The Double Dealer* and *Don Quixote* respectively.[21] London grand jury tried to prohibit posting of play bills about the city. In 1699 the Court of Common Pleas prosecuted several players for profanity (p. 169). The same year King William renewed the licensing orders and asked the Master of the Revels to exercise his authority to scrutinise the plays. The Court of King's Bench prosecuted Thomas Betterton, Thomas Duggett, John Bowman, Elizabeth Barry, Underhill etc. for indulging in acts of profanity on the stage.[22] Queen Anne, soon after ascending the throne, forbade people unconnected with the theatre to enter the green room and the stage. She disallowed women to come in masks to the theatres.[23] Congreve and Vanbrugh were authorised on December 14, 1705 to inspect plays for checking abuses and immoralities.[24] But the Societies of Reformation of Manners approached the Bishop of Canterbury against Vanbrugh's appointment as a Manager of the New Theatre at the Haymarket for he had "debauched the stage to a degree beyond the looseness of all times".[25]

Different playwrights reacted differently to these attacks. Some of them poured forth pamphlets in their defence. Others improved and altered the objectionable passage in their plays. Dryden, in the preface to *The Fables*, admitted his faults but not without asserting that Collier had perverted his "meaning by his glosses", and interpreted his words into "blasphemy".[26] He, rather insolently, defended the *double entendre* in his plays saying:

> What needs Paraphrase on what we mean
> We were at worst but Wanton, he's Obscene.
> I, nor my Fellows, nor myself Excuse;
> But Love's the Subject of the Comic Muse.[27]

Congreve's *Amendments of Mr. Collier's Imperfect Citations* and *A Defense of Dramatic Poetry* published in 1698 are examples of the kind of pamphlets that were written by playwrights in their defence. Admitting some of his 'errors', Congreve stressed that Collier's citations from the plays are the "demonstrations of his own impurity" and are "tainted by his breath". Congreve added that Collier "in the higher vigour of his obscenity first commits a rape upon my words, and then arraigns 'em of immodesty".[28] Defending his characters, he says, "Men are to be laughed out of their vices in comedy... As vicious people are made ashamed of their Follies or Faults, by seeing them expos'd in a ridiculous manner, so are the good people at once both warn'd and diverted at their Expense".[29] Vanbrugh's *A Short Vindication of the Relapse* and *The Provok'd Wife* of the same year tried to absolve the theatre of the charges levelled by Collier. He held that the stage was "a glass for the World to view itself in". He added, "People ought therefore to see themselves as they are; if it makes their faces too fair, they won't know they are dirty, and by consequence will neglect to wash 'em".[30] He claimed that Collier had failed to appreciate satire in *The Relapse* in which Lord Foppington is "design'd for their contempt and not for their imitation".[31] Dennis, a contemporary critic and playwright, finding that Collier's design was against the stage as such, published in 1698 *The Usefulness of the Stage to the Happiness of Mankind, to Government and to Religion* in which he defended the stage saying that "drama arouses the rational passions and is therefore useful to the happiness of mankind". He added that "pleasure in itself is not an evil and mankind lives for happiness"[32] Thomas D'Urfey, in the preface to his comedy *The Campaigners*, complained that Collier not only denounced all drama but also attributed the vices of the characters to the authors who had created them.[33]

The fact is that with all their refutations and denials in pamphlets, prologues and epilogues, the playwrights did realize that their plays had much in them that could disturb a serious and sober reader and, therefore, needed revisions and alterations. Among such authors was Congreve who deleted several phrases from *The Double Dealer*, *The Mourning Bride* and *Love for Love*. He avoided the charge of blasphemy by replacing a particularly offensive Valentine speech of *Love for Love*. He wrote *The Way of the World* as a kind of a reply to Collier. Vanbrugh rewrote a scene in *The Provok'd Wife* in which Sir John Brute, drunk and disguised as a parson, uses lewd words. He referred to this change in the prologue:

> This Play took Birth from Principles of Truth,
> To make Amends for Errors past, of Youth.
> A Bard, that's now no more, in riper Days,
> Conscious review'd the Licence of his Plays.[34]

Referring to Collier, Vanbrugh in the prologue to *The False Friend* (1702) says:

> To gain your Favour, we your Rules Obey,
> And treat you with a Moral Piece to Day;
> So Moral, we're afraid 't will Damn the Play.[35]

Farquhar in the preface to *The Twin-Rivals* says that "there is an Advantage to be made sometimes of the Advice of an Enemy, and, the only way to disappoint his Designs, is to improve upon his invective, and to make the stage flourish by virtue of that Satyr, by which he thought to suppress it".[36] In the preface to *The Constant Couple*, the author pays tribute to priestly critics like Collier as well as shows deference to the changing tastes when he says, "I have not displeas'd the Ladies, nor offended the clergy, both which are now pleased to say, that a Comedy may be diverting without Smut or Profaneness".[37]

The prologues, epilogues and prefaces written in the closing years of the seventeenth century frequently express the playwrights' desire to reform comedies. Still, the old repertory remained unchanged in the theatres. Vanbrugh and Congreve remained the heroes of the theatre, for the great masters had either died or ceased writing comedies, or there was hardly any genius born to cater to the changing popular taste. Old plays went on being staged; *Love for Love* was revived at Drury Lane, and was acted several nights. *The Mourning Bride* drew large audiences whenever it was staged and so did *The Country Wife*. *Don Quixote* was performed successfully twenty-five years after Collier's attack. But, at the same time, there were playwrights like Cibber, Vanbrugh, Farquhar and Steele who were willing to accommodate the changing moods and demands of the audience that was gradually becoming more interested in morality, sanity and refinement of feeling.

NOTES

1. This regulation was not strictly enforced.
2. *The Cambridge History of English Literature*, eds., A.W. Ward and A.R. Waller (Cambridge, 1966), II, p. 94.
3. *The Cambridge History of English Literature*, Vol. II, p. 96.
4. Krutch, *op. cit.*, p. 93.
5. *Ibid.*

6. *Ibid.*, p. 94.
7. *Works,* II, p. 11.
8. Krutch, *op. cit.*, p. 167.
9. J.H. Smith, "Shadwell, the ladies and the change," *Modern Philology* (1948), Vol. 46, p. 31.
10. Krutch, *op. cit.*, p. 96.
11. Hume, *op. cit.*, p. 40.
12. Spingarn, *op. cit.*, Vol. III. p. 227.
13. *Ibid.*, p. 228
14. *Ibid.*, pp. 229-30.
15. *Ibid.*, II, p. 231.
16. A. Beljame, *Men of Letters and the English Public in the Eighteenth Century, 1660-1744* (London, 1948), p. 97.
17. G.F. Lamb, "A Short View of Jeremy Collier", *English* VII (1949), pp. 270-75.
18. J. Collier, *A Short View of Immorality and Profaneness of the English Stage* (New York, 1974), p. 2. Hence onwards references to this pamphlet will be given in parenthesis after each quotation.
19. *Ibid.*, p. 182.
20. Spingarn, *op. cit.*, I, p. 263. (Dryden, *Essay of Dramatic Poesy*).
21. Krutch, *op. cit.*, pp. 168-69.
22. Krutch, *op. cit.*, p. 170.
23. Baljame, *op. cit.*, p. 241.
24. Krutch, *op. cit.*, p.186.
25. *Ibid.*, p. 187.
26. D.C. Taylor, *William Congreve* (London, 1963), p. 122.
27. *The Revels History of Drama*, ed. T.W. Craik (London 1976), V, p. 51.
28. Taylor, *op. cit.*, pp. 131-32.
29. Krutch, *op. cit.*, p. 42.
30. *The Works of Sir John Vanbrugh,* ed. W.C. Ward (London, 1893), pp. 396-97.
31. Beljame, *op. cit.*, p. 242.
32. Krutch, *op. cit.*, p. 136.
33. Taylor, *op. cit.*, p. 129.
34. Beljame, *op. cit.*, p. 242.
35. *Ibid.*, II, p. 9.
36. *The Works of George Farquhar*, ed. Charles Stonehill (London, 1930), I, p. 286.
37. *Works*, I, p. 86.

SECTION II

THE PLAYWRIGHTS

4

Cibber and His Contemporaries

George Farquhar, Sir John Vanbrugh, Colley Cibber, etc., were some of the playwrights who wrote plays in the late seventeenth and early eighteenth centuries. George Farquhar (1678-1707) started as an actor in Dublin but turned playwright when the comedian Robert Wilks asked him to write for the stage.[1] His first comedy *Love and a Bottle* (1698) appeared at a time when Collier's *Short View* had just been published, and the environment was infused with the spirit of reform. The play, accordingly, contains traces of these changes in people's outlook. The chief character of the play, Roebuck is described as a gentleman of wild roving temper. He, like the Restoration rakes, indulges in fashionable vices. He lands in London penniless and is supported by his friend Lovewell who supplies him with money and clothes. Thereupon, he again plunges into love and bottle. From Ireland he has been followed by Leanthe, Lovewell's sister, a virtuous young lady who dons male guise to be with him and who, after a lot of confusion, marries him and converts him to a chaste life. Mrs. Trudge, Roebuck's cast-off mistress, is palmed off, along with his twin bastards, to the fop, Mockmode, and is compensated with the money the reformed rake gets from him. The sub-plot is about Lovewell, as sober and modest lover of Lucinda who has become haughty after inheriting fortune. She misunderstands Lovewell's assistance to Mrs. Trudge and agrees to marry Roebuck. Leanthe intervenes at this juncture, helping her brother in winning over Lucinda. Roebuck is the embodiment of vices and follies for which Collier attacked the Restoration comedy, *viz.*, smuttiness of expression, swearing, profaneness, abuse of the clergy, etc. Leanthe finds Roebuck's follies and vices founded on 'the principles of honour' and she is confident that she "may reclaim him" though he is "wild as wind and unconfined as air". (V.iii). Roebuck is contrasted with Lovewell whose sobriety in love is clearly stated in his speech to Roebuck:

> Those idle hours which you misspend with lewd sophisticated wenches must be dedicated to the innocent and charming conversation of your virtuous mistress; by which mean, the most exorbitant debaucheries, Drinking and Whoring will be retrench'd."
> (I,i)

Smutty jests full of *double entendre* are uttered by Roebuck and also by Lucinda's maid, Pindaress. Still the play emphsises moral values. There is also some incidental satire on the army and the clergy. A disbanded crippled soldier, who after five years of active service has been a beggar for fifteen years, is made to utter the following lines:

> A Captain will say Damme, and give one sixe pence; and a Parson shall Whine out 'God bless me,' and give me a farthing. (I, i)

Farquhar's next play, *The Constant Couple* (1699), exposes the double standard of the conventional morality that allows men the privilege of being whore masters but condemns the whores. The action of the play pivots on Lady Lurewell, a lady of jilting temper which is the result of her resentment against menfolk for having been debauched fifteen years earlier by an unknown Oxford student. Her love for that dissembler has turned to a hatred of the whole sex. She takes revenge on those villains who make attempts on her honour and spares persons of just and honourable intentions by telling them about her resolution never to marry. The way she treates her lovers is quite humorous for she sets them against each other, keeping herself "still virtuous". She believes in the maxim:

> "... though a woman swear, forswear, lie, dissemble, back-bite, be proud, vain, malicious, anything, if she secures the main chance, she's still virtuous.
> (I, ii)

Colonel Standard, one of her admirers, turns out to be her seducer. To test her fideltiy he gives to Sir Harry the ring he had received from her at the time of his parting. The misunderstanding is cleared up in due course of time and she is finally united with her old lover. In Lady Lurewell, Farquhar has created a complex personality, a heroine of sentimental type,[2] with the understandable desire to punish men who believe in and practice different moral codes of chastity. The secondary plot concerns Sir Harry Wildair who considers pursuit of pleasure as the end of life and, therefore, has several love intrigues. Vizard, in order to keep him off Lady Lurewell, introduces him to his cousin Angelica who is described as a whore simply to get him interested in her. After several vain attempts to win her and on learning that she is a lady of virtue and fortune, he proposes marriage to her. His conversion from a licentious fop to a virtuous person is an indirect tribute to women of virtue like Angelica. Vizard, who switches letters to give the impression that Angelica is a whore, is punished by Lady Lurewell by being put in her closet with Smuggler who is disguised as a woman. Clincher Senior and Clincher Junior, former an affected beau and elder brother, the latter a country-bred younger brother afford a contrast between the town affectations and the country innocence. Clincher Senior's preparations for his trip to the Jubilee in Rome, *viz.*, taking pocket pistols against bravadoes and swimming girdle in case of a shipwreck, the farcical scene created by his changing of his coat with a porter's which leads to much misunderstanding, constitute low comedy stuff. His planned trip to the Jubilee provokes Colonel Standard to attack the fools like him thus:

> The travel of such Fools as you doubly injures our Country; you expose our Native Follies, which Ridicules us among Strangers; and return fraught only with their Vices, which you vend here for Fashionable Gallantary.
> (V, ii)

The play is full of satire on women of quality, university education and the army. Reformers too are satirised through Smuggler and Vizard who give financial help to the Collierites to attack the 'Sinful theatre' and though outwardly religious, are, at core, full of lust and greed. Criticism of French morals is found in Sir Harry's use of French for conveying his indecent suggestions to Lurewell and Angelica. Aristocracy is satirised in the play for its peculiar vices, *viz.*, whoring, jilting, duelling, hypocrisy of men and immodesty of women. Virtue and constancy are duly acclaimed. Angelica is "Beauty without Art! Virtue without Pride! and Love without Ceremony," (V, ii). The supposed jilt turns out to be a virtuous lady. Sir Harry Wildair, the "Joy of the playhouse and life of the

Park," a perfect whoremaster is reformed by Angelica's virtue and Colonel Standard, a true lover and a victim of circumstances, is deservedly rewarded. Emphasis is shifted from the common theme of frailty of women to the power of their virtue, as Sir Harry puts it at the end of the play:

> Right Madam, vertue [sic] flows freer from Imitation, than compulsion, of which, Colonel, your conversion and Mine are just Examples. (V, iii)

In spite of the presence of Restoration ingredients here and there, the spirit of the comedy at core is coloured with moral objectives claimed in the prologue:

> The ladies safe may smile; for here's no slandar,
> No Smut, no lewd-tongued Beau, no *double entendre*.[3]

The sequel to the play, *Sir Harry Wildair* portrays Lady Lurewell as a lady of loose morals. She gambles, squanders her fortune at the basset table and has a series of lovers though she has a devoted husband in Colonel Standard. She has intrigues with Sir Harry Wildair too but is scared of his wife's supposed ghost and is reformed with the help of the French Marquis. She tries to blackmail Wildair but her plan backfires. The male lead character is not Colonel Standard, a sober, virtuous passive man, but Sir Harry Wildair, around whom another plot of gallantry is woven. The sprightly Sir Harry of the previous comedy is presented as a devoted husband. He becomes vengeful when his wife shows some lack of faith in him. Consequently, he leaves her but she follows him and causes the news of her death to be conveyed to him. When Sir Harry learns of her (supposed) death and the Pope's refusal to bury her body in the Catholic graveyard he grows so vengeful that he whores the whole nunnery and finally directs his revenge upon Lady Lurewell who has a cynical attitude towards marriage. Angelica, true to her love, follows him and appears twice as her own ghost to reclaim her husband and to reform the erring wife, Lady Lurewell. The moral is aptly given in the words of Colonel Standard who says:

> The Gospel drives the Matrimonial Nail, and the law clinches it so very hard that to draw again wou'd tear the work to pieces. (I, i)

The play ends with due regard shown to marriage ties and extolling of virtue and constancy. Aping of French fashions is satirised through the ridiculous character of the French Marquis and Sir Harry's love for French foppery.

For his next comedy, *The Twin Rivals* (1702), Farquhar used a Restoration motif: a penniless younger brother, Benjamin Wou'dbe, who has been disinherited for villainy towards his elder twin-brother, Hermes Wou'dbe. In order to usurp the estate, he, with the help of the midwife, Mandrake, and his father's steward, spreads the rumour of his brother's death in his absence, leading to the arrest of his elder brother after his return from the travel. Truth prevails in the end as one of the hired witnesses turns out to be Teague, the faithful servant of the elder brother. A letter from Benjamin Wou'dbe, applauding the midwife's perjury further exposes him. The seconday plot concerns Elder the sober Constance and a gay couple in Truman and Aurelia. Richmore, a Restoration rake, has already debauched an innocent girl, Clelia who never appears on the stage, and makes an unsuccessful attempt at kidnapping Aurelia on whom he has his lustful designs. Truman happens to be near the place of her captivity and rescues her and reforms Richmore by his example. Richmore is made to marry his cast-off mistress, Clelia, and the playwright succeeds in bringing in poetic justice. In this play it is not the virtue of a woman but that of a true gentleman that causes the rake's conversion. The hero and other virtuous characters are rewarded with the hands of ladies of virtue and fortune while the villainous young Wou'dbe is exposed. The play ends with the maxim:

> Fortune must yield, Would Men but act like me,
> Chase a brave Friend as partner of your Breast,
> Be active when your Right is in contest;
> Be true to love, and Fate will do the rest. (V, v).

Farquhar's next comedy *The Recruiting Officer* (1706) focuses on the military life – the dishonest enlisting of the recruits, immorality of officers, canting, drinking and whoring sergeants. The plot is concerned with Captain Plume who raises the recruits by wooing women and recruiting their brothers and friends. Kite, the sergent, makes the people drunk and then enlists them. The title character, Captain Plume, is a rake who has discarded Molly with his child, entices Rose to recruit her brothers and lover and tries to win the favours of the virtuous Sylvia. For the love of him, Sylvia enlists herself in Plume's service as his servant but when she finds him flirting with Rose, she makes use of her disguise to lure Rose away from him. There is another love plot, between Melinda, a woman who grows haughty after inheriting a fortune and Worthy, an honest gentleman who finally wins her over. The most comic characters are Kite who pretends to be a conjurer, Brazen, a boastful rival to Plume as a Recruiting Officer, Justice Balance and Bullock. Brazen keeps the action of the play going with his sprightliness. The play depicts a pleasant picture of the country with all the Restoration characteristics with the contemporary mode of army recruitment as its main subject. Rightly does Farquhar dedicate the play to the armymen quartered at Wrekin.[4] Farquhar's last comedy, *The Beaux Stratagem* (1707), has the Restoration stock characters of gallants in Aimwell and Archer, the two friends with the latter acting as a 'servant' to the former who himself is a younger brother and is out to seek fortune. Aimwell passes as his elder brother Lord Aimwell and wins the love of Dorinda. Feigning madness, he is received into the house by the lady (Dorinda) with so much sympathy and sincerity that he feels obliged to reveal his true estate to her. Thereupon she accepts him for his 'matchless honesty', and Providence, through Lord Aimwell's death, rewards him with his brother's estate and title as well. The other love intrigue which touches upon marital incompatibility concerns Mrs. Sullen, and her husband Squire Sullen, an ill-matched couple. Dissatisfied with the ill-treatment of her husband, Mrs. Sullen encourages Archer in his love for her. Archer, hidden in Mrs. Sullen's closet, tries to vanquish her in the most straightfoward scene in the Restoration strain. He, however, is prevented from accomplishing his designs when burglars break into the lady's house at the crucial moment. Aimwell and Archer represent London while Lady Bountiful, Squire Sullen's mother, a benevolent old civil country gentlewoman that cures all her neighbours of all their 'Distempers' but fails to see her son's distemper, represents the Litchfield gentry. Archer's rivals, Foigard and Bellair, exhibiting French manners, represent the army; and Gibbert and his friends, the highwaymen; the demure Boniface, the innkeeper and the sophisticated Cherry, his charming daughter, represent small trades people. Amongst this host of characters is the most prominent one, Mrs. Sullen, the afore-mentioned abused wife who tries to awaken her husband's love by arousing his jealousy. She, failing in her efforts, is forced to seek separation which her husband is too willing to let her have. After this, she is received by Archer and the play concludes with the remark:

> Both happy in their several states we find,
> Those parted by consent and those conjoined
>
> (V, v)

On the whole, the comedies of Farquhar continue the Restoration trend in presenting its stock characters and their licentious life but their cast is genuinely satirical. Farquhar aimed at reforming the people of their follies through his comedies and tried to make them submit to the discipline of love, virtue and good sense. The vices he satirises are the usual ones, *viz.*, drinking, gaming, whoring, etc. His heroes, as Otto Hallbauer, a German scholar, who wrote his criticism of Farquhar in 1880, aptly maintains, have "every taking quality, are Good hearted fellows at the bottom, they are wanton sensualists, but without cynical self-complacency; they would on no account, wrong a person, and relish no enjoyment by great exertions".[5] His heroines are young, difficult ladies, who are virtuous even in the worst of circumstances and who succeed in converting the heroes to their views. There are no love chases or wit-battles but gaiety of the plays is maintained by the display of the sprightly struggle of the lovers. The scenes of all his comedies shift from London to the countryside and thus have the freshness of its cool breeze. The main recurring theme of his comedies is, of course, love, but love not as a mere game, but as genuine and commendable passion. Farquhar's treatment of sexual relationship has a touch of modernity in it as he presents it as a healthy and lasting relationship between the two sexes. Marriage is presented as a union of two lovers who, after wedding, remain true to each other. In respect of two incompatible temperaments, Farquhar suggests divorce or separation through mutual consent. Treatment of such an important aspect of man-woman relationship was generally avoided by the Restoration playwrights. Farquhar gives a new message through his comic material which explicate his views on the end of comedy. In *A Discourse Upon Comedy* he reiterates that "to make the moral instructive" the story must be "diverting"[6] and in this Farquhar has shown his prowess.

Sir John Vanbrugh (1664-1726), Cibber's close contemporary wrote his masterpiece, *The Relapse* (1696) as a sequel to Cibber's *Love's Last Shift* (1696). The main plot takes Cibber's reformed hero, Loveless, and his virtuous wife, Amanda, as his lead characters. He puts the reformed hero in town where, in the face of its temptations, he almost at once relapses into his old rakishness. While he has an intrigue with his wife's widowed cousin, the wife's virtue is put to test by Worthy who tries to molest her forcibly. Amanda is strong enough to resist him and manages to keep herself virtuous both in thought and in conduct. Rather, she converts her would-be seducer to virtue. Clearly, Vanbrugh wanted to make her act as his protagonist to hammer the moral home. This moral plot runs parallel to a stock Restoration plot pivoting on fortune hunting. It concerns two brothers. The elder brother, Lord Foppington, a foolish fop of immortal fame, is a selfish creature who refuses to help even his younger brother, Young Fashion. The younger brother, failing in his attempt to get monetary help from him, tricks him off his betrothed, Hoyden, and her fortune. Hoyden is a stupid country girl, confined into her house by her strict father; but she is eager to escape into the free life of London. Her father, Sir Tunbelly Clumsey, a Jonsonian character, is too clumsy to arrange a match for his daughter and to see through Young Fashion's ruse and impersonation. This clownish country justice is gulled by his daughter and Young Fashion who get married without his consent. To crown this set of comic figures is the fop, Lord Foppington, who is infused with ridiculously aristocratic pretensions. He links the two plots, on the one hand by trying to make love to Amanda, and on the other by indirectly goading Young Fashion into fortune-hunting by denying pecuniary help to him. Lord Foppington, the accomplished town fop and Tunbelly Clumsey, the accomplished country fool are juxtaposed as two caricatures of town *versus* country extremes.[7] Young Fashion is sympathetically drawn, for, in spite of being an impoverished younger brother, he has qualms of conscience before he actually plays the trick of impersonating his brother. But his inner voice is subdued due to the hard-heartedness of his elder brother. The play marks a great advance in treating the problem of marital incompatibility with a commonsense approach unlike the cynical one of the Restoration comedy. The new approach is that incompatibility occasioned by the frailty of human nature can be removed, and adjustment between the spouses can be achieved. This is exemplified in the Loveless-Amanda case. Another case of marital incompatibility is that of Berinthia, a woman of quality and wit who loves town life, and her husband who hates everything associated with the town. Consequently, Berinthia leaves her husband and comes to Amanda's house where she finds Loveless ready to play gallant to her. The Loveless-Berinthia scene gives Amanda an opportunity to question the prevalent double standards of morality which allow men to have love affairs but require women to be chaste and faithful even with the most unhappy marital relationship. This makes chaste Amanda encourage Worthy only to cure her husband's relapse into vice through jealousy.

The problem of ill-matched couples is again subjected to a thorough examination in Vanbrugh's next comedy, *The Provok'd Wife*, produced in 1697. Here the ill-matched couple are victims of marriage of convenience. The lead character, Sir John Brute, is a typical Restoration rake having a cynical attitude toward marriage. His brutish character is reflected in his coming home drunk and filthy and suspecting his wife of being unfaithful to him. Lady Brute had married Sir John for his money although she was in love with Constant. After marriage she shuns her lover, but the husband's brutality and the double moral standards not only drive her into the arms of her lover but also make her justify adultery which, however, she does not translate into action. The husband gets jealous of finding his wife with her lover and, quite unexpectedly, tries to reform himself in order to win her back. The play has also a romantic sub-plot in which, Belinda, Lady Brute's niece, decides to marry Heartfree, a penniless younger brother she is in love with.

Vanbrugh's next comedy, *the False Friend* (1702) is derived from the French translation of a Spanish play *Le Traître Puni* by Le Sage. The plot concerns the love of the honest and innocent Don Guzman for his neighbour Leonora, the daughter of Don Felix, who has arranged her marriage with Don Pedro. Don John the jealous false confidant of Guzman attempts Leonora's rape by hiding himself in her room. His purpose is defeated by Leonora's shouting which brings Guzman to her rescue. Darkness contributes to confusion and Don John accuses Guzman of trying to rape Leonora who is shocked to find her lover as one of her would-be ravishers. Angry Don Pedro tries to kill Don Guzman but by mistake kills Don John who confesses to his offence in his dying moments. In the meantime, Don Pedro, who comes to know of the love between Don Guzman and Leonora, receives the news that his father is dying. He resigns his betrothed to do his filial duty. Thus, eventually, the sincere lovers are rewarded with success in their affairs and the villain is punished. The play has a number of basically good characters, such as, Don Pedro who is a paragon of filial duty and sensibility. In respect of parental authority he tells Leonora, "where a father chooses, a daughter may with modesty approve" (I, i). Another 'good' character is Don Guzman, a true lover facing all sorts of obstacles in his way. He is one who would not even think of taking any undue advantage of a woman in distress. Like him, Leonora is also of modest nature totally different from the gay heroines of Restoration Comedy. She is a young lady with a strict regard for the conventional morality. She is always willing to subordinate her love to her filial duty. The servants in the play are also different from the cunning servants of Restoration comedy who always had their eyes on money. Only one of them, Jacinta, Leonora's maid, makes some lewd statements – such as when she asks Don Guzman to "attack a maid gently, a wife warmly, and be rugged with a widow" (IV, i). But such instances are rare. On the whole, the play is deliberately a moral one wholly in accord with the assurance given to the reformers in the prologue:

> To gain your favours, we your rules obey,
> And treat you with a moral piece today;
> So moral, we're afraid 't will damn the play.[8]

Vanbrugh's next comedy *Confederacy* (1705) is an adaptation of a French play, *Lest Bourgeoises a la mode* of Dancourt. It is about the wives of two wealthy citizens of London – Gripe's wife, Clarissa, an extravagant luxury-loving woman and great admirer of quality, and Moneytrap's wife, Araminta, of the same humour. They plan to trick their husbands to obtain money to indulge in the fashionable vice of gambling. Their husbands are ready to pay off their gambling debts but show amorous inclinations for each other's wives. When all of them come together they realise their faults. The play ends with an epilogue in which, in a non-serious vein, women are exhorted to join hands with one another to achieve supremacy over their husbands. The sub-plot is concerned with the fortune-hunting Dick Amlet, a gamester, passing himself upon the town as a gentleman and trying to win Corinna, Gripe's daughter by his first wife. To live up to his assumed status, and to make presents to his beloved, he steals the diamond necklace of Clarissa which she had pawned with his mother. Dick is a 'rogue', a liar and a cheat who extracts money even from his mother. His cunning schoolmate, Brass, is made to pass for his valet. Dick Amlet courts Corinna through Brass who gains access to her house through Clarissa's maid, Flippanta. Corinna, who has been brought up under the strict discipline of Gripe and is not allowed to commerce with Clarissa or Flippanta, is clever enough to gull him and elope with Dick. They are caught and Dick is charged with stealing Clarissa's diamond necklace. Mrs. Amlet proudly offers her ten thousand pounds, a house and a farm to her son and Corinna adds her share. The play has clever servants as manipulators in both the plots. Flippanta sets Gripe and his wife aquarelling and collects as much money as she can from both. She is impudent as well as lewd in her conversation with Corinna. Her partner, Brass, extracts money not only from Gripe but from Dick also by blackmailing him with a threat to crush his hopes in love and forture. Clarissa is very vividly drawn after the fashionable women of the gentry. She finds a husband "the dullest theme" and loves a coach and a ride. She presents her philosophy of life in the following words:

> What signifies beauty and wit, when one does not jilt the men and abuse the women? (I, iii)

She is fond of gambling, and has set a 'basset-table' in her own house by assuring her husband that this will restrict her going out. She is extravagant just for the sake of being extravagant and all the money her husband gives her to pay her gambling debts is again spent in gaming. There is a significant difference between her attitude towards her husband and that of Araminta who hates her husband for his being miserly and old. Her husband's complaint against her is that she is a spendthrift and is never sober. Vanbrugh criticizes the citizens not because they are 'cits' but because they copy the gentry, as harshly as he does the people of quality for their follies. Corinna's character seems to have been drawn by Vanbrugh with understanding, for any girl of sixteen brought up between two extremes, *i.e.*, the restrictive authority of a strict father and her tutors, and the waywardness of a 'libertine' step-mother, will inevitably follow the course of her own choice. She marries a 'rogue' yet she does it quite nobly; she offers him her share of fortune and seeks his mother's blessings.

Vanbrugh left an incomplete comedy *A Journey to London* (1697) which was later completed and partly re-written by Cibber under the title *The Provok'd Husband*. The main plot of this play concerns a country bumpkin, Sir Francis Headpiece, who has come to the metropolis as a Member of Parliament. The clash of temperament is seen in Headpiece's being thrifty and his domineering wife, Clarissa's fondness for the extravagant ways of the ladies of quality. Besides, their son, who is dull and stupid and is fascinated by the first pretty girl he meets, is juxtaposed with his sister who is pert and forward and always thinking of her shape, clothes and suitors. As soon as they arrive in London, they are cheated of their belongings but their craze of the town life blinds them to the loss. Vanbrugh is as critical of the extravagance, gaming etc. of the fashionable London and its gulls and cheats as he is of the country bumpkins. The underplot treats the theme of marital incompatibility presented through Lord Loverule and his wife, Lady Arabella, a sophisticated woman of London. While the husband, as his name suggests, is a lover of orderly life, his wife is fond of gaming, gambling and late hours which the husband objects to. She is also contrasted with her friend, Clarinda, who has a sober approach to life. The unfinished play concludes with Lord Loverule's determination to offer his erring wife one last chance to renounce her obnoxious way of life with the alternative of final separation. How Vanbrugh would have completed the play can be guessed from Lord Loverule's words:

> Physick's lothsome thing, till we find it gives us health; and then we are thankful to those who made us take it. Perhaps she may do so by me....

Vanbrugh's treatment of marital incompatibiliy and his commonsense approach to problems cropping up in such situations show his genuine concern for conjugal felicity. Another problem that conditioned his approach and portrayal of characters is that of the younger brother, treated elaborately in his play *The Relapse*, in Cibber's *Love's Last Shift* and in Farquhar's *The Twin Rivals*. Vanbrugh's treatment of this problem has a touch of originality about it as the Restoration dramatists hardly ever introduced it in their comedies. He has imbued the younger brothers with 'scruples' and 'qualms' of conscience when they are forced to resort to tricks. This highlights the indifferent and callous attitude of the elder brothers towards their fates. Another notable feature of his comedies is that one finds in them a shift from the town people to the country gentry and from the courtiers to the citizens who are rather sympathetically portrayed. He, however, objects to their copying of the manners of the Court people. Vanbrugh has presented positive norms in his sensible couples like Belinda and Heartfree in *The Provok'd Wife* and Clarinda and Sir Charles in *A Journey to London*. These pairs of lovers demonstrate a commonsense attitude towards love, marriage and conjugal relations. Vanbrugh, no doubt, is a thoroughly down-to-earth playwright who tries to instruct the audience in such serious matters. His approach in this respect is stated by Sir Charles of *A Journey to London* when he says:

> 'Tis true; for bad examples (if they are bad enough) give us a useful reflections as good ones do.
>
> (II, i)

Colley Cibber (1671-1757) bridged the gap between the Restoration comedy of the Court Wits and the moral comedy of Sir Richard Steele. He got associated with the theatre as an apprentice actor when he was hardly nineteen, and was the actor-manager of the Drury Lane Theatre from 1711 to 1731. He wrote comedies for the audiences he was well acquainted with. On the one hand his plays appealed to the "kind city gentlemen of the middle rows,"[9] on the other hand he also catered to the lewd tastes of a part of his audience by depicting characters, situations and using language reminiscent of the Restoration comedy. In the dedication to *Lady's Last Stake*, he makes a favourable reference to Collier and says that "a play, without a just moral, is a poor and trivial undertaking."[10] He also expresses his belief in entertainment as one of the ends of comedy. Later, in the prologue to *The Rival Fools*, he addresses the audience in the following words:

> Not Set-dress Morals form'd in't to affright you,
> From the dear modish Follies, that delight you,
> Unblushing Vice in fairest Forms may Lurk,
> Nor fear the Smart of our keen Satire's jerk.[11]

Thus, as stated earlier, he caters to the moral sense of the citizens as well as the lewd tastes of the people in the gallery. For this he usually presents two sets of characters, the basically good ones and the stock characters of the Restoration Comedy, *viz.*, the rakes, the fops,[12] the fools, the wits, gay and witty heroines, and the women of quality, etc. The main plot of his first comedy, *Love's Last Shift* (1696), deals with the theme of marital reconciliation. It concerns the rake hero, Loveless, who, soon after his marriage, leaves his wife to lead the life of a libertine on the continent and now returns to England penniless after ten years of absence. His friend, Younger Worthy, tells him of his wife's supposed death and tricks him into 'seducing' her. Shocked by the horror and remorse at his perjured love and guilt, he is reformed and starts extolling the blessings of virutous love. One of the sub-plots (with which the sub-title is related) concerns Sir Novelty Fashion, a coxcomb and a direct successor to Sir Fopling Flutter. He has a mistress in Mrs. Flareit and is an unsuccessful suitor to Hillaria who encourages him in order to rouse the jealousy of her lover, Elder Worthy. Mrs. Flareit, tempestuously vengeful, runs at him with a sword. Somehow he manages to free himself of her by paying her off. There is yet another sub-plot which hinges on fortune-hunting and is concerned with the two Worthy brothers who assist each other in their love pursuits. Sir William Wisewood, uncle of Hillaria, has planned a marriage between his daughter Narcissa and Elder Worthy because he is a man of fortune. Young Worthy wishes to marry Narcissa because of her wealth. He gains access to her on the pretext of wooing his beloved for his elder brother. He succeeds in marrying Narcissa and helps his brother in marrying his own beloved, Hillaria, and at the same time, brings about reconciliation between Loveless and Amanda. Along with the supposed seduction of Amanda by Loveless, there is the real seduction of her maid by Snap, the servant of Loveless who is forced to marry her by his master. The play is marked for its depiction of the fifth-act reformation of the rake, Loveless. Young Worthy ascribes Loveless's licentiousness to "an affectation of being fashionably vicious" (I, i). The masque at the end celebrating the glory of conjugal love is indicative of the moral tone of the play.

The plot of Cibber's next comedy, *The Woman's Wit* (1697), is concerned with the love intrigues of two friends, Lord Lovemore and Longville who love Leonora and Olivia, a coquette and a virtuous lady respectively. Longville, a faithful friend, cannot stand Lord Lovemore's wasting his love on a woman who trifles with him. Besides, he finds that his sister Emilia is in love with his friend. Therefoe, he plans to woo Leonora in Lord Lovemore's presence and thus to expose her as a flirt. Leonora, a woman of extraordinary wit, turns the tables upon Longville and discovers him to Lord Lovemore as his secret rival which results in challenges and drawing of swords. In order to prove his innocence, Longville pledges never to meet Leonora but she uses the trick of the mask and makes him talk to her which adds to the misunderstanding between the friends. He is accused of the breach of faith by his friend, his sister and even by his beloved, Olivia. This compels him to show them Olivia's letter of assignation which Leonora has tampered with, changing the place of the meeting. His innocence is established and his constancy in love and friendship is rewarded. The sub-plot concerns a typical Restoration satirical character, Mrs. Manlove, Leonora's mother, an amorous old lady with her designs on Longville. The comedy offers another amorous old person, Major Rakish, who is in love with Leonora's mother. There is also Dominic who tries to entice Master Jonny, Mrs. Manlove's son, to become a monk so that he may have no wish to assert his claim on her fortune. As the plot unfolds the characters of the vicious and the fashionable 'fools' are exposed and the virtuous characters of Emilia and Olivia get their due recognition. The former is really a 'sentimental' character who endeavours to establish her brother's innocence and suppress her love for Lord Lovemore. Nothing but "tears of Madness" can express her joy on finding innocence, constant love and friendship rewarded.

Cibber's another sentimental comedy with a moralising tone, *Love Makes a Man* (1701) deals with the pros and cons of marriage of convenience and the marriage based on love. The main plot relates the affairs of two brothers, Carlos and Clodio. The former, an elder brother, is an Oxford scholar "weddéd to books" while the latter is a fashionable fop. Their father has arranged a marriage between one of his sons with Angelina, the daughter of his rich neighbour, Charine. Since the elder brother shows his aversion to matrimony, the younger one is to marry her. However, the former's faithful servant and his uncle succeed in arousing his interest in the girl. He also refuses to renounce his claim to ancestral property in favour of his younger brother. Discarding his 'humour', Carlos proposes to Angelina who is quite willing to accept him. On failing in their attempts to marry with their parent's consent they elope to Lisbon. There they get separated by accident and it is only after several complications that they succeed in their goal. The sub-plot concerns Clodio, who after reaching Lisbon in pursuit of his brother, supposedly kills the boastful Don Duart and hides himself in the house of the victim's sister, Elvira, a virtuous lady. She saves him but gets him arrested when she learns that he is the 'murderer' of her brother. Don Duart appears at the right moment to prevent the arrest and Clodio is rewarded with the hand of Elvira by her brother for curing him of his 'evil humour'. There is another episode in which Louisa, a woman of quality and affectation, becomes jealous on finding Carlos, her lover, in the company of Angelina. Don Manual, a sincere lover of Louisa, had at one stage rescued Angelina who, in return, agrees to stay at Louisa's place to promote his love for her. Hearing the woeful tale of the two lovers, Carlos and Angelina, Louisa is cured of her jealousy and love for Don Manual is kindled in her heart. Louisa, a Restoration type, is ridiculed and reformed, while Angelina, a virtuous lady, is made to triumph over all obstacles to show the victory of virtue and good sense over intrigue and folly. The play is marked by its being heavily inclined towards morality and sentimentality. Religion and virtue receive their due tribute, true love is rewarded and foppery and affectation are fully exposed.

Cibber's next Comedy *She Wou'd and She Wou'd Not* (1702) deals with the love intrigues of Octavio, a young gentleman. Don Manual, the father of his beloved, Rosara, had earlier agreed to have him as his son-in-law but has now changed his mind. Instead, he has contracted a marriage alliance of his daughter with Don Phillip, the son of a rich friend of his. Octavio's sister, Hippolita, loves Don Phillip but dissembles and gives him a "cold reception" so much so that Phillip, despairing of her love, agrees to his father's arrangement for him. The quadrangle of lovers meets at Don Manual's house; Don Phillip coming to marry his daughter according to the settlement, Hippolita, reaching there impersonating Don Phillip in order to woo Rosara and Octavio, in response to a letter from Rosara. Hippolita easily deceives Rosara's father for she has with her Don Phillip's letters of credentials which she had got stolen from his servant's possession. The real Don Phillip, not received warmly by Rosara's father, takes Octavio, disguised as a friar, as his rival. Octavio discards his disguise when he confronts Rosara's father. This only serves to increase the antagonism of Don Manual towards him. In the meantime, a person known to Don Phillip identifies the real suitor. Hippolita, convinced of Don Phillip's love for her, reveals herself as required by the situation. Everyone is taken by surprise, including her brother who is happy to know that she really loves his friend, Don Phillip. At the end, love and friendship are suitably rewarded. Hippolita, like the typical intelligent heroines of Restoration comedy, is sprightly and witty, while Rosara is a sentimental woman of suffering nature.

Cibber's next major comedy *The Careless Husband* (1704), treats the theme of marital incompatibility in the main plot which is concerned with Sir Charles Easy's love intrigues with Lady Graveairs and Mrs. Edging, his wife's waiting-woman. Lady Easy, the wronged wife, is tolerant beyond limits, for she fears that a display of "jealousy may tease him to a fix'd aversion" (I, i). Later, when she finds her husband and Mrs. Edging asleep together she thinks of "waking" him in his guilt but, true to her character as a devoted and faithful wife, she takes her scarf and covers his head lest he should catch cold. On waking up, he comprehends the whole situation and is filled with remorse. He is greatly impressed with his wife's love for him which has remained unabated in spite of his aberrations. The sub-plot concerns the wooing of the attractive coquette, Lady Betty Modish, by a worthy young noble, Lord Lovemore, a friend of Charles Easy. Lady Betty Modish, a sprightly woman of wit of the Restoration type, exhibits traditional reluctance to matrimony and unabashed pleasure in bestowing favours on a fop, Lord Foppington. She spurns her sober lover for his criticism of her conduct. Lord Lovemore, in order to arouse her jealousy, makes a show of love to another lady. His strategy succeeds when Lady Modish, realising her mistake, expresses her preference for her faithful lover. Lord Foppington, a typical vain and affected Restoration coxcomb, apes French pronunciation and, though already married, talks boastfully of his several amours. In the end he too realises his folly. Besides Charles Easy's repentance, Lady Betty's assurance of giving up flirtation to avoid giving Lord Lovemore any uneasiness and her begging pardon of Sir Foppington for taking undue freedom with him constitute the sentimental elements in the play.

Cibber's next comedy *The Lady's Last Stake* (1707) was a great success because of its stock Restoration characters, *viz*., a rakish hero, women of quality and an amorous old lady. The hero, Lord Wronglove, loves his wife dearly but finds her unconquerable. As a consequence he starts spending his time in pleasurable pursuits but this is resented by her. He, however, indulges in these activities more and more deliberately. This pushes the couple to the brink of separation but the timely arrival of their well-wisher, Sir Friendly Moral, brings about reconciliation between them through tears, apologies and pardons. Sir Moral advises her to "lure him home with soft affection" and the husband is asked to think of the "long-watched, restless hours she has already endured" (Act V) on account of his misdoings. The other plot of the play attacks the fashionable vice of gambling. Lady Gentle, of impregnable virtue and with a deep love for her husband, is addicted to card-playing. Lord George, in order to be considered a successful gallant, gambles with her and tries to seduce her. Lady Gentle reaches the point of staking her virtue but is saved by the timely intervention of Sir Moral and Lord George's beloved, Mrs. Conquest, who helps her with money and at the same time courts her in the disguise of a gentleman to wean her away from him. Lord George challenges Mrs. Conquest in her disguise, and wounds her but is amazed and overjoyed to discover her identity and her great love for him – in this way her constancy in love is duly rewarded. Double standards of behaviour between the sexes are condemned in the play. Cibber, trying to placate the critics of *The Careless Husband* who had judged Lady Easy as an insipid and poor-spirited character, has created in Lady Wronglove a virtuous character who is at the same time most spirited too. The husband-wife conflict in this play is not due to a clash of temperaments but is based on misunderstandings caused by the husband's resentment at what he considers to be undue interference in his affairs.

The Double Gallant (1707) presents humour characters besides Freeman Atall, a rakish hero of the Restoration descent and Sylvia, a sprightly young lady. He carries on his love intrigues by following the strategy of assuming different names to court different ladies. His libertine conduct, his attempt to gull his father, his figuring in closet scenes, his discomfiture when meeting the concerned ladies together constitute some interesting situations. The girl his father has chosen for him is none other than the one he loves, that is, Sylvia. The fact that he remains ignorant of this for long heightens the comic element in the play.[13] Another strand in the play concerns the marital discord between Sir Soloman Sadlife, a miserly merchant and his young and gamesome wife. He is a typical absurd Restoration figure ridiculed for his miserliness and his fear of being cuckolded. In a closet scene he is put in an extremely comic situation when in the darkness he is made to hold his wife's maid. In another situation he assists his wife in writing a love letter to her gallant, giving the impression as if it is from the maid. The play satirically presents the consequence of marriage-de-convenience, which are referred to by Lady Sadlife thus: "But consider, Sir, What a perpetual discord must a forc'd marriage probably produce" (I, i).

In *The Provok'd Husband* (1728) Cibber added sentiment to Vanbrugh's incomplete Comedy, *A Journey to London*, and emphasised the repentance and reformation of an erring wife.

On the whole, Cibber's plays present a fair number of virtuous characters who contend against distress and are finally rewarded. These characters, with their virtues and exemplary behaviour, reclaim those who have been erring. As Parnell says, his rakes and flirtatius ladies and, on rare occasions, lewd situations and dialogues were intended to please the low tastes of a part of his audience while the fifth-act reformation of erring characters was designed for those who believed in Christian morals.[14] The heroes and the heroines of his comedies profess true love and sincere friendship, and do not indulge usually in lewd talk or immoral actions. If actual seduction is presented it is mostly concerned with the servants or with a husband who mistakes his wife for another lady. There are rakes, libertines, fops, etc., but they either revert to virtue or are thoroughly exposed and ridiculed. The fair sex is treated with respect and there are hardly any whores or mistresses. Matrimony is given due regard, though rakes are there to flout it. The dialogues are coarsely witty as well as full of sententiae. Cibber became a trend setter[15] for presenting exemplary characters in pathetic situations and for showing the reformation of dissolute characters. The reformed rakes and erring women are basically good at heart and their licence and innocent freedoms are the mere veneer to conceal virtue and goodness which triumph over vice and roguery in the fifth-act. Cibber's plays are morality dramatised, presenting such problems as the evils of parental tyranny and marriage-de-convenience. In spite of abundant intrigue, the serious tone of the plays, the presence of exemplary characters wedded to the moral conduct, their sufferings bordering on the thresholds of tragedy and the unmistakable moral aim of the playwright win sympathy and applause of the audience. What Thomas Davies says in his *Dramatic Miscellanies* about Cibber's first comedy, is true of the rest of his comedies also:

> ....never were spectators more happy in easing their minds by uncommon and repeated plaudits and... honest tears.[16]

It is no wonder he ranks as a pioneer of sentimental comedy in the late seventeenth and early eighteenth century for it was he who opened up the path for Steele and others to follow and his own plays retained popularity for a fairly long time for that very reason.

NOTES

1. F.S. Boas, *An Introduction to Eighteenth Century Drama* (London, 1968) p. 32.
2. E. Bernbaum, *The Drama of Sensibility* (Massechusetts, 1958), p. 85.
3. *The Works of George Farquhar*, ed., Charles Stonehill (London, 1930), I, p. 87.
4. Farquhar was posted at Wrekin when he was in the army.
5. James, E. Nelson, *The Development of George Farquhar as a Comic Dramatist* (The Hague, 1972), p. 27.
6. *Works*, II, p. 338.
7. J.L. Loftis, *Comedy and Society from Congreve to Fielding* (California, 1959), p. 71.
8. *Works*, II, p. 9.

9. Epilogue to *Love's Last Shift* in *The Dramatic Works of Colley Cibber* (New York, 1966), I, p. 68.
10. *Ibid.*, p. 195.
11. *Ibid.*, II, p. 99.
12. Cibber often acted the roles of the fops.
13. The play bears resemblance with Steele's *The Lying Lover* (1703) and appears to have inspired Sheridan's *Rivals*.
14. Paul E. Parnell, "Equivocation in Cibber's *Love's Last Shift*," *Studies in Philology*, L, vii (1960), pp. 519-34.
15. Revel's History, V, p. 222.
16. Bernbaum, *op. cit.*, p. 1.

5

Steele's Comedies: *The Funeral*

Richard Steele's first stride towards making use of stage for moral reformation was his first Comedy *The Funeral* (1701). The theme of this play is the husband-wife relationship which was quite a familiar subject with the contemporary stage, specially in picturing the perfidy of a wife. Steele depicts a wife who is faithless to a loving and considerate husband. Lady Brumpton has already been secretly married to Cabinet and remarries Lord Brumpton only for the sake of his money. The honourable and gentle Lord Brumpton has fallen into the hands of this wicked schemer who, taking advantage of the eight year long absence of her stepson, Lord Hardy, persuades her husband to disinherit him so that she can acquire all his wealth. Lord Brumpton falls into a fit and is taken as dead, and when he regains his consciousness his faithful servant, Trusty, persuades him to take advantage of his seeming death to test his wife's fidelity. The ruse works. Lord Brumpton overhears his wife's conversation with her maid, Tattleaid, in which she exhibits her unseemly rejoicing over his supposed death, her machinations against her stepson and her intention to dispose of his wards, Lady Sharlot and Lady Harriot, profitably. She finally prepares herself for the funeral according to the fashionable conventions but finds that Lord Brumpton's coffin has been seized. This sends her post haste to Lord Hardy's lodging to which place it has been brought by Trim, Lord Hardy's servant. Lady Brumpton is shocked to find Lord Brumpton's ward, Sharlot, in the coffin in place of her husband's body. Her husband makes his appearance at this stage and all the remnants of his feelings for her are removed when he intercepts her letter to her brother asking him to commit rape upon Lady Sharlot. Moreover, Cabinet's confession that Lady Brumpton had been secretly married to him six months before her marriage to Lord Brumpton completes her exposure. Since her marriage with Lord Brumpton turns out to be an irregular one she loses her position as the wife of a lord as well as the money she had her eyes on.

Besides the main plot, there is a sub-plot consisting of two young loving couples. Lord Brumpton is guardian to two beautiful and virtuous young orphaned sisters, Lady Sharlot and Lady Harriot. After the supposed death of Lord Brumpton, his 'widow' has taken control of them and forbids them to commerce with Lord Hardy and his friend Campley, the young gentlemen they love respectively. The girls are imprisoned in Brumpton House with an old maid Mrs. Fardingale, who is more interested in singing and dancing than keeping a vigil over her charge. Campley comes disguised as the woman attendant of Mademoiselle D'Epingle and escapes with Harriot who, to disguise herself, puts on the dress of Madamoiselle D'Epingle. Lady Sharlot is handed over to Trusty who helps her to escape from the house. In accordance with Trusty's plan, she is put in the coffin that was supposed to carry the body of Lord Brumpton. Trim, Lord Hardy's servant storms the 'House' and rescues his mistress Mademoiselle D'Epingle. Finally all the three couples, including the servants, are united in the presence of Lord Brumpton.

That Steele felt agitated at the sight of vice in the world is evident from the concluding lines of the preface to the play where he defends his satire directed at Lady Brumpton who deserves full exposure and condemnation.[1] The preface expressly states Steele's moral commitment through the ridicule of other social vices, *i.e.*, the heartlessness of the undertakers, the hired mourners' grief, etc. which he presents at their basest, removed of all traces of humanity. Besides these scenes there are other satirical scenes interspersed in the serious plot, *viz.*, the recruiting scene, the ladies' visiting scene, Lady Brumpton's mourning over the dead squirrel, etc. The comic scenes include the ones showing the escape of Lady Sharlot and Lady Harriot, Campley's stealing into the house in a woman's guise, Mrs. Fardingale's unmusical singing, Trim's parodying the kitchen love-song, eavesdropping by Trusty and Lord Brumpton and the latter's appearance at the crucial moment to punish the guilty. These are some of the familiar farcical devices that have been used with adroitness. In spite of the comic and satirical scenes the play has melodramatic overtones because the hurdle in the lovers' path is not a foolish rival but a calculating villainess. Still the play ends as a comedy for the extreme ordeals faced by the 'good' characters while highlighting their virtuous qualities lead them to a happy and successful life which they richly deserve.

In the love plot, Lady Sharlot and Lady Harriot are drawn on two different patterns. Lady Sharlot represents the sober, mute and self-effacing platonic love of the heroic plays and Lady Harriot the gay, sprightly and flippant one of the Restoration Comedy. The former, though silent and sober, sees Lord Hardy's name in "Every line of the Book" that she happens to read. She is earnestly devoted to her man. Whereas Lady Harriot "delights in the vanity of being pursued with sighs, with flatteries, etc." (II, iii). She likes to be wooed and chased but looks at matrimony with pretended aversion. She finally emerges as a woman of good sense and reason as a result of the plain-speaking Campley's lecture on her flippant behaviour. Lady Sharlot inspires the dream of marital felicity while lady Harriot arouses a sense of pleasure in her lover. The characters of these two women were sketched by Steele to present in Lady Sharlot an embodiment of his own moral precepts for the sober middle class, and in Harriot, as some one who, besides offering a foil to Lady Sharlot, could be subjected to conversion; one who at heart adores virtue but needs some inducement to exhibit it.

Of the two lovers, Lord Hardy and his friend Campley, the former faces the threat of disinheritance. He is too good to devise any way out and, therefore, allows himself to be led and assisted by Campley and his servant, Trim. These lovers have nothing of the sex-oriented dialogue of the earlier comedy for they enshrine in themselves Steele's ideal of young gallants. No carefree love-game is to be indulged in by them for they are basically good and conscientious. In this respect Lord Hardy, in particular, anticipates Steele's exemplary hero, Bevil Junior of *The Conscious Lovers*. When he is seen in the Ladies' chamber, he is asked to hide in a closet. He refuses to do so and, unlike the Restoration gallant who used every possible means to escape from such situations, boldly faces his adversary, *i.e.*, Lady Brumpton. Campley, though more sprightly and spirited than Lord Hardy, is not a frivolous person. When Mademoisella D'Epingle asks Lady Harriot to change clothes in his presence, which the latter refuses to out of modesty, Campley approves of her conduct saying, "What a delicate Chastity she has" (III, iii). Campley, the gallant, is so attracted by her physical charms that he eagerly wishes to "fold" his "Arms about the waste [sic] of that Beauteous Struggling [sic]..." (II, ii) and employs all the stock tricks of the Restoration lovers. He chases her and scruples enough not to injure her sense of honour by behaving rudely. Instead, he acts as her mentor and makes her see reason and be aware of faults. Occasionally his head runs too much on the "Wedding-Night" and "Yielding Fair" to allow him to think seriously about the ensuing years of marital bliss, a flaw for which Lord Hardy chides him. But with all his light-hearted gaiety Campley is not a libertine of the Restoration comedy. He appreciates Lady Harriot's modesty, treats women with due regard and is on the whole a good-humoured and good-natured gentleman. To set off Lord Hardy as a platonic lover it was but incumbent on Steele to create some difference in the temperaments and attitudes of the two lovers. He had to make Campley a lover of earthly sort but he kept him free from dishonourable practices. Campley and Harriot's courtship remains innocent and amiable throughout the play.

Juxtaposed to this pair are Lady Sharlot and Lord Hardy. They belong to a different order of lovers. In the words of Lady Harriot they are of that "high Order of Lovers, who know none but Eloquent Silence, and can utter themselves only by a Gesture that speaks their Passion Inexpressible" (II, iii). They take the whole procedure earnestly. Steele has created in them two exemplary characters, two serious lovers of heroic drama type who are too shy to give expression to their genuine feelings. Their idealism is mocked by Harriot when she affirms that "we Gay People are more Sincere than you wise Folks. All your Life's an Art" (II, iii). They may dream of each other and speak in raptures when alone, but until the very climax they stutter when they come face to face. Lady Sharlot longs to meet the "excellent man", her lover, and he too keeps his mind "fixed on the Married state". What kind of conjugal life he is looking forward to, is expressed by him in the following words: "I expect my Felicity from Lady Sharlot, in her Freindship, her constancy, her Piety, her Household cares, her Maternal tenderness" (II, i). It is impossible for him to think "lightly of a woman" he loves with honour. These lovers of meditative type do ont open their hearts to each other. Instead of railing at each other and talking like the gay couples of Restoration comedy, they avoid love talk and, instead, talk about Lord Hardy's travels in Mantua, Italy and England. Lady Sharlot indirectly refers to "a lady in Italy" very like her in order to elicit proof of his love for herself. They supplement their mutual adoration with noble sentiments. Their style of courtship is totally different from that of the other team of lovers. Whereas Lord Hardy and Lady Sharlot are always sober and reserved, Campley and Harriot are all gaiety and relaxation. This gaiety, however, is not of an irresponsible kind; it is always accompanied by a certain degree of reason and restrain. Lady Harriot, frank and outspoken though she is, will obey reason as soon as she sees it. The portraits of the two ladies drawn by their respective lovers also differ – one is idealised and the other, of the conventional Restoration cast. This is shown in the following dialogue between them:

Lord Hardy: But my Ladly Sharlot, there's a Woman – So easily vertuous ! [sic] – so agreeably severe ! Her Motion so Unaffected, yet so Compos'd ! Lips breath [sic] nothing but Truth, Good sense, and Flowing wit.

Campley: Lady Harriot ! there's the Woman, such Life, such Spirit, such Warmth in her Eyes – Such a Lively Commanding Air in her Glances... her lips are made up of Gum, and Balm – There's something in that Dear Girl that fires my Blood....(II, i).

To their respective lovers, one is all virtue and the other all physical charms.

In Campley's character Steele has presented a model of male friendship. He is so noble that though he has come by fortune lately he is not vain about it. He stands by Lord Hardy through thick and thin. He helps his friend with a bill of three hundred pounds which he hands over to Trim in order to avoid making the receiver feel humiliated or the giver proud of it. His nobility is highlighted when he assigns no importance to his success in his own amours and places the interest of his friend at the top. He feels miserable at the sight of his friends' predicament. He is also ready to postpone his marriage till Lord Hardy's affairs are smoothened. His joy gets redoubled when he finds his friend's love duly rewarded. Their friendship is reciprocal as Lord Hardy also warmly shares the joys and sorrows of his friend. Whenever Campley errs Lord Hardy chides him mildly out of love for him to make him realise his mistake. The sprightly good-natured Campley and graceful gentle Lord Hardy present an amiable duo in the comedy. Their sunny friendship dispels the clouds of distress.[1] He extols his friendship with Lord Hardy in the following words : "Continue Heav'n, a grateful Heart to bless With Faith in Friendship, and in Love Success" (III, iii).

Steele has created another exemplary character in Trusty, the old servant of Lord Brumpton. Lord Brumpton and Lord Hardy find in him a friend, a counsellor and a well-wisher of the family. Trusty manipulates the exposure of Lady Brumpton with a sober dignified and benign steadfastness. He succeeds in making his master realise his mistake in being so attached to Lady Brumpton and also his folly in disinheriting his son. He persuades his master to do a bit of evesdropping to be convinced of his wife's villainy. It is through this clever, though unethical device that he succeeds in saving his master's family, property as well as his honour. Benevolence is ingrained in him. He had helped Lord Hardy eight years earlier with "fifty guineas" when the latter was turned out by his father at the instigation of his wicked wife. Trusty is still ready to offer him his life's savings. The emotional outpouring of his love for Lord Hardy in a sentimental scene in Act IV is an evidence of his affectionate attachment to his master's family and interests. He "indulges in telling fond tales that melt him and interrupt his story" and even "weeps" and "hugs" Lord Hardy. (IV, ii). He revels in the memories of the past and "confounds" Lordy Hardy with his tenderness and generosity. But this paragon of faithfulness is not a sentimental fool; he is practical too. He not only manipulates exposure and discomfuture of Lady Brumpton, whom he goes to the extent of calling a 'strumpet', but also protects Lady Sharlot from a possible rape by arranging her escape from Lady Brumpton's custody.

Trim is another basically good character with certain conventional traits of the Restoration Servants. He apes his master, Lord Hardy, in love as well as in military manoeuvre, which produces much comic fun. Likewise, his courting of Madam D'Epingle, mimicking her French manners and pronunciation, his kitchen parody of the tender love-song composed by Lord Hardy and singing it with a pair of tongs appropriate to his lady love, the kitchen maid, make him a comic character full of wit and fun. But at heart he is as sincere and faithful as Trusty is. It is sincerity towards Lord Hardy that prompts most of Trim's actions. Even his amour with the kitchen maid is designed to further the cause of his master. When he storms the Brumpton House it is to rescue his mistress as also to remove the coffin in which Lady Sharlot is concealed. He says, not totally in a vainglorious vein:

> When I rush on, sure none will dare stay;
> 'Tis Beauty calls, and glory leads the way.
> (IV, iii)

Besides serving as a manipulator in the love plot Trim provides good humour and mirth in the rescue and recruiting scenes through his deliberate parody of his master Lordy Hardy's style as a lover and a military man. Trim, through his tom-foolery burlesques the exemplary characters which is an evidence of Steele's inclination to blend old-styled laughter with new sober melodramatic strokes. Trim's swaggering like a general immediately after Lord Hardy's enlisting of soldiers; his bellowing of his kitchen parody accompanied by a pair of tongs immediately after Lord Hardy's tender love song and his "going to storm for his Statira" to save his mistress in a heroic manner produce the effect of a burlesque and thus provide good deal of fun and frolic. The credit for "many a comic strokes" in the play, much applauded by the audience, goes to the convivial Trim.

Lord Brumpton too is to be classed with the 'good' characters of the play. He no doubt acted foolishly when he fell into the trap of a designing and immoral woman. Yet even this foolish act reveals the very goodness of his character – a goodness that almost verges on weakness and is exploited by his worthless wife. Trusty describes him rightly though critically in these words:

> That very Lord — that very Lord Brumpton, The very Generous, Honest, and Good Lord Brumpton who spent his strong and ripe years, with Honour and Reputation, but in his Age of Decay declin'd from Virtue also. (I, i)

It is more of an eulogy than a pin-pionting of his folly for Trusty knows that his master is too simple minded to guage the true character and motives of the woman he was marrying. Taken in by her false appearance, he soon came to love her so sincerely that he refuses to believe what Trusty tells him about her. Hence it is that Trusty thinks of the ruse, his master's supposed death, to open his eyes in respect of her perfidious character. But even after her exposure the kind-hearted man cannot "hate that woman".

Juxtaposed to the good characters is the set of villainous ones comprising Lady Brumpton and Cabinet. Lady Brumpton is a hypocritical calculating woman who with the connivance of her real husband, Cabinet, marries Lord Brumpton after his first wife's death. With an eye on his wealth, she dissembles love and feigns fits which she considers "a mighty help in the Government of a Good natur'd Man" and succeeds in getting his son disinherited. On her husband's supposed death she gains control over his household and the two wards too. The very first scene of the play shows her mourning her husband's death in the fashionable style of the heartless woman who looked for nothing so eagerly as the "joys of the widowhood"(I, i). She is devoid of all feelings for Lord Brumpton and is immensely pleased at becoming the widow of a rich Lord. The first thing that she does in her new capacity is to imprison the two innocent wards of her husband and to try to get one of them dishonoured by her brother. Her concern for a suitable mourning dress and her grieving over the loss of her pet squirrel (more keenly felt than her husband's death) reveal her true character. She is happy when she learns that the 'corpse' of her husband has been forcibly carried away as this will save the charge of internment. Even when she is fully exposed, she does not admit defeat. She is undone finally when Cabinet's letter reveals that she had committed bigamy by marrying Lord Brumpton. She is chastised and dismissed with shame and thus poetic justice is meted out.[3] She remains an unrepentant sinner and accuses Cabinet for the failure of her designs.

In Cabinet, Steele has created a character who appears to be a villain but basically is a good person. Born a gentleman, brought up as an idle prodigal, debauched by luxury, he is led astray into an alliance with Lady Brumpton whom, it seems, he never loved.

His need for money makes him believe in her (false) promise that she would make him a partner in Lord Brumpton's estate after she becomes a widow. The first scene reveals him as a critic of the tricks of the undertaker which earns him the audience's sympathy. But his accepting some money from Campley and letting Mrs. Fardingale act as a watch over the young heroines expose the sordid side of his character. Occasionally the good peeps through the veneer and a morally weak Cabinet is seen frightened of the 'ghost' of Lord Brumpton which causes penitence in him.[4] He feels so much of contrition that he readily acknowledges a private marriage with Lady Brumpton and thus assists in the exposure of the wicked woman. Quite deservedly he is pardoned by all except his wife who promises to make his life a hell. In Cabinet's character Steele has illustrated a moral precept; good prevails over evil. Except for the expected mercenary gains, Cabinet shows least concern for the infidel woman or her affairs. He despises making a fortune from so "chimerical" an act as that of the undertaker's who suborns "others to do by Art, what they (the relatives of the dead) should be prompted to by Nature" (I, i). Steele lays emphasis on moral reformation and on basic goodness of man.

A number of professional people are satirised in the play, namely, Puzzle, the lawyer; Tom, his clerk; Sable, the undertaker; the unnamed grave-digger, Dr. Passport, the quack, and the clergy, etc. The army is satirised through the recruitment scene. The lawyers are represented by Puzzle and his nephew, Tom. Tom lacks professional training as well as aptitude but is inducted into the profession in order to keep the lawyer's job in the family. Puzzle's coaching of Tom is a reflection on the corruption prevailing in this profession. To Steele, who was beset with legal difficulties in his personal life, such lawyers who prostitute themselves for hire appear quite mean for their falsehood introduces injustice which is contrary to what they ought to stand for.[5] Puzzle is clever, false, avaricious and heedless to justice itself. To him to be a lawyer is to be learned in verbal jugglery, eloquent in gibberish and drawing the documents in such a manner that no one can make out anything. He teaches several tricks of the trade to Tom, particularly how to cheat his clients with the help of legal jargon. His maxim is "a True Lawyer never makes any man's Will but his own, and as the Priest of Old among us got near the Dying Man, and gave all to the Church, so now the Lawyer gives all to the Law" (I, i). Puzzle makes no appearance after this scene nor is he punished or exposed.[6] A reference to the professions that had become a nuisance for the society is made in the Preface of the play where it is said:

> Ridicule is partly levell'd at a sett [sic] of people who live in Impatient hope to see Us out of the World, a Flock of Ravens that attend this Numerous City for their Carkases [sic].[7]

This set comprises the undertaker and his hirelings, including a grave-digger who is also a body snatcher and who keeps his master informed of the impending deaths. Sable, the undertaker, calls his profession a solemn and magnificent job, which is to embalm the deceased and to satisfy the vanity of their survivors. He calls his income a hard earned money for he labours for others, keeps a record of all their lives, employs people for the same, and when they die it is he who arranges for their funerals, providing mourning furniture and even mourners. He complains that people are not grateful to him as they should be. Sable's defensive moves expose him as an animal of prey.[8] Another vulture like him is the grave-digger who is suborned by the undertaker as to the burying or removing of the dead-bodies from their graves. He not only removes the belongings of the deadbodies but even cuts their fingers to have their rings. Another professional class satirically noticed by Steele is that of the physicians. Dr. Passport, a quack, is supposed to have promised Sable some six or seven deaths with the help of his bogus medicines. He is in touch with the centres of medical profession such as the Royal College of Physicians in Warwick Lane and the Country Farm at Kensington Gravel-pits which in the eyes of Steele and other satirists of the period functioned not as seats of learning but as headquarters of quackery. These quacks are shown as being hands in glove with the undertaker and his team. They prepare people for untimely deaths and engage women like Goody Trash, to get information about impending deaths. Steele has satirised the complete network of the inhuman persons who wished for untimely death of the people in the prime of their lives.

Grief a-la-mode, a vice common among the quality, is satirised in a scene between Cabinet, Sable and Campley to highlight the lack of feeling for the dead on the part of the 'mourners' that are engaged "to grieve, lament and follow" the dead instead of their near relatives who are busy in more rewarding pursuits. The satire becomes more pointed in another scene (III, ii) in which Steele refers to the same subject, grief a-la-mode. The women who visit Lady Brumpton to condole with her spend their time in drinking and match-making, thus exposing the hypocrisy of their pretended sorrow. The mourning brings new opportunities to the widows like Lady Brumpton to put on the black because it suits their persons and is a good mask to their real intentions and feelings. Lady Brumpton is more concerned about a ride in a coach than about her dead husband. Her mourning for him is all false, just for the sake of appearances whereas her sorrow for a pet squirrel is ridiculously genuine.[9] Thus Steele has thrown light on women's affectations and their regard for appearance, a vice which he was never tired of attacking ruthlessly in his essays.[10]

The recruiting scene showing a medley of ill-clothed, unpaid, starving and ignorant recruits drawn from all walks of life, and Trim as their commander, was designed to reflect on the state of the army. These "ragged fellows" are ready to die for the king whom they have never seen and, as Trim says, are not to "enquire what you are going to do, 'tis only for us commanders" (IV, iii). These wretched men get enlisted as soldiers for reasons which are not in the least heroic or patriotic. Matchlock has been "whipt from constable to constable" for being poor and has finally joined Lord Hardy's troop to escape this inhuman treatment. Bumpkin, a perfect countryman, has been "cross'd in love" and therefore seeks refuge in the army. Trim tries to ape his master, Lord Hardy, and orders them like a "perfect general". The whole scene is permeated with genuine humour but at the centre of it, there is a great deal of realistic criticism of the army affairs based on Steele's personal experiences as an ensign. The manner in which Trim attacks the "House" to carry away what he supposes to be Lord Brumptons's corpse is just pure fun. Lord Hardy's approval of the poor, starving and disabled persons as recruits burlesques the contemporary methods of recruitment as well as the condition and quality of men enlisted to defend the honour of the country.

The recruits that are selected are social anamolies and most unfit for military service.[11] A hint to this situation can be seen in Lord Hardy's otherwise condescending comments:

> Well I've seen enough of 'em, if you mind your Affair, and Act like a wise General, these Fellows May do...Well Gentlemen do your Business Manfully and nothing shall be too good for you. (IV, iii).

As soon as the noble captain, Lord Hardy, leaves, Trim swaggers before the recruits with his hat on his stick adding last strokes to the comic scene.

General hostility towards France due to long period of war with it is reflected in the burlesque of the French manners as also in the attitude of the majority of characters towards France. Ragg joins Lord Hardy's troop in order to pull down the French. Mademoisella D'Epingle assumes a French name, apes the French manners and says: "all Women of Quality en France are Dress and Undress, [sic] by a Valet de-chamber...." (III, iii). These observations of Mademoiselle D'Epingle are designed to satirise and reflect on the French people and their manners.

To sum up, the play has a number of stock situations and devices used by the comic dramatists of the Restoration era. There is the perfidious wife, young lovers meeting and overcoming obstacles of the familiar sort, people aping foreign manners, servants copying the style and manners of their masters and being useful to them, use of disguise and closet scenes etc. Yet the play is cast in a different mould. It has a seriousness of purpose that was rarely the concern of the Restoration playwrights. Steele's first play can in fact be called a sermon on goodness of heart and virtue presented in the form of an entertaining story. Steele took great care in fixing the targets of his attack as well as in choosing the objects of his commendations. He has lashed out freely against the hypocritical pretensions and manners of the upper-class, the immorality of the widows, the unethical and even inhuman conduct of the representatives of the two noblest professions, medicine and law. At the same time, he spares himself no pain to bring out and extol the good that he found in human behaviour – the sincerity of friends, the devotion of faithful servants, and the nobility of virtuous love and its attending bliss of a happy married life. There is no licentiousness nor any cynical treatment of women, love and marriage. No bawdy can be seen anywhere in the play.[12] Moreover, the dialogue of the play is sprinkled with sententious pronouncements and moralisations by serious-minded virtuous characters. The expression of tender sentiments and distress over the suffering of the virutous add to the moral effect of the dialogue. Lord Brumpton's fortyone-line lecture on proper behaviour of young men is perfectly in tune with Steele's abiding interest in and concern for moral values. Too much of moralising and preaching normally affect the popularity and appeal of a comedy.[13] But Steele's play in spite of its rather excessive 'moral' contents, not only met with more than expected success when it was first staged but continued to be a favourite with the London play-goers for several years.[14] This goes to prove that the play has certain intrinsic qualities that appealed not only to his fellow soldiers[15] but to wider audience.[16]

According to A. Nicoll, *The Funeral* "shows the main tendencies of Steele's Art."[17] G. Salgado goes a step further when he says that the play "lays down the lines to be followed by comedy throughout most of the century: It's ranging of 'good' and 'bad' characters less severely regarded in Restoration Comedy and it's high-minded didacticism are typical."[18] As the first moral comedy, *The Funeral* was indeed a trend-setter for the Eighteenth Century Sentimental Comedy.

NOTES

1. In *The Spectator*, No. 286 he again condemns the conduct of such women which excites "Horror and Aversion".
2. Steele's idealization of friendly ties through Campley and Lord Hardy is a dramatic presentation of his own friendship with Addison.
3. So far as Lady Brumpton is concerned Steele's claim in *The Spectator*, No. 422 that satire is directed against the 'Fault' or 'Vice' only and not against the criminal is untenable.
4. It may be noted that in Restoration comedies a villainous character hardly ever shows any sign of repentance. Congreve's Maskwell (*The Double Dealer*) never reprents, nor does Lady Touchwood, who, for selfish interest is prepared to injure a virtuous character. In this respect also Steele's comedies are different from the Restoration Comedies.
5. These views are expressed by Steele in *The Spectator*, No. 370. Again in No. 372 he presents a group of lawyers who are expert in cheating and exploiting their clients.

6. Steele as a rule was more concerned with his exemplary characters than with subjecting bad characters to a ruthless treatment. Moreover, Steele believed in exposing and reforming the individual. The lawyer represents a class whose roguery is deep-rooted. His reformatiôn alone would not reform the class.
7. *Plays*, p. 19.
8. Sable's men are beaten up bu̇t he is neither exposed nor punished which Gildon, a contemporary critic found contrary to the law of comedy. But this also is due to the reason mentioned in the preceding note on lawyers.
9. Pope also refers to the affected sorrow of the widows in *The Rape of the Lock*. Fielding's Lady Booby of *Joseph Andrews* belongs to this class of widows.
10. In *The Tatler*, No. 74, Steele reiterates that a satirist has a right to lash 'the reigning Vices' so long as he kept to "the true spirit of Satyr", and particularly in "prosecution of such Persons" who are 'not to be reclaim'd by making 'em only ridiculous'.
11. This ..cruiting scene is similar to the one in George Farquhar's *The Recruiting Officer* where innocent poor country people and unhappy men are enlisted by Captain Plume. Steele's scene is drawn on his personal experience as a Captain. Steele himself was recruiting people of Essex and Norfolk in 1702 and the scene throws light on the corrupt methods of recruitment under the Enlisting Act which required a Captain of the army to recruit his own troops.
12 Campley's passionate speech to "fold these Arms about the Wast (sic) of that Beatiteous struggling — and at last yielding Fair." was modified by Steele later as he found it too suggestive.
13. F.W. Bateson finds the ending of the play "difficult to take seriously" on account of its somewhat forced inclusion of séntentiae and profuse emotions. *English Comis Drama,1700-50* (New York: Russell & Russell, 1963), p. 48.
14. According to Cibber, who played the role of Lord Hardy, the play was so successful that for once Mr. John Rich, the manager of the Drury Lane Theatre, paid the actors; nine days wages for one week's work. (*Apology*, p. 137).
15. This is mentioned in the Prologue, 11.26-27.
16. Steele shows his patriotic fervour repeatedly through his praise of the king as also through the eagerness of certain characters to fight for the defence and honour of the country. His patriotism is also expressed obliquely through the fun that is made of the French people and Frenchified English men and women.
17. A. Nicoll, *A History of Early Eighteenth Century Drama, 1770-1750* (Cambridge, 1966), p. 191.
18. G. Salgādo, *English Drama* (London, 1980), p. 163.

6

The Lying Lover

For his next play, *The Lying Lover: or, The Ladies' Friendship* (1703), Steele draws on Corneille's *Le Menteur* (1642) which, in turn, was based on Ruiz de Alacórn's *Le Verded Sospechosa.* In Corneille's play the liar of the title, Dorante, fabricates tales of his absurd exploits, succeeds for a while in fooling people but eventually gets caught in the web of his own lies. In the last Act, however, his virtuosity as a liar saves him from public embarrassment. Steele follows the model closely but the tone of his play is serious while that of *Le Menteur* is comic. In Alacórn's play the liar has to marry a girl other than the one he loves, while Corneille's Dorante does get the lady of his choice,[1] just as Steele's hero does.

The plot of *The Lying Lover* is typically a Restoration one: a hero facing the problem of wooing and winning a lady of great beauty and wealth. Young Bookwit, an Oxford Scholar just out of the University, is an expert liar. As soon as he comes to town he sets out on an 'expedition' of intrigues, and behaves like a town-bred fop. As convention requires the presence of a servant, Young Bookwit casts lots as to decide who, between the two, Bookwit himself and Latine, his friend and classmate, should play that role. It falls to Latine's lot to be his friend's attendant. Thus the foundation of the plot is laid on the comic selection of Latine as a servant. Young Bookwit dresses himself in a military garb to impress the fair sex with his supposed adventures, for he thinks that "the name of a soldier bids you better welcome (I, i). Besides, he decides to practise the philosophy he learnt at Oxford, *i.e.*, the government of passions" concentrating on "one dear passion, Love" and "to keep company with none but the ladies – bright ladies" (I, i). Fortune helps him soon and he sees Penelope and Victoria, women of wit, beauty and fortune. He tries to impress them with his "fine talk" of fields, travels and adventures. His lies impress them so much that they turn rivals in their love for the supposed soldier while he himself loves Victoria whose name he confuses with that of Penelope. Young Bookwit arouses the jealousy of another friend of his, Lovemore, who is in love with Penelope. When Young Bookwit's father, Old Bookwit, talks of settling him down by arranging his marriage with a beautiful daughter of a rich friend, Young Bookwit, in order to avoid the arranged marriage with a girl he had never seen, tells a lie that he was already married to Matilda, a girl he had met at Oxford. He does not know that his father wanted him to marry the very woman he was in love with, namely Victoria. Lovemore accuses Penelope of injuring him in her regard for another person. He also challenges his supposed rival, Young Bookwit, to a duel, who, in his drunkenness gets unduly provoked and wounds Lovemore fatally (so it seems to him). For this he is arrested. In the jail when he becomes sober a sense of guilt dawns on him and he repents the supposed death of his friend at his hand. His friend-*cum*-servant, Latine offers to take the blame of the supposed murder of Lovemore on himself but his offer is turned down by Young Bookwit. At this stage Lovemore who is still alive appears on the scene and overhears the above conversation. He is greatly impressed by their sincere friendship and pardons them. Frederick, Lovemore's friend from Oxford, tells Old Bookwit about Young Bookwit's lying about his marriage with a non-existent Matilda. The play has a happy ending as Penelope returns to her sincere lover, Lovemore, and Young Bookwit's marriage with Victoria is settled by his father.

The plot of the play is woven round Young Bookwit who is presented as a sparkish gentleman given to drinking and lying. Like his Restoration forbears, he is out in the town along with his friend to seek the "gay pursuits" the town would offer him. His words, "No, hang Business, – hang Care, let it live and prosper among Men" (I, i), echoes Bellmour's attitude to life (*The Old Bachelor*).[2] This aspect of his character is summed up by Steele in the preface to the play where he descirbes Young Bookwit as a character "without the Circumspection and good-sense which should always attend the Pleasures of the Gentleman." Steele has purposely introduced these weaknesses in Young Bookwit's character in order to provide a basis for his future repentance and reformation. Though the plot is woven round his skill of lying, the later half of the comedy concentrates on his drinking and duelling for which too he is to repent later on.

Young Bookwit's lying is the product of good humoured mirth without the slightest trace of malice in it. To him lying is "wit", "fable, allegory, fiction and hyperbole" and as to his lying to his mistress, he considers it not strange for " 'tis what all the lovers upón earth do" (I, i). He has the Restoration blood in his veins: he hates the marriage of convenience and prefers to marry the girl of his own choice. He does not care what means he adopts to achieve this end and is determined to "obtain the woman he pitches upon" no matter how "artfully" he may have to act. It is only in the fifth. Act that he discards the guise of the Restoration rake and emerges finally as a sentimental character repenting his defiance of his affectionate father and his cruelty to Lovemore and pledging to give up his habit of lying whose harmfulness he has himself experienced. Yet even in the earlier acts, he differs from the Restoration rakes. Though lying is an adventure to him and drinking a habit, his mental make-up is of a fabric superior to that of the Restoration sparks. He regards a woman with the eyes of a scholar, sees "her Mind by her Eye" and considers her "a Being between us and Angels", a person who gives "Awe and Invitation" (I, i). When he is in the company of women he shows moral rectitude in his speech and behaviour. He is full of regard for his father too. When his father grieves, his heart also bleeds. His lying to his father is not a gesture of impudence but an expression of good-humoured mirth and, sometime, a necessity. His youthful sallies lead him to trouble which is necessary for his eventual reformation and moral awakening.

Latine, like Campley in *The Funeral*, is the ideal of friendship in the play. He had been a companion to Young Bookwit not only at Oxford but at the school too. He is ready to make sacrifices for his friend. He willingly accepts the role of a servant though he also belongs to the genteel class. He warns Young Bookwit against lying lest it should prove "a dangerous sport" but sparkish humour of his friend pays no heed to it. For the sake of his friend he acts as an errand boy to Penelope's house to give Young Bookwit's letter addressed to Victoria and endures the ignominy of being kicked out. For sometimes he participates in his friend's intrigues but he shows his true character in the prison scene. Seeing Young Bookwit's contrition over the supposed murder of Lovemore, Latine feels so distressed about his friend's plight and his father's grief that he takes the guilt of murdering Lovemore upon himself. For a good cause, that is, to save his friend's life, he resorts to lying, the 'art' that he had decried before. Young Bookwit, amazed by his freind's love and nobility says: "But all my Mind is seiz'd with Admiration of thy stupendious Friendship" (I, iii). Latine's eagerness to sacrifice his life causes an inner awakening in Young Bookwit who feels that "Death's more welcome than a life so purchas'd" (V, iii). Just as Frederick cures Penelope of vanity and Lovemore of jealousy Latine cures Young Bookwit of his fashionable follies. The noble sentiments thus expressed by the two friends have contagious effect on Lovemore, who was not dead and is now in a disguise to test the love of Penelope. He also joins the two friends and praises their "transcendant Virtue". The exemplary situation shows Steele's concern for presenting to the audience models of virtue for their emulation and it is no wonder that such scenes won great applause from all quarters.

Lovemore, Young Bookwit's friend at Oxford and supposed rival for the hand of Penelope, was purposely created by Steele as a foil to Young Bookwit. He is a typical sentimental lover whose jealous nature creates a misunderstanding between him and his friend. But at heart he too is a good man. Rightly drawing his character, Penelope says, "He is indeed a Man of an honest character,... He is so wise a Fellow, always so precisely in the right, so observing and so jealous, – he's blameless indeed, but not to be commended" (Act. I). However, Lovemore lacks the mein and grace of conversation that Young Bookwit possesses. Lovemore's constancy and concern for his beloved make him behave like a jealous lover. Even Penelope, who enjoys teasing and tormenting him, admits that "his person was as free as his Mind was honest, nor had he Imperfection but his Love of me" (V, iii). His friendship with Frederick is an evidence that he is a man of sterling qualities. That he is generous even to his foe is evidenced when he forgives his supposed rival and killer, Young Bookwit. Eventually when his love is rewarded he appears as a noble and good-natured gentleman.

Like Young Bookwit's Latine, Lovemore has his faithful and truly sincere friend in Frederick who follows "the dread laws of Friendship".[3] Frederick, a man with stoic temperament, is a well-wisher of Lovemore. Though a minor character, Steele has created him to solve Lovemore's love tangles: to dispel the clouds of misunderstanding between Lovemore and Penelope, as well as between Lovemore and Young Bookwit. He enacts a situation in which he breaks the news of Lovemore's "death" and delivers his 'last' letter to Penelope. The ruse works; Penelope is cured of her vanity and expresses her true feelings for Lovemore. Lovemore, watching the scene in disguise, is impressed by his friends' sincerity. Frederick feels amply rewarded in his friend's happiness. Steele's desire to make stage a means of moral reform by providing exemplary characters is fully expressed through these two pairs of true friends.

Old Bookwit is portrayed differently from his counterparts in the plays of Restoration era. He does not confine his only son to his estate but sends him to Oxford and hopes that the son "brings from a College the Mein and Air of a Court" (II, i). He loves him "entirely" with a desire to have him properly and decently "settled". He has chosen a fair, witty, prudent and rich young lady as his life companion. Unlike his predecessors, Old Bookwit belongs to a different generation of benevolent guardians. This is revealed from his actions and words when he says:

> I scorn to hoard what I only now can gaze at, while your Youth and person want those Entertainments you may become and tast [e]. – All your just pleasure mine also.– In you my youth and gayer years methinks I feel repeated. (II, ii)

When he learns of Bookwit's supposed marriage, with tender feelings he wishes to contact his wife and accept her as his daughter-in-law. He does neither chide nor threaten his son. He says:

> That I most blame is that you conceal'd it from me, your best Friend. I'll instantly to Penelope's Father and make my apology. (II, ii)

The sight of Young Bookwit in chains is something that the kind-hearted old man cannot bear and he swoons. This pathetic, heart-touching scene was designed to provide the picture of an ideal, loving father completely different from the unreasonably authoritative cantankerous 'fathers' of the earlier drama.

Steele has, among the women characters, portrayed Penelope as a typical Restoration lady – vain, jealous and fickle-minded. She is eager to see the man she is going to marry and, therefore, writes an assignation to that purpose and plans to meet Young Bookwit as Victoria. When Lettice, her maid, tells her of a gentleman dying for her and writing pure verses, the vain reply she gives is characteristic of a lady in a Restoration Comedy. She says:

> Whoever writ'em, he's not the first poet I have made. They may talk, and say Nature makes a Poet, but I say Love makes a Poet. (II, i)

She points out her lover's lack of warmth and life and shows her preference for "a Man that has agreeable Faults rather than offensive Virtues". (I, i). She does not want her lover to be a paragon of virtues but one who has "fire" of love which Lovemore wants badly. She is cruel to him, teases and tries him to "rack his very heart-strings", and plays upon his jealousy. She is highly pleased at his loquacity when he accuses her of her inclination toward Young Bookwit and she says in an aside:

> A little ill Usage, I see, improves a Lover Strangely; I never heard him speak so well in my life before. (II, i)

The Restoration woman in her is humbled in the fifth act when Victoria accuses her of insincerity towards Lovemore. Her reformation reaches platonic heights when she suffers genuine pangs of love and remorse on receiving a letter from Lovemore after his supposed death. In an apostrophe to the letter she exclaims:

> Thou shalt live her fore'er, Here, thou dearest Paper, mingle with my life's stream; Either the Paper bleeds anew, or my Eyes weep Blood. (V, iii)

She is sentimental like the heroines of heroic plays and curses all worldly possessions once she has lost her lover. "Curse on all Wealth and Fortune! he, he is gone who only deserv'd all." (V, iii). Steele lets sincere feelings and inherent virtue shine through the thin layers of vanity put on by Penelope.

To set off Penelope, Steele has created Victoria, a Sober woman. Both of them find Young Bookwit attractive and witty. Victoria's "wary Carriage, and Circumspection have been a Safety against Errors" for Penelope. They are two incompatible tastes vexing each other. At heart Victoria does not like Penelope who, she thinks, has "no gesture in the least", and Penelope considers the other an encroacher upon her love. In their portraits Steele has tried to reflect on certain feminine weaknesses such as malice and hypocrisy in relation to one another. Out of jealousy, they blight each other's beauty by applying powder and pathches the wrong way. Their friendship is threatened by "the sudden intruder, love" (II, i) but eventually Penelope repents of her vain and jealous behaviour. Her realisation that "Simplicty is the Dress of honest Passion" carries a wholesome lesson for the gay and fickle minded young women who would not recognise and reward constancy in their devoted lovers until much unnecessary trouble has been created for all concerned. A chastened woman in the final act of the play, she changes her attitude towards Lovemore and accepts him saying, "if Lovemore can forgive my late ill usage, – I need say no more" (V, iii).

The two ladies are crucial to the main plot. It is the confusion of their identity which creates complications that lead the hero to fight a duel with Penelope's lover. The hero mistakes Penelope as Victoria, praises her beauty and has an assignation with her which she plants as Victoria. Still some good humoured fun is provided through this confusion which the two ladies do not bother to resolve but rather prefer to prolong the hero's discomfiture. Old Bookwit is seeking Penelope's hand for his son and Penelope does not miss this golden opportunity of meeting Young Bookwit under the assumed name of her cousin. It is Old Bookwit who withdraws the marriage proposal when he learns of Lovemore's devotion to Penelope. Besides Young Bookwit and Latine, it is the sprightly Penelope and good natured Victoria who give life to the otherwise too sentimental a play.

Introduction of several comic scenes and situations in the serious fable of the play exhibits Steele's genius as a comic writer. He weaves brilliant comic strokes into an inherent moral fabric designed to some extent after the morality plays. The comic touches include farcical, sometimes low and satirical scenes which give vivacity to the play. Ample comic fun is found in the scenes dealing with Latine, the supposed servant of the hero. This young Oxonian dazzles Lettice, Penelope's maid, with his brilliant verbal display and keeps up the appearance of a servant successfully. Latine's licentious behaviour towards Lettice is the means of the author's satire on the morals of the servants of the people of quality. Lettice weeps copiously whenever she reads a romantic story and dreams of marriage and children. She does not encourage Simon, Penelope's servant, for she does not find in him a suitor of the type that she had become familiar with after reading romances. Her love of 'romances', generally found among the young wards of the rich families, makes her different from the other members of her class. This is enough to make her behaviour, in fact her whole character, look ridiculous. On the one hand she wants Latine to seduce her and on the other, she asks her mistress to rescue her from his amorous advances. She is as eager as her Restoration forbears to have "the gentleman's pretty man" but dissembles well "for the servants must do as they are bid".[4] At heart she is the cunning maid of the Restoration type who welcomes amours. Her provocative pleadings to Latine are exactly of the same texture as of female attendants in those plays. The instant she is discovered in a compromising position she acts very cleverly and starts accusing Latine of flirting with her. But when she is asked to beat him, she reveals a throbbing heart and her scruples. She cannot hurt him as she has "bowels" for him. She is a prude superficially but humane at heart. Steele, it seems, did not care much for the "low" characters like Lettice. Here again he was being realistic. Maid servants of this type are found in the works of other eighteenth century writers. As a rule they were supposed to be women of easy virtue. Moreover, Steele's focus was on the characters and manner of the genteel society.[5]

Another comic situation is Old Bookwit's display of absurd delight when at the sight of the young ladies he describes his abilities at courtship as less rusty than what he had hitherto believed. He recalls how he wooed Young Bookwit's mother and, recounting her physical charms, he gets so excited as to become oblivious of the beauty of the lady he is seeking for his son. His verbal picture of his deceased wife's beauty has traces of sensuality in it. He highlights her physical features thus:

> Her complexion was charming, but not indeed with all your sweetness, Her Neck and Bosom were the softest pillows, her shape was not of that nice sort....But 't was the work of Nature, free, unconstrain'd, healthy and... (II, i)

He soon realises his lapse and starts extolling Penelope's beauty but it is in abstract terms and in tags only, giving the impression that he was making love on behalf of his son.[6]

The gulling of Young Bookwit by two young ladies, his joining them and making fun at his own expense, his lying before Lovemore, his criticism of Penelope unknowingly in her very presence and the ladies jealousy are some interesting comic strokes in the play. The first four acts of the play have such elements in abundance. Young Bookwit with his ingenious lying surprises Penelope and Victoria and then Lovemore and Frederick and sweeps the floor with his mirth. He, with an amazing grace and ease, weaves yarns of bottles, fires, music, dance and feasts, etc. The ladies are impressed with his wit and gallantry whereas Lovemore and Frederick, with his tales of midnight feasts. The jealousy of the blind lover does not let Lovemore see through his lying and Young Bookwit glories in his art of extempore lying so much so that his own confidant is wonder-struck at it. The comic spirit lies not so much in his false stories but the way he applies his scholarship to his gay pursuits, employing the noble arts and sciences. Even when Young Bookwit and Latine are drunk they put the precepts of philosophy into practice and talk of body, mind and soul. Even in the prison his ingenuity and learning help him impress the other mates and keep him merry. The most comic situation caused by his extempore lying is his being gulled and mocked at by Penelope and Victoria (III, iii). The two young women have an assignation with him. He pours romantic dialogue before his beloved and draws an ugly portrait of Penelope. He is ignorant of the fact that the person he is talking to is Penelope herself. He laughs with them not knowing that the laughter is at his own cost. A part of their dialogue is worth reproducing:

Both:	Ha! ha! ha!
Young Bookwit:	I hold myself oblig'd to be of the same humour ladies are in, – Ha ! ha ! ha ! – Now pray do me the Favour to tell me what I laugh'd at.

Comedy of a farcical kind is found in the Lettice-Latine scene. Latine, drunk, goes on an errand to penelope's house. In order to gain access to the mistress of the house, he courts Lettice.

Lettice's behaviour in accepting the advances mady by Latine as well as in kicking him out belong to low comedy. Lettice shows a soft corner for him but as soon as she learns that he has brought a letter for Victoria, not for her mistress, she beats him with a broom and kicks him out of the house.

One of the best satirically comic scenes is the one between Penelope and Victoria. It demonstrates and makes fun of feminine jealousy. Each of the two women, the supposed rivals for Young Bookwit, feels attracted towards him and tries to put the other out of her way. In their heart they hate each other for this reason and determine never to be a minute away from the other. Under the garb of friendship they walk arm in arm but actually keep a watch over each other. This hatred and jealousy are exhibited when they prepare to visit Young Bookwit. Victoria pretending to arrange Penelope's hood deliberately displaces her hair-do and comments:

> That's something. You had before a fearful silly
> blushing Look.— Now you command all Hearts.
> (III, i)

Similarly Penelope spoils Victoria's face by applying a patch at a wrong place, saying:

> Hold still, my dear, I'll place it just by your
> Eye.— (Aside) Now she downright squints.

Victoria too applies a patch near Penelope's temples and then near her lips, while Penelope puts it on the former's forehead. Both try their best to undo other's make up. Beneath the thin layer of friendship lies a deep current of hatred between them – a fact which does not escape the discerning eyes of Betty whose comment is, "How civily people of Quality hate one another" (II, i). The satirical implication of the ironical sub-title of the play, *The Ladies Friendship*, is exhibited further when the two women meet Young Bookwit. Each is charmed by his wit and learning but dissembles indifference towards him in order to deceive the other. Each feels "I begin to hate her so – I'll never be a Minute from her." Their pronouncement that "there is nothing like a sincere friend" sounds hollow and hypocritical in the context of their conduct. They are just a contrast to Latine and Young Bookwit, the very reverse of sincere friendship. Steele has satirised through these two 'friends' women's vanity, affectation and lack of constancy – something which he never felt tired of doing.[7]

Steele has introduced a few songs and some verse in the emotionally surcharged scenes. Remorse and repentance are expressed in verse so that its music along with its sentiments moves the audience. The songs in the play are mostly love songs in consonance with the tone of the play. The first song ('To Celia's Spinet') is of conventional type in which a devoted lover addresses his cruel beloved. It feeds Penelope's vanity and shows how fashionable wealthy women love listening to songs made on them. The other song ('Venus has left her Grecian Isles') is sung with full flourishes by Young Bookwit who pictures Victoria as Venus. But he sings a sad song in the next act which reflects his changed mood. The pessimistic note of this song is due to his remorse and gloom over Lovemore's challenge. The last song ('The rolling years the joys restore') relieves the heavy and tearful scenes. It also shows Steele's patriotic favour and contains lavish praise of Queen Anne. Patriotic sentiments are repeatedly exposed in the preface and the Epilogue to the play. The inclusion of the songs, can also be attributed to Steele's patriotism; to his desire to provide indigenous diversion to his countrymen to check their increasing fascination for Italian Operas.[8] It was, again on patriotic considerations that he made use of the talents of the contemporary musicians like Richard Leveridge and Daniel Purcell.[9]

In Act four, scene five Steele takes the audience to a prison. The picture of Newgate inmates provides ripples of humour and comic relief.[10] In Restoration comedy an actual prison scene has not been presented although some stray allusions to it are made. In *The Squire of Alsatia*, Belfond Junior, the hero goes to jail but this is only referred to. It is Steele's *Lying Lover* that exhibits vividly and realistically the different aspects of life in the contemporary jails. Young Bookwit is arrested for murder in a state of drunkenness and, therefore, he is oblivious of what is happening to him. But when he becomes sober (in the next scene) on the following morning, he broods over his impulsive action and the pain that it must have given to his father and friend. While he is under the influence of alcohol he enjoys himself with the other hardened 'gaol-birds', who are very crafty and unscrupulous. For example, Storm, as his comic name suggests, overwhelms Young Bookwit with his self-glorification and self-justification as a martyr when he refers to his imprisonment as "the Portion of the Virtuous, and the Gallant" (IV, v). Steele has euphemistically pictured the profession of a highway-man and a forger of coins who justify themselves with their amusing arguments. The inmates of the gaol have sympathy for one another and call the world ungrateful for not rewarding them for their talents; for example, Storm for his gallantry and the forger Charcoal for his "Melioration of metals" (IV, v). Charcoal's professed expertise in his ability to convert iron bars of the prison into gold and his request, on the other hand, for half a crown for wine render him quite a ridiculous figure. Even on the threshold of death, he is non-serious and befools others into giving him wine and money. The climate of the place with death sentences hanging over the heads of the condemned is depicted comically but still quite realistically.[12] The condemned prisoners want to enjoy life to its last drop. The psychology of such criminals is vividly shown throughout this scene. Death does not frighten them and Newgate has become a place for merry-making for them. These hardened criminals show least trace of grief or repentance. Rather, they balance the world and glorify themselves for their 'talents'. The following conversation between Young Bookwit and Charcoal reveals their attitude towards death:

> Young Bookwit: When pray, Sir, are you to be immortal?
> Charcoal: On Friday next. — I'm very unhappy our Acquaintance is to be short. — I'm very sorry your Business is not Over, Sir, that if it must be, we might go together.
>
> (IV, v)

Similarly, Storm, even when a sword is hanging over his head, is making merry at the cost of others, dispelling the clouds of gloom. He enjoys teasing Simon, Penelope's servant, who has been arrested with others for being found roaming on the roads at midnight. Storm mirthfully says:

> We'll drink his Coat off. Come, my little Chymist, thou shalt transmute this Jacket into Liquor, Liquor that will make us forget the evil Day, — And while Day is ours, let us be merry.
>
> (IV, v)

There is another prison scene in the play which contrasts the repentant prisoners with hardened criminals. This scene gives a moral touch to the play by presenting a picture of Newgate different from the earlier one. It is, as it ought to be, full of gravity, suspense and moving stillness. The Young Bookwit of this scene is completely different from that of the previous scenes. He emerges as a basically good man, thus showing the real reformation of an outwardly rakish character. Young Bookwit expresses sincere repentance and Latine grieves at his friend's sorrow, and in order to save him, makes a false confession of murdering Lovemore who is brought in to witness Latine's nobility and to pardon the sincere penitents.

Steele introduced these two scenes into his play purposely to convey his moral convictions. One example of this is found in Latine's words that show his genuine concern for his friend:

> How quietly he rests ! Oh that I could by watching him hanging thus over him, and feeling all his Care, protract his Sleep !

Similar objective is noticeable in Latine's speech when, as an ideal and sincere friend he tries to boost up Young Bookwit's morale and wishes that he could save his life. His wish: "How do I pity that returning Life, which I cou'd hazard thousand Lives to save!" is fulfilled and he takes the blame on himself.

One thing that makes the play remarkable is the way the hero feels pangs of repentance as soon as he shakes off his drunkenness and realise the enormity and tragic consequences of his acts of indiscretion. Steele expresses his own feelings against duelling when he makes Young Bookwit condemn it, as is clear from his essays on duelling.[13] Latine's warning note to Young Bookwit when he tells him that it "may prove dangerous sport, and may involve us in a Pack of Troubles" (I, i) comes true. It is only after suffering that Young Bookwit realises his fault. He denounces drinking, the root cause of all evils – thus: "Oh this senseless drinking! To suffer a whole week's Pain for an Hour's Jollity." (V, i). It is a genuine inward awakening, a kind of moral rebirth different from the patterns of pity and benevolence provided by other characters. In this respect one interesting point is to be noted. Young Bookwit and Penelope's reformation is entirely due to their own sense of remorse not, as in some other dramatists, due to the influence of a virutous and loving person. In the Preface Steele says that Young Bookwit's anguish and sorrow in the prison scene are "perhaps an Injury to the Rules of Comedy; but I am sure they are a Justice to those of Morality..."[14] His denunciation of "senseless drinking" and "the horrid application" of duelling against friends provide the playwright ample opportunity to reflect on those contemporary social vices. His play "instructs" the audience as does the motto from the classics which, in English, reads as follows: "To have seen this is salvation to the Young."[15]

In Act V the portrait of exemplary friendship is given a noble touch. Latine's sacrifice for his friend is not wasted as it arouses inner awakening in Young Bookwit who applauds his freinds thus:

> Who cou'd believe that any pleasing Passion cou'd touch a Breast loaded with Guilt like mine; But all my Mind is seiz'd with Admiration of thy stupendous Friendship. (V, iii)

The noble conduct of Latine and Young Bookwit produces a healthy effect in Lovemore who, abandoning his jealousy, says, "let me grasp you both, who in an Age Degenerate as this, have such transcendent virtue." (V, iii). Sincere friendship -- as the Preface of the play, Steele's essays and his own friendship with Addison illustrate, was one of Steele's favourite themes

Besides, these prison scenes exhibit Steele's concern for social and moral reforms. On the one hand friendship, spirit of sacrifice, virtue etc. are extolled and on the other Newgate is pictured as an end to which the evil paths lead. A career of vice inevitably takes one to Newgate – this warning is designed to be conveyed through these scenes. Persons who repent and reform deserve pardon whereas hardened criminals get the punishment which they deserve. Steele has referred to the hero's moral reform and the concept of a morally clean comedy (a result of Collier's criticism) in his Apology thus:

> 'I was ... a great Admirer of his (Collier) Work, and took into my Head to Write a Comedy in the severity he required. In this play I made the spark or Hero kill a Man in his Drink, and finding himself in Prison next Morning, I give him the contrition which he ought to have on that occasion.'[16]

Quite a few aphorisms, amply sprinkled in the play, enhance the moral tone of the play. The following statements are to be noted in this connection.

> There's nothing shews a Man so Much as the Object of his Affections.
>
> ...
>
> There's consolation when a Friend laments us, but when a Parent grieves, the Anguish is too native, Too much our own to be called Pity. (V, iii)

Young Bookwit's concluding words are the best guideliness for the moral conduct of the youth. He wishes to instruct them through his own experience:

> Since such deserv'd misfortunes they must share
> Who with gay Falsehoods entertain the Fair:
> Let all with this just Maxim guide their Youth,
> There is no Gallantry in Love but Truth.
> (V, iii)

The play has several emotional scenes. The fainting of Young Bookwit's father when he sees his son being tried for murder; the dialogue between Young Bookwit and Latine about who should take the blame for the supposed death of Lovemore, and the inevitable repentance scene at the end – are all typical characteristic of Steele's pen. These sentimental scenes add pathos to the inherently comic plot. The comic spirit of the first four acts is made to blend with the pathetic arousing pity, remorse and repentance, etc. The hero's grief is two-fold; one over the "loss" of his friend Lovemore, the other, over the grief of his affectionate and aged father.[17] The hero's mirth and gaiety that led him to "senseless drinking", and to duelling has eventually landed him into Newgate. Now, reviewing his irresponsible way of life he feels unsupportable remorse which he expresses in the following words:

> I cannot bear the rusting of New thoughts,—
> Fancy expands my Senses to Distraction,
> And my Soul stretches to that boundless Space,
> To which I've sent my wretched, wretched Friend.

He denounces his 'art' of lying and curses himself thus:

> Oh this unhappy Tongue of Mine!
> Thou lawless voluble destroying Foe
> That still run'st on, nor waitest Command of Reason:
> Oh! I could tear thee from me. (V, i)

His grief does not end here. It is enhanced at the sight of his old father grieving for him. He finds that by his mirthful lying he has inflicted acute pain on his affectionate father. His grief knows no bounds he cries:

> — Oh big unutterable Grief — Merciful Heav'n,
> I don't deserve this ease of Tears to melt,
> With Penitence — Oh sweet, sweet Remorse,
> Now all my Powers give way,
> To my just sorrow, for the best of fathers.
> (V, iii)

His remorse and repentance must have been a treat to the middle class that loved conventional morality. This sentimental element, very much like that of Cibber's comedies, is reinforced by the grief of another good character. Old Bookwit's grief for his only son adds to the pathos of the play. His grief is too deep for words. Young Bookwit, in whom his father sees his own "youth and gayer years" repeated, is imprisoned for killing Lovemore and is waiting for an impending death sentence. This sentimental situation is filled with unbearable grief of a loving father and moves Young Bookwit's soul as it must have moved many a heart among the audience. His heart-touching words are of genuine sentimental kind:

> Oh Tom! are all thy aged Father's Hopes then come to this.... Thy Mother's happy that liv'd not to see this Day. ....Oh my Son! rise and support thy Father! I sink with Tenderness, my Child, come to my Arms while thou art mine. (V, iii)

Rightly does he voice the feelings of a father when he says to Lovemore: "You know not what it is to be a Father" (V, iii). This sentimental statement full of parental grief must have gone well with the eighteenth century audience. Latine's friendly concern for and grief over Young Bookwit's plight in the prison also have traces of sentimental comedy. He shares his friend's distress as he shared his gay pursuits. His concern for the friend's welfare and his watching Young Bookwit like a nurse, his prayers to heaven to give courage and composure to face the calamity and finally his noble gesture all exhibit virtue triumphing in distress.[18] Besides, remorse and repentance are not restricted to male characters only. Penelope who had inflicted pain upon her devoted lover finds herself in a pathetic situation; the news of her lover's death breaks her heart and feeling the pangs of genuine grief, she repents and finally reverts to virutous ways. She curses wealth, vanity and fortune, and weeps copiously for Lovemore. As Young Bookwit cries for his fainted father, Penelope cries for her lost lover:

> Oh ! cou'd I see him now to press his liv'd lips,
> And call him back to Life with my Complaints,
> His Eyes wou'd glare upon my Guilt with Horrour,
> That us'd to glote and melt in love before me, —
> Let mine forever then be shut to joy,
> To all that's bright, and valuable in Man! (V, iii)

Her resolve that:

> I'll to his sacred Ashes be a Wife,
> And to his memory devote my Life. (V, iii)

bestows upon a vain modish woman the stature of a sentimental heroine. All these sentimental scenes and situations show Steele's moral concern. There is no dearth of evidence in the play to show that Collier's concepts of comedy were very much in Steele's mind while he was writing this play.

The characters, their tone and intrigues, gulling of the spark and making assignations, mistaken identities, servants with licentious ways are all according to the pattern of the Restoration comedy. Steele can be accused of impropriety in presenting some lewdness in Latine-Lettice scenes but it seems to be a reflection of the public desire for a bit of this kind of diversion. However, Steele associates not his protagonists but the characters representing the lower strata of society with such actions. In consonance with his didactic bent of mind, the focus of the play is on the repentance of the hero after he realises his faults and weaknesses. In the Preface Steele claimed that it was his "honest Ambition to attempt a Comedy, which might be no improper Entertainment in a Christian Common Wealth" and to present "simplicity of Mind, Good-nature, Friendship, and Honour."[19] He added that in the play he has attempted "to strip Vice of the gay Habit in which it has too long appear'd and has clothed it in its native Dress of Shame, Contempt and Dishonour".[20] It was, he felt, for his convictions and his avowed moral aim, that the play was damn'd. It was "damn'd for its piety."[21]

NOTES

1. Aitken, *op. cit.*, Vol. I, p. 93.
2. Bellmour, deplores business (Serious work) and says:

   Leave Business to idlers, and Wisdom to Fools: they have need of 'em; Wit be my Faculty, and Pleasure, my Occupation; and let Father Time shake his glass .... (I, i).
3. *Plays*, p. 117.
4. Latine though a representative of the upper class is allowed to act as a typical modish servant. The servant's aping their masters in dress and manners, and their becoming vain and spend-thrift is considered objectionable by Steele. He elaborated this point later in *The Conscious Lovers* and in his periodicals essays.
5. In *The Spectator*, No. 88 Steele makes the following observations on the servants:

   They are in a lower degree what their Masters themselves are; and usually affect an imitation of their Manners... It is a general observation, that all Dependents run in some measure into the Manners and Behaviour of those whom they serve: You shall frequently meet with lovers and Men of Intrigue among the lacqueys.
6. Sheridan has used this situation in *The Rivals* in which Sir Beverley praises Lydia's beauty on behalf of his son.
7. For example, see *The Tatler*, No. 86, and *The Spectator* No. 478.
8. In *The Spectator* No. 278 Steele expresses his dissatisfaction with the present state of music and how operas have given a blow to his art. In *The Censorium* started in 1715 he tried his best to encourage this art by organising music concerts.
9. Mr. Richard Leveridge, a song-writer, composer and singer employed in the Drury Lane Company perhaps sang two of these songs while Mr. Daniel Purcell had set Young Bookwit's song.
10. Comic relief is basically a feature of tragedies and its incorporation in a comedy can be correctly deemed as a kind of new development in English drama. The inclusion of sorrow, a feature of sentimentalism, justifies the existence of comic relief in a play. In this respect Steele's role was that of a pioneer.
11. For the presentation of this scene Steele drew on his personal experience already referred to on p. 91.

12. Similar prison scenes are present in some other works of contemporary writers. Gay's *Beggar's Opera*, Fielding's *Jonathan Wilde* and Defoe's *Moll Flanders* depict life in Newgate and the attitude of the hardened criminals.
13. Steele's views on duelling will be discussed in the later chapters.
14. *Plays*, pp. 24-25.
15. *Ibid*, p. 392.
16. Cited from Steele's *Apology* in *The Tracts and Pamphlets*, p. 311.
17. Nicoll, commenting on the tragic potential of the scene, finds it too revolutionary for its time for it "moves into a sphere that is nearer tragedy than comedy proper." (A. Nicoll, *op. cit.*, p. 192). Nicoll seems to forget Steele's theory of comedy which allows "anything" that has "its foundation in joy." The more the distress, the greater the joy is in store for the virtuous characters as well as for the audience.
18. Acclaiming the sentimental elements of the repentance scene and overt didacticism F.T. Wood says:

    The Lying Lover gave an impetus to sentimental comedy which urged others to follow in the same path as Steele... Sentiment was rapidly gaining a foothold, and moralising began to take the place of manners upon the stage. "The Beginning and Significance of Sentimental Comedy", *Anglia*, XLIII (1931), p. 388).

    The fact is that now onwards most of the comedies, specially Mrs. Centlivre's, followed sentiment and kept it in view from the very beginning of the play.
19. *Plays*, p. 115.
20. *Ibid.*, p. 116.
21. Apology, *The Tracts and Pamphlets*, p. 312.

7

The Tender Husband: Or, *The Accomplish'd Fools*

Soon after *The Lying Lover* was performed, Steele, still in the army, started writing *The Tender Husband* because of the former play's being 'damn'd for it's piety' and his being in a tight condition financially.[1] In *The Tender Husband* he has taken certain hints and ideas from Molière's *Les Précieuses Ridicules* and *Le Sicilien* and presented them in a totally different manner. The basic theme of Steele's play is conjugal happiness and the factors that so often destroy it.

The nature of the plot and the characters of the play are described by Addison in the Prologue to the play:

> Out Author, to divert his Friends to-Day,
> Stocks with Variety of Fools his play;
> And that there may be something Gay, and New,
> Two ladies Errant has expos'd to View;
> The First a Damsel, travail'd in Romance;
> The other more refin'd, she comes from France;
> Rescue, like Courteous knights, the Nymph from Danger;
> And kindly Treat, like well-bred men, the Stranger.[2]

The main plot concerns the reformation of the modish wife, Mrs. Clerimont, whose inclination towards 'infidelity' is fully impressed upon the audience through her husband's lips. Clerimont Senior, the husband of this female fop, finds that his wife is copying French manners too much going to the brink of immorality and impropriety. He complains of her admiration for the male sex and depreciation of every viture in her own. What annoys him is the fact that her addiction to fashionable follies, mainly gambling, costs him a lot of money. The turning point in their relationship is reached when he can neither live with her at ease, nor discard her, and, therefore, he has to "catch" her enlarging her "innocent freedoms". Hence, he seeks the help of his mistress, Lucy Fainlove, who disguises herself as a young gallant and tries to seduce Mrs. Clerimont. Lucy Fainlove gambles with her but returns the money she wins to Clerimont Senior. According to the plan, Fainlove kisses Mrs. Clerimont during an assignation and the husband, who is hiding himself in the closet, comes out with a sword drawn, which results in his wife's swooning. When she regains consciousness she finds her husband embracing Lucy and now she starts chiding him and banishes him from her sight and bed. Clerimont Senior shows her the letter of assignation she had written to Lucy supposing her to be a man. This makes Mrs. Clerimont weep and repent over "the thing she was" and promise to improve her ways. Still in the last scene she is seen praising everything French which indicates that her reformation is not complete. In this play Steele has used the same plot pattern, *i.e.* a husband testing the fidelity of his wife, as he had done earlier in *The Funeral*. However, while in the earlier play the faithless wife is publicly exposed, in *The Tender Husband* the exposure is restricted to the bedroom only in the presence of the husband's mistress. When Clerimont Senior succeeds in convincing his wife of the enormity of her misdemeanour he happily concludes with a maxim:

> They only who gain Minds, true laurels wear:
> 'Tis less to conquer, than convince the Fair.
>
> (V, i)

The sub-plot concerns the fortunes of a rich city heiress, Biddy Tipkin, who lives in a world of romances and does not fancy an arranged marriage for herself. She is being forced to marry her country cousin, Humphry, who, in his turn, is averse to marrying a blood relation.[3] Eventually, unknown to her guardian, she marries Captain Clerimont, younger brother of Clerimont Senior, who has just returned from war and is on the look out for a rich heiress. Pounce, the lawyer, resolves the matter by arranging a meeting between him and Biddy after instructing him in respect of the likes and dislikes of the latter, and by informing Humphry that he has come of age and can afford to disobey his tyrannical father who is forcing him to marry his cousin for the sake of her money. In the process, Pounce is able to palm off Clerimont Senior's mistress, who happens to be his sister, to Humphry who gladly accepts her as his bride. What makes the plot remarkable is the younger brother's assuming the garb of a knight of the romances to impress and win Biddy and to bring her to the world of common day light. In another scene he disguises himself as a painter, gets admittance into her house, and succeeds in eloping with her. Humphry assists Captain Clerimont and himself marries Lucy. Both the couples come back married and the elders are stunned to find the tables turned upon them. Tension is eased when Sir Harry Gubbin learns that Lucy comes of a rich family and Tipkin is highly pleased to see his daughter Biddy well disposed of. The play ends with dance and music like Steele's other comedies. Captain Clerimont, the younger brother and fortune hunter, weds an heiress, Biddy, who succeeds in averting marriage to a country clown by marrying a supposedly romantic husband, and Humphry Gubbin succeeds in averting marriage with his cousin. Thus, each one of them gains his or her ends. The elders are duped and their calculations and dictatorial methods prove of no avail. The sub-plot is interspersed with scenes of comic fun the best of which is the proviso scene between Tipkin and Sir Harry. The attempted barter of the children through marriage and Humphry's ridiculous appearance in his father's antique suit add to its comic effect.

Biddy, the "damsel" of the prologue, is the central character of the sub-plot. Steele has satirised, without bitterness, this "city nymph" who lives in the world of romances. Her whimsical character is thus explained to Captain Clarimont by Pounce:

> The young lady by being kept from the world, has made a world of her own... She has spent all her solitude in reading *Romances,* her head is full of shepherds, knights, Flowery Meads, Groves and Streams, so that if you walk like a Man of this World to her you do nothing.
>
> (I, i)

She considers her name contemptible and unbecoming to a heroine of romances and, therefore, would like to have "something soft and engaging in Her Name – Something that gives us a notion of the sweetness of her Beauty and Behaviopur" (II, ii). Her concept of marriage and living comfortably is different from that of her aunt who believes in conventional marriage of economic convenience. Biddy is not averse to elopement as it has something romantic about it but she cannot think of abridging her fantastic day dreaming by "cutting off all farther decoration of Disguise, Serenade, and Adventure". Her dilemma whether to elope with

Captain Clerimont and thus cut the courtship short, or to refuse him for the thrill of romance and be obliged to accept the country booby under duress is resolved when she agrees to resign herself to Captain Clerimont. In Captain Clerimont's words she is "A perfect Quixote in petticoats" (II, i). She is upright and virtuous, and does not hide Captain Clerimont in the closet when her aunt comes. Instead, she talks boldly of her admiration for him. What makes her different from the Restoration heroines is her excessive predilection for romances and total lack of exuberance and complete disinterestedness in using wit and repartee and indulging in love intrigues. Whatever Restoration attributes are present in her are not of much significance. Though she is distracted by her literary tastes, she is amusing, innocent and likeable. She is a victim of the contemporary taste for French Romances which reaches its apex in Lydia Languish in Sheridan's *The Rivals*. Steele attacks the love of romances but Biddy escapes unscathed for she is basically a good and virtuous character. She is criticised by none except her old aunt, a target of ridicule herself. Moreover, Biddy, as soon as she steps out of the world of romances, which happens in the final Act, is rewarded with the hand of a deserving youngman.[4]

That Biddy is portrayed sympathetically does not mean that she is approved of by Steele as his protagonist. Through her Steele has satirised the contemporary craze for romances among the artistocratic women. Biddy's sketch is a reflection on the harmful effects that the excessive fondness for such fantastical and irrational works had on the immature minds of the young girls. How this kind of reading turned their heads and how the wonder world they identified themselves which alienated them from real life is amply illustrated through her character. In the early eighteenth century the young girls of aristocracy did not have formal education in schools; but had recourse to lending libraries which supplied them French romances.[2] It is Steele's concern for reform that urged him to satirise this contemporary phenomenon through Biddy.

The set of immoral characters shown in certain lewd situations comprises the "erring" wife, the 'tender' husband and his mistress. The errant woman, as already noticed, is Mrs. Clerimont, who has been to France and Italy and, therefore, as Mr. Clerimont tells his mistress, has "improved her perfections" so much that she has learned "to lose her Money gracefully, to admire every Vanity in our Sex and to contemn every Virtue in her own (I, i). She has abandoned, as her husband testifies, her household responsibilities, regard for the posterity, and fear of poverty out of her excessive love for the modish game of cards. Like a vain lady of quality, she enjoys the company of a minor and a dog. She considers herself a pioneer in setting the fasion of "colouring" and is pleased to find other ladies imitating her. She loves fine talk and abhors sullen English tempers, and looks upon English women as "mere talking barometers" whose discourse consists of nothing but questions and answers. She prefers a spinet-master to the company of the dull English women. She presents herself as a true Francophile when she asks the spinet-master to sing an English song the French way, she says, "I wish you'd give more into the *French* Manner" (III, i). She sings and dances with Captain Clerimont and Humphry Gubbin, though, without any dishonourable intentions. She treats her husband like a slave. He has to obtain her permission to enter her room, cannot share her bed-chamber, is always carrying out her commands and to cap it all, has to pay off her gambling debts. This clearly shows that she badly needs correction. This is done through the Lucy Fainlove episode which convinces her of her faulty behaviour. She is candid enough to confess that she has "erred", but only in "intention" not in deed. In spite of her fashionable vices and follies, she is, as her husband says, "guilty of nothing but what my indiscretion led her to" (V, i). When Lucy, in male disguise, criticises Captain Clerimont she not only chides her but goes on to denounce the fops as "pert-Billy Butterflies", "things proper for hours of daliance" but unfit for competition with "a man whose name one would wear" (VI, i). She is so angry with Lucy that she does not let her kiss her. Why Steele did not provide a man-seducer to Mrs. Clerimont was perhaps because he did not want to make the threat to her virtue real. Besides, perhaps, Steele had in his mind Queen Anne's proclamation of January 1704 prohibiting the play houses from staging "anything that is not strictly agreeable to religion and good manners."[6]

The responsibility for Mrs. Clerimont's follies and innocent freedoms lies mainly with her husband who believes in double standards of behaviour. He is a husband of old Restoration type, wife to reform without even thinking of giving up his own immoral practices. His "honest art", *i.e.*, using his mistress as a means to his end, his playing innocent, and frightening his wife with a sword, making a feigned attempt on his supposed rival's life, his embracing and kissing of his mistress during his wife's swooning and using her letter of assignation as a trump card are the means that he unscruplously employes to 'reform' his wife. The recurrent references to his wife's gambling debts show his concern for money. His attitude towards his mistress shows want of feeling on his part; he debauches and ruins her and is ready to discard her. He considers her only as a necessary "tag in the pedigree of a wealthy House."[7] He feels relieved when he finds her married to Humphry.

His design that his mistress should act as a "seducer" of his wife carried on diplomatically, reveals him a very clever and practical man. This is clearly revealed in the following speech of his:

> I should have the whole sex on my Back, should I pretend to retrench a Lady so well visited as mine is – Therefore I must bring about, that it shall appear her own Act, if she reforms; or else I shall be pronounc'd Jealous, and have my Eyes pull'd out for being open. (I, i)

Clerimont Senior has planned to reform and reclaim his wife, not through reasoning things out with her, but through a stratagem that will make her feel shame and remorse and give up her foolish pursuits.[8] In reality he is the least concerned about her feelings. He is tender of is own reputation rather than of her sentiments. His wife's unrestrained conduct hurts his ego but he is blind to his own vicious and unscruplous conduct. It is his own double standards that do not allow him to indulge in any plain dealing. His social pretensions force him to pose as a 'tender' husband, but there is not much of tenderness in his attitude towards his wife.

Clerimont's mistress, Lucy Fainlove, is a women of a different cast. She is definitely a better woman than Mrs. Clerimont. Lucy's devotion to her seducer and keeper is sincere and genuine. Hence it is that she is always willing to assist him in every scheme of his. She acts as his agent and disguises as a gallant to 'seduce' his wife to please him but at heart she is convinced that she would make a good wife of Clerimont and, therefore, is desirous of being instrumental in his separation from his wife. She often regrets for having allowed herself to be taken in by his sweet words and losing her honour and happiness. She is determined to "gain him" from his wife forever and save her reputation. Moreover, she believes that her 'seducing' of Mrs. Clerimont is not an immoral action. There is no trace of bitterness in her for the person who had ruined her life. Only mildly reproaching him she says, "Now am I rubbing up my memory to recollect all you said to me when you first ruined me" (V, i). At this stage she is not after fun but sincerely wants herself to be socially and financially settled. As Steele was writing for an audience favouring reform in society he was desirous of presenting a penitent wife and also, an honest mistress who is to be rewarded in one way or the other since she is not a depraved woman at heart. As Clerimont Senior cannot give her the status of a wife without divorcing Mrs. Clerimont, which is impossible, she is quite willing to have Humphry as her future husband.[1] She surely deserves a better deal but it is out of regard for the contemporary social norms that Steele does not let her have all her wishes fulfilled. After all she is a fallen woman.

Other characters of the play include fools and a person of wit. The young gentleman of wit is a younger brother, Captain Clerimont, who is a soldier and has to resort to fortune-hunting after leaving the army. The relationship cemented with complete accord and understanding between the two brothers, Clerimont Senior and Captain Clerimont, marks a new note in comedy. In order to settle down in life as a gentleman, the younger brother wishes to have "a fine Woman, pretty Equipage, good Company and a clear Habitation" (I, i). Biddy Tipkin, the rich heiress is suggested to him and he readily capitalises on the girl's love of romances. His knowledge of the lending libraries furnishes him with sufficient material to play the role of a lover as well as a painter. Eventually, he succeeds in convincing her that a short courtship is preferable to a disagreeable marriage (that is, with her cousin). His motives are not wicked though his eyes are fixed on Biddy's fortune. Steele does not portray him as an extravagant libertine but as a victim of the law of primogeniture. He, like others in similar situation, joins the army and after the war is in need of a settled source of income. Being himself an army man, Steele's sympathies naturally rest with another army man now rendered jobless.

Another man of wit in the play is Peter Pounce,[10] a lawyer, who frequents Cheapside, Convent Garden as well as St. James. As he avows, his profession is "to assist a Free-hearted young Fellow against an unnatural longlived Father, to disencumber Men of Pleasure of the vexation of unwieldy Estates, to support a Feeble Title to an Inheritance", etc. (I, i). With his sharp legal eyes he sees through everything and pounces on the best of all the opportunities. He manoeuvres Biddy's marriage with Captain Clerimont and appears to have obliged Humphry as well by averting his forced marriage with his cousin. Showing similar dexterity, he manipulates his sister's marriage with Humphry. To allow sufficient time to Captain Clerimont to win Biddy, Pounce goes through the ordeal of wooing her amorous aunt. It is he who introduces Captain Clerimont as a painter. He befools the elders and helps the young in distress without pretending to be altruistic. The services that he renders to others are all inspired by self-interest. It is due to his prudence that Captain Clerimont gets Biddy and her fortune, Lucy a husband, and Humphry and Biddy an escape from the elders' stranglehold.

In Humphry Gubbin, Steele has presented the Restoration stock character, the country booby, drawn after Shadwell's Young Heartford in *The Lanchashire Witches*.[11] The tyranny of forced marriages is exemplified in his case as in that of Biddy. Humphry has his own scruples about marrying a relation which invites his father's wrath. He is treated by his father "like one of his hounds." He is ashamed of being displayed like something on sale but, cowed down by his father's crab-tree cudgel, acts like "a docile dunce, a fellow rather absurd, than a direct fool." (I, ii). He is too insensible to feel distressed by his inability to walk like a fop but is quite conscious of the humiliation he has to suffer at the hands of his domineering and hectoring father. Expressing his feeling on this point he says grumblingly:

> Why, Sir, would it not vex a Man to the Heart, to have an old Fool, snubbing a Body every minute after Company. (I, ii)

As soon as he learns through Pounce that he has come of age and need no longer be under his father's thumb, he becomes a changed man. He gathers enough courage to defy his father and marry Lucy. He realises that now "he is quite another thing" (I, ii). He sings and dances in Mrs. Clerimont's house, and trying to be useful suggests to Biddy to elope with the young man of her liking. He is honest, virtuous and honourable in motive as well as in conduct. He gets a rich wife, though she is a cast-off mistress. He is in affinity with Biddy for both are 'accomplished fools' in their respective spheres; Humphry in his country ignorance and Biddy in foolishly living in the world of romances. Neither of them has any regard for the society which is compelling them to contract a marriage of economic convenience.[12]

Steele has satirised two more Restoration stock characters through Humphry's guardian, Sir Harry Gubbin, the country gentleman, and Biddy's uncle. Mr. Tipkin, the rich city merchant. Among the traders Mr. Tipkin is known as "Sly-Boots". To Pounce he seems to have "a very good Credit, and very bad conscience" (I, i). In the bargaining scene he reveals his true self when he demands a "discharge from all retrospects as Biddy's guardian, and One Thousand Pounds" for disposing her of (I, ii). He is the true representative of the early eighteenth century city-merchant class which weighed husbands for girls on the principle of frank barter, and often sent them to places to seek husbands at cheaper rates.[13] Business has gone to his marrows to such an extent that he has lost all concern for Biddy's welfare and future happiness. In the end he loses his niece and the "retrospect" discharge as well and no one feels sorry for him.

Tipkin is juxtaposed with the country squire, Sir Harry – who is a cruel, callous, niggardly, with a crab-tree stick to complete his portrait. This country squire cannot raise himself above his rustic level and equates his son with his cattle and hounds. He has brought up his son away from all city temptations and demands abject obedience from him. He has decided that his son will marry and live according to his instructions, *i.e.* to marry a fortune, "go down into the country" and live with him (*i.e.*, the father), not touching "a farthing of money but having all things necessary provided they (*i.e.* Humphry and his wife) shall go tame, about the house" (V, ii). He is shocked to learn that the fine city ladies' clothes become old "not by being worn but by being seen", and, therefore, he decides that Biddy's expenses, after her marriage, are to be reduced to a minimum. He says, "I'll warrant her she shall not appear more in this wicked town, where clothes are worn by sight" (V, ii). Just as Tipkin's love of money has made him barren of humanity, Sir Harry's strict discipline has killed affection in him. The values of Mr. Tipkin and Sir Harry are clearly revealed in their clash – which depicts one between the city merchant class and the country gentry. Through their verbal tug of war in which each tries to get the maximum profit out of the marriage settlements between their children. Steele bitterly satirises the commercial attitude towards matrimony common in his days.[14] The two guardians in the play are not in the least concerned about the double crime they are about to commit. In the end these two money-conscious guardians get their due punishment at the hands of their son and ward. Pounce's pronouncement expresses an average man's reaction to their discomfiture:

> This is dear delight to gall[sic] these old Rascals and set 'em at variance about stakes which I know neither of 'em will ever have Possession of. (V, ii)

Steele, like the other thinkers of his time, ascribed the moral degeneration of the English to the influence of the French ways of life. This is illustrated in his satire on the French in general, and in his denunciation of the French romances and French manners in particular. Biddy and Mrs. Clerimont are the characters swayed by the French morals and manners which are contrasted with the English ways of Humphry and the aunt. Biddy is turned into a denizen of the world of romances and Mrs. Clerimont is a francophile. Biddy and Mrs. Clerimont are the characters through whom Steele wanted to warn his audience against the harmful influence of the French and the Italian ways of life. Mrs. Clerimont's vices, her desire to have French servants, French food and French dances have been highlighted throughout the play. Her preference for chirping like the French is voiced when she condemns the "English Sullen Tampers", saying that:

> Abroad (that is in France) the People of Quality go on eternally, and still go on, and are Gay and Entertain —. In England discourse is made up of nothing but Questions and Answers. (III, i)

The satirical sting can be felt in Mrs. Clerimont's preference for and praise of French food habits as well as for foreign music and dance. Her hatred for the English food habits and her liking for the French dishes comprising frogs and sallads are, in turn, mocked at by the aunt. Their conversation is worth reproducing.

Mrs. Clerimont:...	When I first went into *France*, I was mortally afraid of a Frog, but in a little time, I cou'd eat nothing else except Sallads.
Aunt:	Eat Frogs, Have I kiss'd one that has eat Froggs (sic) Paw (V, ii)

Her wish to sing the song in the French manner (III, i) is juxtaposed with Humphry's inability to perform Courant, Boree and Coupe in pure French manner, and Tipkin's remarks on it are in consonance with Steele's views expressed in his other writings. Obviously, Steele's sympathies lay with the English. This is illustrated by Humphry's following conversation with Mr. Tipkin:

Tipkin:	I see, Sir Harry, you han't set him a Capering under a French Dancing-Master: He does not mince it: He has not learn't to walk by a Courant, or a Boree – His Paces are natural.
Humphry:	I don't know, but 'tis so we walk in the West of England. (I, ii)

Steele's satire on aping foreign manners and morals is deeper and more pronounced in *The Tender Husband* than anywhere else.

The Tender Husband is a severe satire on the aristocracy given to fashionable vices and extra marital relations. Steele denounces such people through Mrs. and Mr. Clerimont. In order to be modish Mrs. Clerimont is infused with all the fashionable follies common among the women, *viz*., gambling, flirting, kissing her lap-dog, and spurning conjugal love. Her humiliating treatment of her husband, whom she commands like a servant and makes him seek her permission before entering her room are the glimpses of some of the unhealthy aspects of the fashionable world. In order to be deemed modish she asks her husband, "How did you sleep last night? (Aside) if I had not asked him that Question, they might have thought we lay together (III, i)". Her fondness for "modes of visage" and for lap dogs[15] goes with her character of a gay woman and is a prominent target for Steele's satire.

Steele has attempted to describe the psychology of women through Captain Clerimont's study of Biddy's character and Pounce's tactful handling of the aunt. According to them, to win their favour one has to feed their vanity and whims. Pounce's "tickling" the vanity of the old aunt is a common feature of the Restoration Comedy whereas to win a girl living in the world of romances, Captain Clerimont has to comply with her humours. He explains his views in the following words:

> I know none but the Coxcombs think to win a woman by any desert of their own – No, it must be done rather by complying with some prevailing Humour of Your Mistress, than exerting any good Quality in yourself. (II, iii).

Summing up his assessment of a woman's nature, he says:

> 'Tis not the Lovers' Merit wins the Field, But to themselves alone the Beauteous Yield. (II, iii)

From the learned professions Steele has satirised that of the law in the character of Pounce who is presented as a very discerning and practical man, as all lawyers generally are, well versed in the ways of men in all walks of life, *viz.*, Cheapside (business world), Covent Garden (pleasure haunt), St. James (world of fashion), and Westminster (Law), etc. Having worldly wisdom and a morally unscrupulous but pleasing personality, he is much sought after by the people in distress. He has several law suits on his hands but has time to spare for promoting love intrigues of Captain Clerimont since his and his sister's interests are also involved. As a lawyer he cleverly sets Mr. Tipkin and Sir Harry Gubbin "at stakes so that none of them have possession" of Biddy's fortune while he sees his sister Lucy Fainlove well settled finanically. He represents the class of the clever opportunistic lawyers to whom the interest of their clients are matters of secondary importance. He is promised ten thousand pounds by Clerimont Senior if he succeeds in getting Biddy and her fortune for his younger brother. This he readily agrees to do since the amount offered exceeds the one given by Mr. Tipkin for promoting Humphry's marriage with the same girl. "My character is helping the Distress'd" is Pounce's boastful claim but it is not based on altruistic or moral considerations. No doubt he does help the 'distressed' Humphry, Captain Clerimont and Biddy Tipkin, but in so doing he is motivated by personal considerations. He secures money for himself and a foolish rich husband for his sister, who, as already noted, is a fallen woman. When all is said and done, the fact is to be admitted that Steele's Pounce is not as rascally a character as Steele's own Sable[16] or as Fielidng's Peter Pounce.

Besides serious satire noted above, there is much fun too in the play. This is found in the scenes between Captain Clerimont and Pounce and Mr. Tipkin and Sir Harry Gubbin. On one occasion we find Pounce and Captain Clerimont praising the qualities of Biddy Tipkin; the former her fortune, the latter her physical charms which apparently look like Old Bookwit's praise of his wife. Captain Clerimont has never seen Biddy Tipkin but dwells on her beauty which he is ready to grant her as, being a fortune hunter, he is looking for wealth not for physical charms. It is, therefore, Biddy's wealth which makes her appear so attractive to him. This piece of comic dialogue, about Tipkin and his niece, Biddy, is worth quoting:

Captain Clerimont: No — But the Noble Captain would have Treasure out of his Hands — You know his Niece.

Pounce: To my knowledge Ten thousand Pounds in Money.

Captain Clerimont: Such a Stature; such a Blooming Countenance, So easy a Shape !

Pounce: In Jewels of her Grandmother's five thousand —

Captain Clerimont: Her Wit so lively, her mein so alluring!

Pounce: In Land a thousand a Year.

Captain Clerimont: Her Lips have that certain Prominence, that Swelling Softness, that they invite to pressure; (I, i)

The fact that all these 'charms' of Biddy are endowed by her money takes the fun to its apex. Similarly, the barter scene between Sir Harry Gubbin and Mr. Tipkin for two 'commodities'— the son and the niece — ridicules the money-minded guardians. Pounce's presence during the encounter heightens the comic effect. A part of the dialogue reproduced below shows how the two stock characters are ridiculed by Steele.

Sir Harry	– And as to what you demand, I tell you, Sir, 'Tis Extortion.
Tipkin	Sir Harry, do you accuse me of Extortion?
Sir Harry	Yes, I say extortion.
Tipkin	Mr. Pounce, write down that – There are very good laws provided against scandal and Calumny – loss of Reputation may tend to loss of Money –.
Sir Harry:	Why then Mr. *Pounce*, and Mr. *Tipkin*, you are both Rascals.
Tipkin:	Do you call me Rascal, Sir Harry?
Sir Harry:	Yes Sir.
Tipkin:	Write it down Mr. Pounce – at the end of the Leaf.
Sir Harry:	If you have room, son of a whore, Curmudgeon, - Hunks and Scoundrel.
Tipkin:	Not so fast, Sir Harry, He cannot write so fast, you are at the Word Villain – Son of a Whore, I take it, was next – You may make the account as large as you please, Sir Harry.

This produces pure sunny laughter and scenes like these lie interspersed throughout the play.

Some lewd and promiscuous expressions are also found here and there. Clerimont Senior's words to Lucy Fainlove savour of this element when he says: "No, no, you must not go near men – I don't design you to personate a real man, you are only to be a pretty Gentleman – Not to be of any Use or Consequence in the world, but merely as a property to others" (i, i). Captain Clerimont's instructions to Biddy Tipkin during the painting scene also have immodest suggestions. For example, when he tells her, "Please Madam, to uncover your Neck a little; a little lower still – a little little lower" (IV, ii). Further, Mrs. Clerimont's addresses to her 'seducer' Lucy Fainlove show lack of propriety: "Welcome my Dear, My Tender Charmer – Oh! To my longing Arms –

Feel the Heart Pant, that falls and rises as you smile or frown – Oh !, the Extatick Moment" (V, i).

That a moralist like Steele, who had modified some similar expressions in *The Funeral* should use or exhibit such things again can only be explained in the context of Steele's desire to portray apparently depraved characters. But, more than that, it was, probably the fate of his earlier play (damn'd for piety) which forced Steele to introduce this bit of vulgarity in *The Tender Husband*. Although the overall tone of *The Tender Husband* is satirical yet Steele has endeavoured to give it a sentimental touch in consonance with his pronounced moral objectives expressed in the Prologue and the Epilogue. But this element is confined to Mr. and Mrs. Clerimont Senior and, except for the latter's tearful repentance, there is not much of that.[17] Since the threat to her honour is not real and serious the sentimental situation is shorn of its poignancy of remorse and self-awakening like the one we find in *The Lying Lover*. Moreover, the person (her husband) who exposes and chides her for her misconduct is himself a philanderer needing self-reformation. Further, the 'seductuion' as well as the compromising position that she is punished for, deflates into a comic situation as we know her ravisher is a woman disguised as man.[18] Since the objective of reclaiming her is apparently fulfilled, the tears that she sheds may be considered as genuine and springing from her heart.[19] However, the scene between Clerimont Senior and his wife fails to touch our hearts.

Mrs. Clerimont:	You laid that Train, I'm sure, to alarm, not to betray, my Innocence – Mr. Clerimont scorns such Baseness! Therefore, I kneel – I weep – I am convinc'd (kneels).
Clerimont Senior	(Takes her up embracing her). Then kneel, and weep no more. – My Fairest – my Reconcil'd! Be so in a moment, for know I cannot (without wringing my own Heart) give you the least Compunction – Be in Humour – It shall be your own Fault, if ever there's a serious Word more on this Subject.

Mrs. Clerimont: I must correct every Idea that rises in my Mind, and learn every Gesture of my Body anew — I detest the thing I was.

(V, ii)

What made Steele give this scene a sentimental colour is perhaps his faith in marital reconciliation and conjugal love. The benign moralist makes the husband speak in maxims:

> They only who gain Minds, true laurels wear;
> 'Tis less to conquer, than Convince the Fair.
>
> (V, ii)

In the play Steele has also tried to present an objective assessment of certain facts of life. He shares the contemporary bourgeoise conscience and believes in the importance and value of money. The sketches of Humphry Gubbin and Captain Clerimont drawn somewhat sympathetically illustrate Steele's viewpoint. How sudden possession of money makes a man a different person is shown through Humphry's exuberance and confidence after he learns of his independence of his father from Pounce. Almost instantaneously he finds himself capable of great deeds. His timidity gives place to confidence and to a zeal to enjoy life. He says:

> Now I am flush of Money — A Man's quite another thing with Money in his Pocket. (I, ii)

Steele reiterates the same opinion through the character of Captain Clerimont. He is a discharged soldier who was at Blenheim. But his "trading in the Noble Mart of Glory", as Pounce defines patriotism, will not help him. Once the red coats are out of job, he will have no means of livelihood except that of marrying a fortune. It is a situation that had a parallel in Steele's own life.[20] It is money not Biddy's wit or beauty that attracts Captain Clerimont. It is money that makes her beautiful in his eyes. Like the Restoration Comedy, early eighteenth century comedy, too, considered fortune as a necessary qualification in a woman.[21] Lucy Fainlove's eagerness to have Humphry Gubbin as her husband is also related to the question of financial stability. What money means is best known to Mr. Tipkin who is a merchant. His belief in thrift and a sensible way of spending money seems to have Steele's approval. He expresses his opinion thus:

> Let the Girls be what they will – a Thousand Pound a Year, is a Thousand Pound a year, and a Thousand Pound a Year is neither Girl nor Boy.
>
> (I, ii)

He loves money because it has its practical value and not because he wants to amass it, as Squire Gubbin does. Mr. Tipkin's thrift and prudent way of life typical of his class, is advocated by Biddy's aunt when she says, "to live with Prudence and Frugality, which the traders in Lombard Street do," is the only way "to live comfortably." (II, ii). Steele shared the views of the trading class which practised frugality, a quality which Steele applauded in others – such as in Mr. Sealand (*The Conscious Lovers*) – but himself did never possess.

Some vital issues of the time are touched upon by Steele in the course of the play. These relate to the question of the improper upbringing of the children by the money-minded self-centred parents and guardians. Like Shadwell in the *Squire of Alsatia*[22], Steele has decried application of strict discipline to grown up children (V, ii). This idea was subsequently reiterated by Steele in his essay where, referring to the effect of merciless flogging on young boys in schools, he says:

> Many a brave and noble spirit has been there broken; others have run from thence (schools) and were never heard of afterwards.
>
> (*The Spectator*, No. 168)

Besides this he has denounced repeatedly marriages based on mercenary motives of the parents who treat their marriageable children like livestock to be disposed of to the highest bidder. How the feelings of the children are not taken into account in such marriages is depicted vividly in Biddy-Humphry episode.

The play, on the whole, despite its apparent resemblance with the comedies of the preceding age, is in essence a moral comedy. The well-known Restoration features, *viz.*, amorous intrigues, erring wives, licentious husbands, short-sighted strict guardians, country boobies, mistresses, etc., are no doubt the staple of this play too. Nevertheless, Steele's play shows that the Restoration seeds grown in the Augustan soil could give results different from those of the past.[23] Here the emphasis is on the reclamation of the erring wife. Whereas the Restoration dramatists were chiefly concerned with the mere depiction of these vices and weaknesses, Steele's emphasis is on the correction and reformation of the wayward and the wanton as also of the misguided or ill-managed individuals. The play is marked by its emphatic use of satire which is directed at the contemporary social and moral vices, like card-playing and gambling of the fashionable women which led them to the squandering of their money and neglect of their household duties besides putting their honour at stake. Steele, the admirer of domestic virtues of a sensible wife devoted to her husband, house and children, could hardly approve of the conduct of a reckless woman like Mrs. Clarimont. Yet Steele does not go to the extent of exhibiting the extreme danger that such women were courting. The moralist in him who always envisaged a woman as an embodiment of chastity and virtue, would never let him present her in an openly immoral situation. No wonder the play with its Restoration satirical tone as well as pronounced moral objectives, honest and basically good characters and a basically 'sentimental' situation retained its popularity next to *The Conscious Lovers*.

NOTES

1. Steele's financial difficulties and rift with Rich, the Manager of the Drury Lane, started somewhere in 1703 and culminated in 1705 when Rich refused to pay him the profits of the first two nights.
2. *Plays*, p. 212.
3. The situation makes one think of Congreve's *Love for Love* where Ben refuses to marry Miss Prue, a girl chosen by his father.
4. That Steele had conceived the character of Biddy very clearly is evident from the title he had initially chosen for the play, *The City-Nymph*; Or, *The Accomplish'd Fools* which was subsequently changed probably because this title and the sub-title both referred to the main plot only to the neglect of the other.
5. Biddy's Love for these romances is like that of the heroines of Molière's *Les Précieuses Ridicules* but the emphasis on their harmfulness for women is wanting in Molière. Like Biddy, Cathos and Magdelon call themselves as Aminta and Polyrena, after the names of the ladies in romances.
6. Krutch, *op. cit.*, p. 184.

7. He is equally conscious of his own squandering of money on costly wenches. (IV, i)
8. A similar situation is found in Mrs. Centlivre's *The Basset Table* (1705) where a female gamester, Lady Reveller, is reclaimed through a similar stratagem by her lover who sends his friend to assault her honour
9. Steele was quite considerate towards the unfortunate 'fallen' women. In *The Spectator* No. 274 Steele accuses "the crafty men" for their "gallantries" and "pruriency" which make women resign the characteristic of their sex, "Modesty". He could never forget his affair with Elizabeth Tonson.
10. Peter Pounce reappears in Fielding's *Joseph Adrews*, but this time as a caricature of a real scoundrelly lawyer, Petre Waters.
11. Young Heartford is as averse to marrying his cousin as Humphry is
12. Nevertheless, Biddy and Humphry are not recalcitrant and refractory like the young wards of the Restoration comedy. Their politeness and respect for their guardians is a marked feature of Steele's comedies.
13. Trevelyan, *Social History*, p. 36.
14. In *The Spectator*, No. 268, Steele has published for general consideration a letter which questions the justice of marriage de convenience. Steele condemns such marriage contracts that couple two incompatible temperaments. In this connection, in *The Spectator*, No. 437, he says, "A parent who forces a child of liberal and ingenuous spirit into the Arms of a Clown or a Block-head obliges her to a Crime too odious for a Name."
15. Pope has repeatedly satirised the fondness of the fashionable women of the early eighteenth century for lap dogs:

    Not louder Shrieks to pitying Heavens are cast,
    When Husbands or when lap-dogs breath their last.

    (*The Rape of the Lock*, Canto III)
16. In *The Tatler*, No. 61 Steele shows his determination to satirise such malefactors as would, in the normal course of life, escape unscathed. In the same essay he further says, "we shall therefore take it for a very moral Action to find good Apellation for Offenders, and turn 'em into ridicule."
17. F.T. Wood finds fault with Steele on this score. According to him although (the play) held out ample opportunities for a sentimental development, Steele failed to make the best of them. (F.T. Wood, *Anglia*, p. 389).
18. Such a situation is found in Cibber's *The Lady's Last Stake* which presents a real threat to the lady's honour. Lady Gentle's gambling makes her put her honour at stake which Lord George wants to assault. She is saved by the timely arrival of Lord George's beloved, Lady Conquest. Lady Gentle eventually realises her folly and resolves to mend herself. Steele, however, would not let even Mrs. Clerimont go to such extremes.
19. Similar scenes in which errant wives are reclaimed are found in sentimental comedies such as in Colley Cibber's *The Lady's Last Stake* and Mrs. Centlivre's *The Basset Table* and *The Gamester*.

20. Steele was always in need of money. On leaving the army in 1705 after the victory of Blenheim, he pursued the aging rich widow, Margaret Ford Stretch, whom he married soon after finishing *The Tender Husband.*

21. Old Bellair, while talking of the girl chosen for his son, expresses similar views in the following words:

    A wife is no curse when she brings the blessing of a good estate with her. (*The Man of Mode*, II, i)

22. Sir Edward Belfond in the concluding lines of the play says:

    You that would breed your Children well, by Kindness and Liberality endear 'em to you; And teach 'em by Example. Severity spoils ten for one it mends: By gentleness and Bounty make those Sons your Friends. (*Works*, II, p. 281)

23. It will be useful to remember what F.T. Wood says about this comedy:

    The play is really a combination of the comedy of manners and farce, with an underlying strain of sentiment.

    (*Anglia*, p. 389)

8

The Conscious Lovers

The Conscious Lovers conceived sometime before 1714[1] and finished by 1719 could not be produced at Drury Lane before November 1722 because of Steele's dispute with the Duke of Newcastle, the Lord Chamberlain. Financial stringency caused by his expulsion from the Parliament in 1714 and his increasing debts,[2] didactic cast of his mind and the prevailing reforming spirit of the Drury Lane theatre itself were some of the factors that gave to this play the shape that it has.

The basic theme of the play seems to be the pleasing passions which arise from watching the conduct of the virutous sensitive and honourable lovers. The main plot concerns the love of Bevil Junior, a paragon of virtue, for Indiana, a virgin in distress helped by him. But his father has arranged his marriage with Lucinda, the beautiful daughter of a rich merchant, Sealand. But, contrary to the wishes of her husband, Mrs. Sealand wants their daughter to marry a relative of her, Cimberton. The play opens with Sir John Bevil who finds himself in a dilemma as he has come to know about Bevil Junior's concern for Indiana whom he had carried to a secure place after she had fainted at a masquerade. This has created suspicion in the mind of Sealand and he wishes to break off the match between his daughter and Bevil Junior. Sir John Bevil pretends to be keen on Bevil Junior's marriage with Lucinda to keep his word with Sealand but actually he is anxious to know his son's actual inclinations. Complications arise when Bevil Junior is unable to disoblige "the best of fathers" because of his filial devotions and gets dressed suitably for the marriage ceremony. On the other hand, to avert his marriage with Lucinda, he writes a letter to her describing his interest in Indiana. In the meantime Lucinda's father tries to investigate the veracity of the rumour caused by the masquerade scene by meeting Indiana himself. He discovers in her his long-lost daughter, which is confirmed by the presence of his long-lost sister, Isabella, and of a bracelet that he had given to his first wife. He learns how his family was involved in a ship-wreck, how his daughter and his sister had been rescued by the Captain of the ship, and how Bevil Junior had been their benefector after rescuing them from the clutches of the wicked brother of the Captain. This sentimental reunion helps Indiana marry her virtuous and constant lover, Bevil Junior, with the approval of his father.

The sober tone of the main plot is lightened by the introduction of a sub-plot concerning Myrtle's love for Lucinda. It has several features of Restoration comedy such as, the light-hearted love intrigue, a contemptible suitor in a pedantic coxcomb and a social climber. Myrtle, basically good-hearted but jealous and hot tempered, challenges Bevil Junior, whom he takes to be his rival, to a duel which the latter with his characteristic cool-headedness averts by explaining to him his whole conduct, particularly his love for Indiana. Phillis, Lucinda's maid, and Tom, Bevil Junior's servant, help Myrtle in seeing Lucinda by disguising him as Sir Geoffery, Cimberton's uncle. When Sealand on finding his long-lost daughter gives half of his estate to her, Cimberton shows his true colours. He refuses to marry Lucinda who will now inherit only half of her father's fortune. The tension created by the threatened arranged match is relieved and everything ends happily.

The play has another pair of lovers in the servants, Tom and Phillis, who ape the polished foppish manners of their superiors. Since the dialogue of the serious-minded hero and the sober young heroine in pathetic circumstances is not witty and jestful, the characters of the lower strata, suffering from no constraints, compensate for this with their wit-battles and quips.[3] It is said that Steele had added these two comic characters on Cibber's advice to lessen the gravity of the play[4] and true it is that their frank and straight-forward love-making does provide that kind of pleasure which was traditionally associated with the 'low' characters of earlier comedy.

Steele had selected Terence's *Andria* as his model for this play. Steele's play has quite a few parallels with the original. The main plot and the concerned characters are as grave as those in the original. The rumour of Bevil Junior's love for Indiana arising out of their behaviour at the masquerade which becomes the root cause of the calling off of the match between Bevil Junior and Lucinda is similar to the one in the Roman play. Bevil's friend Myrtle is the counterpart of Pamphilius's friend Charinus who loves Chremes's daughter Philumena, the lady Pamphilius is supposed to marry. Like Pamphilius, Bevil assuages the jealousy of his friend. The characters of Tom and Phillis in Steele's play are based on Davus, Pamphilius's servant and Mysis, Glycerium's maid servant. The recovery of the long-lost children brings about a happy ending in both the plays.

There are, however, certain significant departures too which can be ascribed to Steele's didacticism. For example, in Terence's play there is no paragon of virtue like Bevil Junior, and of chastity and modesty like Indiana. In *Andria* the hero has illicit relations with Glycerium who is presented as the sister of a prostitute and who gives birth to his child. Chremes is made to see a child brought from Glycerium's house and placed on Pamphilius's threshold which makes him turn against the match. In the original a traveller from Andros appears and reveals that Glycerium is the long-lost daughter of Chremes. Steele has replaced the traveller with Indiana's aunt and has used the bracelet, Sealand's gift to his wife, as an identification mark. The challenge to a duel by Myrtle and Bevil Junior's refusal to take it up are some of the crucial departures necessitated by the moral concern of the playwright.

To encourage good morals and manners for the emulation of the young people of the gentry, Steele has created a perfect moral specimen in Bevil Junior. This hero exemplifies Steele's concept of a fine gentleman.[5] Bevil Junior is brought up liberally by his father, Sir John Bevil and, thanks to his dead mother's legacy, is a man of independent means. He could have lived a life of fashionable debauchery but he is an upright man with strong convictions. He is an embodiment of good manners, goods sense, reason, kind-heartedness and honesty. His sober temperament, filial devotion and "tender obligations" to his father have conditioned his behaviour so much that he is always found sedate, decorous, obedient and obliging. He has taken an oath not to marry without the consent of his father. He makes his position clear when he tells Humphrey, "You may assure yourself, I never will Marry without my Father's Consent" (I, ii). To please his father he has dressed himself for the wedding, but he has, in the meanwhile, conveyed his feelings to Lucinda and thus hopes that eventually he will be saved from the painful necessity of opposing the wishes of his father. However, the proposed match with Lucinda is telling upon his nerves and he has to strive to maintain his calm to steer "his actions with conscious honour." Throughout the play his actions are governed by reason and not by passion or wordly considerations. This clearly is a departure from the Restoration tradition where the hero never bothers about his guardian's (father or uncle) sentiments and commitments. Bevil Junior's rational conduct is further revealed when jealous Myrtle, who misunderstands Bevil Junior's correspondence with his beloved Lucinda, challenges him to a duel. He, exercising utmost self-control, takes the challenge as a product of a lover's over-jealous mind. He evinces active interest in Myrtle's affairs and helps him in securing his beloved. Thus, he succeeds in establishing his innocence and regaining the love and esteem of his friend.[6] Bevil Junior has no trace of vanity in him. He is unassuming and gentle even to his inferiors. This is shown by his conduct towards his servant Tom and his father's steward Humphrey, but more particularly by what he says about the music master he had called to entertain Indiana. He explains his treatment of the latter to Indiana in words which deserve to be quoted:

> I think it's not enough barely to pay those, whose Talents are superior to our own (I mean such Talents, as would become our Condition, if we had them.) Methinks we ought to do something more than barely gratify them, for what they do at our Command, only because their Fortune is below us.
>
> (II, iii)

His attitude towards Tom is of good humoured authority and he treats his father's servant, the aged Humphrey, with that kind of courtesy and respect that Shakespeare's Orlando had for Adam (*As You Like it*). It is Humphrey who Bevil Junior confides in. This reveals Steele's regard for the faithful servants of old type who were so different from the modish ones of the contemporary society – a type that was often criticised (though not severely) by him.[7]

Bevil Junior is an "unfashionable lover". Though a lover of Indiana's beauty he has been a "parent to her honour". He is always careful to protect her reputation and hence it is that he visits her only in the presence of her aunt. Whenever he happens to be alone with her he talks about myriad things of life, *viz.*, opera, theatre, morality, etc., but never about love as his counterparts in Restoration Comedy do on such occasions. This again shows Steele's concern for morality and regard for women. Bevil Junior is so unfashionable a lover that he has never probed into Indiana's feelings for him nor has he openly declared his love to her or his desire to marry her. His dealings with her have all along been like those of an emotionally disinterested person, doing good for its own sake instead of a reward or recognition. He is ready to sacrifice his love for her at the altar of his filial duty which, again, a Restoration lover would never have done.

However, his obedience to his father does not mean that he is prepared to surrender his individuality totally. He has very strong views about marriages arranged by parents who do not take the feelings and sentiments of their children into consideration. This trait adds to the complexity of the situation he is placed in. Obviously, Bevil Junior's character was sketched with utmost care by Steele since he wanted him to be a model for the young men of this time. Steele has, therefore, deliberately made Bevil Junior what he is, a dutiful son, a sincere friend and a virutous lover who is never swayed by passion, anger or any vulgar desire. His reluctance to marry the girl chosen by his worldly wise father is due to his abhorence for the prevailing practice of making material gains as the sole object of marriages. He, however, will not openly rebel against the authority of his father[8] because he is confident that he can manipulate things and finally have his way. Moreover, he is confident his want of warmth for the match arranged by his kind and considerate father, which Sir John Bevil surely is, will not be overlooked by him. And this is what actually happens eventually.

Steele has substituted the libertine Dorimant with Bevil Junior and the gay and witty Harriet with an exemplary character, Indiana, who has all those qualities which Harriet lacks.[9] The moralist in Steele would not let him have characters like Dorimant and Harriet. Bevil Junior and Indiana, as also Myrtle and Lucinda, belong to altogether a different class. His young lovers are not libertines nor young ladies gay coquettes. Indiana has got an impressive personality, and her sad experiences right from her childhood have given her a gravity and a grace that win our heart. Sir Bevil himself is struck by the uncommon air, noble modesty and dignified conduct exhibited by her at the masquerade. Her inherent sense of a woman's natural decency does not allow her to express openly her feelings for her lover and benefactor. But, in his absence, she cherishes his amiable image which her aunt, who has lost all her faith in man, wants to tear off from her heart. But, despite her aunt's persistent efforts to change her opinion in respect of Bevil Junior, she understands what his motives are and, therefore, remains devoted to him. How deeply she loves Bevil Junior is shown by her words – "All the rest of my life is but wanting till he comes. I live when I'am with him" (II, ii). When provoked by her aunt, she throws the garb of "natural decencies" and becomes desirous of knowing Bevil's feelings for her. She introduces the subject indirectly through a discussion of imaginary characters. Convinced of Bevil Junior's seemingly "disinterested respect of virtue" and understanding the genuine concern of a father for the welfare of his daughter she is prepared to sacrifice her interests for the sake of Bevil and Lucinda's happiness. She will not demean herself and beg for love but will rather resign herself in a most philosophic manner:

> if he takes me forever, my purpose of Life is to please him, if he leaves me (which Heaven avert) I know he'll do it nobly; and I shall have nothing to do but to learn to die... (II, ii).

Sealand's humiliating treatment of her adds to her misery. Her heart, hungry of love, bleeds at this unfair attack on her virtue and denial of love to her. Her sufferings, constancy and sacrifice are rewarded by Providence when she is reunited with her long-lost father and gets the man she loves and secures love, honour and respect of all concerned.

Another virtuous character that Steele has presented is Sealand who upholds, as his name symbolises, the dignity of his class, the rich trading class. Sealand, who belonged to an ancient family, was a younger brother and, therefore, had adopted trade as his profession which brought him both fortune and social status. But his business life has seen several ups and downs which have affected his domestic life also. On one occasion he lost his wife daughter, sister as well as all his fortune. After this tragedy he had to change his name from Danvers to Sealand for reasons which now be considers as "too tedious" to narrate. May be, it was the loss of fortune that compelled him to start anew with a new name in Indies where fortune again helped him in his trade over sea and land. He retains his new name even after coming to England which, along with a long lapse of time, makes it difficult for his daughter to search him out. After the loss of his first wife, Indiana's mother, he had married for a second time and was again blessed with a daughter, Lucinda.

As a member of the rising merchant class, Sealand is proud of his social condition and makes fun of Sir John Bevil, a representative of the idle 'gentry', for his absurd obsession with "geneology and descent" and class status. He has agreed to marry his daughter off to Bevil Junior not because of his pedigree but because of his merit. But the moment he grows suspicious of Bevil's character he decides to break this match off. He is, however, a sensible man and therefore he would investigate the matter thoroughly before taking any action. When he meets Indiana he further reveals himself as a respector of virtue; he finds her "so worthy an object, so accomplished a lady" as her "sense and mein bespeak" that all his hostility is changed into admiration. After the discovery that Indiana is his long-lost daughter he agrees to promote her alliance with Bevil Junior once he satisfies himself in respect of his character. He admires constance and virtue and is always ready to reward them.

In Mr. Sealand's character Steele has shown that the class represented by him deserved respect equal to that of the gentry. In *The Spectator*, No. 218 he voices the feelings of the early eighteenth century society which viewed the merchant as a person "who every day he lived literally added to the value of his native country". The prosperous merchants were generally anxious to ennoble their line by getting their children married into the gentry. Steele's sympathetic treatment of this class was clearly a departure from the Restoration comic tradition which presented the 'cits' in most ludicrous colours. Mr. Sealand expresses Steele's conviction when, defending his class, he says:

> We merchants are a species of Gentry, that have grown into the world this last Century, and are as

> honourable and almost useful, as you landed Folks, that have always thought yourselves so much above us. (IV, ii)

He is juxtaposed to Sir Bevil who is materialistic even in respect of his only son's marriage. These two fathers with their different motives and attitudes and values have a confrontation, like that of Tipkin and Sir Harry in *The Tender Husband*, over finding a suitable match for their respective children. But in *The Conscious Lovers* the treatment is substantially different for Steele's sympathies seem to lie with the merchant rather than with Sir John Bevil.[10] Sir Bevil and Sealand are kind, sympathetic and understanding fathers whose utmost concern is their children's welfare. But the former is still at heart a squire lured by fortune which he considers as a necessity for a happy life, whereas the latter has more regard for man's character and is conscious of the fickleness of fortune. Steele has created, in Sir John Bevil, a character who is an alloy of the elements of the Restoration and the sentimental comedy that was to come later. He is an amalgamation of kind, considerate and liberal guardian of *The Squire of Alsatia* type and the fortune hunting one of the Restoration type. As a sensible father he has allowed full liberty to his son to live "after his own manner" because he believes in liberal upbringing and not in the policy of restraint and intimidation. Mutual understanding prevails between him and his son and each fears giving pain to the other. Sir John realises that there is something behind his son's disinterestedness in Lucinda but does not suspect anything unbecoming on his part in the absence of a positive proof. However, he cannot bear the idea of losing a daughter-in-law like Lucinda. The temptation of her wealth is too great to be overcome. He says, "... great Wealth, and the Merit of his only Child, the Heiress of it, are not to be lost. .. (IV, ii). He asks Humphry not to let Bevil Junior stir out of the house from fear of meeting Sealand and thus causing a break of the match. This shows that his love of riches is so excessive that for once he is ready to abandon his laudable principles and exercise the restrictive authority of a father. But his apparently mercenary outlook is a product of his love for his only son. It is his concern for Bevil Junior's material welfare that makes him so keen to get him married to Lucinda. Still, he is "the kindest father" who would like to have that kind of frank and congenial relationship with his son which Steele had been talking of in his essays.[11]

Another exemplary character in the play is Humphrey, the old servant of Sir John, who is almost equal in age to his master and has been serving him since his childhood. He is honest, sincere, sober and affectionate like Trusty in *The Funeral* and represents the faithful servant class of the old days.[12] He is seen exchanging quips with Sir John Bevil at their age, gravity and their difference of status. Poverty has imposed premature gravity upon him while wealth has kept Sir John Bevil younger. Humphry's "ingenuous nature" has made him his master's confidant and, therefore, he shares his secrets and tries to resolve his problems. He understands both Sir John Bevil and Bevil Junior and tries to avert the impending breach between them. Where the father fails, he succeeds in persuading Bevil Junior unravel the mystery of the "woman of the masquerade". While he advises Bevil Junior to pretend to be willing to marry Lucinda, he tells Sir John to be patient with his son. The happiness of the master's family is the sole object of his life.

Another basically virutous character painted most vividly is that of Myrtle, Lucinda's lover. He is a typical lover of the sentimental romantic type and, accordingly, suffers from jealousy, a fault which he admits and repents of, but, from which he is unable to free himself completely. However, his jealousy is understandable and most natural under the circumstances since it is due to the news that his closest and most trusted friend, Bevil Junior, is going to marry his beloved. Overcome by anger, he takes it as an act of perfidy on the part of his friend and feels honour-bound to challenge him to a duel. What he does not know is the fact that Bevil Junior is averse to this match and is in fact secretly promoting his cause. When Bevil Junior shows him Lucinda's letter and dispels the clouds of jealousy, good-hearted Myrtle apologises readily and expresses his gratitude to Bevil Junior. After this he feels so spirited that he enthusiastically welcomes Phillis' suggestion to disguise himself as Cimberton's uncle and, in a typical Restoration style, get access to Lucinda. Once there, he feigns fainting in the presence of Mrs. Sealand and Cimberton and dupes both of them. His jealousy and hot temper give place to cheerfulness and serenity. But this does not mean that his nature and temperament are permanently changed. Myrtle is a man of fluctuating moods, governed by impulses and not by reason. Steele has deliberately given him this trait to distinguish him from his ideal young gentleman Bevil Junior. In spite of all this, he is basically a good human being. He does not covet fortune and loves Lucinda only for her worth.[13] He says, "No abatement of fortune shall lessen her value to me", and accordingly, unlike Cimberton, accepts happily Lucinda when the discovery of Sealand's another daughter implies a reduction of her share in her father's possessions. Here again Steele shows a departure from the traditions of Restoration writers in making a true gentleman solely concerned with virtues rather than with the fortunes of a woman. In Restoration Comedy a young man of the town never feels inclined to marry a woman who would not provide him with the means (that is wealth) to carry on his amours with other women.

Unlike the gay fun-loving heroines of the Restoration Comedy,[14] Steele's Indiana is virtue and modesty personified. His concept of womanhood is exemplified in her character. She is richly endowed with wit, beauty and virtue and is thus the source of "pure delight" and "guiltless joy" to her lover. She is a woman of culture and refinement and has a taste for operas, music, philosophy, etc. Her conduct is always correct and courteous. When she is with Bevil Junior she never gives vent to her passion. Exercising puritanical restraint, she suppresses her true feelings and talks to him about various matters with utmost calm. Every thought and every action of hers bears a stamp of decency and modesty. She is so virtuous and accomplished that even Sealand and Sir John Bevil have to admit that she has an "uncommon Air, her noble Modesty, the Dignity of her Person" (I, i). Her faith in Bevil Junior's good nature is so strong that the persistent efforts of her aunt fail to shake it off. On the contrary, she defends him on all occasions, before her aunt as well as Sealand. Reason and sense govern her thoughts and actions. She understands Bevil Junior's dilemma and his inability to declare his love openly to her. Her statement before her aunt – "but by his Behaviour I am convinc'd he will offer it (marriage proposal), the Moment 'tis in his Power, or consistent with his Honour, to make such a Promise good" (II, ii) – reveals her conviction that Bevil Junior is in every respect an honourable fine gentleman. She herself is an example of nobility and sacrifice. When she realises that she is the cause of unhappiness to Sealand as well as to Bevil Junior's father she at once makes up her mind to sacrifice her love and self-interest to help the distressed parents. But she knows what this loss will mean to her. Isabella's final assessment of the characters of the two lovers is indeed a tribute which they rightly deserve. Her words are:

> I must own, if they are both what they seem, they are made for one another, as much as Adam and Eve were, for there is no other, of their kind, but themselves.
> (V, iii)

Steele has shown a marked departure from the Restoration tradition by presenting Indiana as an exemplary character drawn after Collier's concepts. He has created her character for the emulation of the young women and it embodies and exhibits the precepts which he had been often presenting through his essays.[15] It would not be a far-fetched observation if one finds a close affinity between Indiana and the heroines of the Heroic Play, such as Aurelia, Graciana, Palmyra, the Queen of Sicily, etc.[16] Indiana never crosses the threshold of modesty and decency to woo and win her lover as the heroines of Restoration comedies do. Through her Steele seems to preach that women, in all circumstances should be modest, innocent and virtuous for Providence always rewards such women.

Like Indiana, Lucinda is also a virtuous lady but somewhat of a sprightly nature. The former is a victim of circumstances, the latter has to undergo the tribulations attending on the custom of arranged marriages of convenience in which the feelings of the girls concerned are treated as of no consequence. Lucinda is considered a commodity for sale and is exhibited to "awkward boobies" and "wealthy coxcombs". She expresses her helplessness and indignant disapproval of the sordid custom in the following words:

> To be bartered for, like the Beasts of the Fields,
> ... but for encrease [sic] of fortune. (III, i)

She is disgusted with the whole affair at being "surveyed like a steed at a sale" and when she finds that Cimberton takes her not as a human being but a machine capable of producing "a colony of heirs" she starts hating him more strongly. However, like other young girls of her time, she is in no position to do anything at this stage. Later on, when Myrtle comes to her disguised as

Cimberton's uncle, she is overjoyed and receives her lover with open arms. Her sprightly nature comes to the fore and she co-operates fully with him in his intrigue. Her love for him deepens when she finds him interested only in her and not in her fortune. Providence rewards her constancy and virtue by seeing that she is happily married to Myrtle.

The play has some absurd characters ridiculed in Restoration manner yet it has no downright vicious characters like Lady Brumpton of *The Funeral*. Cimberton is just a pedantic coxcomb and a pretender to wit and learning but not a detestable villain. He approaches marriage cold-bloodedly, and is more interested in Lucinda's dowry than in her other assets and qualities. When half of Sealand's estate is given to Indiana he at once shows his disinclination for the match because he is "in treaty for the whole, but if that is not to be come at, to be sure, there can be no bargain" (V, iii). In every respect he is true to the portrait drawn by Myrtle.

> Cimberton! .... under the direction of great Vanity and very little Judgement, shows his strongest bias [sic] in Avarice.... that he will examine the limbs of his Mistress ...as if she were a mere breeding Animal.
> (V, i)

This is what actually happens when under the very nose of Lucinda's mother, he passes the following comments on her:

> The speaking Invitation of her Shape, the gathering of herself up, and the Indignation you see in the pretty little thing – how, I am considering her, on this occasion, but as one that is to be pregnant..... And pregnant undoubted she will be yearly. I fear, I shan't for many years, have Discretion enough to give her one fallow Season. (III, i)

Myrtle does not consider this pedantic coxcomb a real threat to his earnest love. Cimberton's repeated talk of gratification of hunger, thirst and propagation of species is an evidence that the animal dominantes the human in him. His dwelling on Lucinda's physical charms and on the chances of her proving to be very fertile in the most lascivious manner reveals his sensuality. This kind of lewdness is not common in the play of Steele. In presenting this, Steele may have been motivated by his desire to depict a character considered contemptible by the early eighteenth century audiences. Of the three suitors of Lucinda, Cimberton, in spite of his pretensions (which are admired only by Mrs. Sealand's), is on the lowest plane of values and is rightly abhored by her.

Mrs. Sealand is a female fop of the Restoration type. Steele makes her a ridiculous character who is vain of her supposed intellectual powers and envious of her daughter's youth and beauty. Coming from the gentry, she is dissatisfied with her present middle class status. She disregards her husband's choice of Bevil Junior as Lucinda's bridegroom and proposes Cimberton, a kinsman of hers, as a match for her, thinking that it is an honour to "return" her "Blood again into the Cimberton's" (V, i). To live up to her social pretensions she is ready even to disregard her daughter. She expresses her grudge against her daughter thus:

> I'll live no longer in anxiety for a little Hussey [sic] that hurts my Appearance wherever I carry her: and, for whose sake, I seem to be not at all regarded, and that in the best of my Days. (V, iii)

When Phillis flatteringly says to her that she "might be taken for Mr. Sealand's daughter" she feels greatly flattered. Her personal limitations – a married women's status, the presence of a grown-up pretty daughter and the middle class sensibilities – would not let her live a life of gallantry as she wants to. She considers it a good riddance when she finds that her daughter is to marry not her favourite, Cimberton, but the man whom she (the daughter) loves. Her jubiliation over this shows how strongly the mother in her is dominated by the woman. She shows no sign of penitance or any inclination to reform herself till the very end. This seems rather odd in view of Steele's predilection for such reformations. Obviously, he wanted Mrs. Sealand to be what she is – a stupid woman to be ignored, if not despised, by one and all.

There are some characters which show Steele's efforts to blend the serious with the comic. The gravity of Bevil Junior's dilemma and trials of a distressed virgin are depicted in sentimental scenes which are juxtaposed with the lighter ones. Here also, Steele was following Cibber's advice who knew the taste of the audience better than Steele.[17] The comic element in the play is provided by a pair of lovers both of whom belong to the lower class. They are Tom, attendant-*cum*-confidant of Bevil Junior and Phillis who is to Lucinda what Tom is to Bevil Junior. Both of them have their prototypes in Restoration comedy.[18] Tom is a typical foppish Restoration servant having pretensions, dreams and aspirations of thé gentry. He considers himself as a superior being belonging to a class of servants totally different from the vulgar "domestic ordinary Drudges that do Business" (I, i). In a boastful vein he calls himself as a "Man-of-quality", having all the requisite traits. To establish this, he says:

> We are false Lovers; have a Taste of Musick, Poetry, Billet-deux, Dress, Politicks, ruin Damsels, and when we are weary of this lewd Town, and have a mind to take up, whip into our Master's wigs and Linnen, and marry Fortunes.[19] (I, i)

Tom is vain and foppish as well as witty and debonair. Humphry calls him "the prince of poor coxcombs" and he is proud of being the servant of a "single gentleman" that is, a bachelor. He is no more the bashful Tom of the past as now he has acquired "follies and vices enough for a man of ten thousand a year." (I, i). Servants in Restoration comedy followed their masters in having amours of their own. Likewise, Tom has an affair with Phillis. He loves "to fret and play with little wanton", who, unlike the hypocritical 'civilized' people, frankly justifies love-play between herself and Tom on the ground that "we vulgar take it (kissing) to be a sign of love. We servants; we are poor people that have nothing but our persons to bestow" (III, i). Though Tom apes the manners of the men of quality he claims to be, at heart, a man of "prodigious nice honour" Phillis by herself is a fortune to him. He says" One Acre with Phillis, wou'd be worth a whole country without her" (III, i). He plans to have a small tenement in young Bevil's house where he may live with Phillis after marriage. This clearly shows not only his honest motives and virtuous intentions but also the author's whole-hearted approval of alliances based, not on mercenary considerations, but on genuine affection.

Phillis, his beloved, also hates to be a slave and loves aping the women of quality. She lives in higher orbs of female fops; wishes to be carried in a coach or chair and considers it "a sad thing to walk". She is livelier and more ingenius than Tom. It is she who suggests to Myrtle to gain access to Lucinda by disguising himself as Sir Geoffrey. But, she, in spite of her foppish airs, is a virtuous woman at heart, as is her lover, Tom. She would not let Myrtle kiss her but to her lover, Tom, she allows this favour for she thinks that among servants kisses serve as seals to the contracts which are oral but more dependable than the legal parchments of the people of quality.

Steele allows Tom and Phillis to talk freely and frankly about love without exhibiting prudish inhibitions. But, at the same time, their behaviour is within the bounds of propriety. Though the people of lower classes were not to be governed by the same code of conduct as the people of quality, yet Steele's concern for morality would not permit the servants and attendants to indulge in acts of indecency.[20]

Steele, in the Preface, defended the tears shed on the reunion of long-lost father and daughter on the grounds that "anything that has its Foundation in Hapiness and Success" has its spring in "Delight" and is, therefore, an appropriate object of comedy. The sentimental scenes, showing a virtuous innocent virgin in the most pathetic situations, her having a silent passion for her benefactor and protector, and being tormented by false allegations are all an attempt on the part of the playwright to highlight the hero's essentially selfless goodness and benevolence to her and her own admirably exemplary qualities. The turn in her fortune with the unexpected happiness showered upon her from Heaven must have appeared as edifying to the contemporary audience as Pamela's fate did to a later generation.

In the play Steele has attacked certain social evils; particularly that of marriage of convenience (as opposed to one based on mutual love and understanding). According to him more often than not it plays havoc with the lives of the people concerned.[21] This is illustrated through the characters of Sir John Bevil and Sealand who have a materialistic approach to matrimony. True enough, to them their children's welfare is of paramount importance and it is for this reason that they are interested in money matters. Between the two fathers, Sir John Bevil is more materialistic than Sealand. Both of them are attracted by the merit of the other's child but Sir John gives equal (if not more) importance to money. He knows fully well "how useful Wealth is, and how necessary, even to those who despise it...."(IV, ii). He is keen to exercise his authority over his son in this connection because he wants to guard him from "being imprudently engaged" as he himself had done when he was young. Moreover, his experience has taught him that love-based marriages cause inconvenience even though they bear the stamp of social approval. Sealand, on the contrary, considers the boy's merit of paramount importance since his daughter's future happiness rests on it. To him, however, a marriage no matter how prudently arranged, can never be a success unless the husband is as virutous as the wife. He quotes Dryden to show the kind of life a virtuous woman is made to lead if she is forced into marrying a libertine:

> And while Abroad so prodigal a Dolt is,
> Poor Spouse at home ragged as a Colt is.
>
> (V, ii).

Steele's views in respect of matrimony are in consonance with those of the trading class of his time which knew the fickless of fortune as well as the enduring quality of worth and merit.

Closely following Sir Bevil and Sealand is Cimberton who is too gross and materialistic to show any regard for worth or love. He considers matrimony as a business contract, a bargain meant for multiplying one's fortune as well as progeny. The girl's merit of compatibilty is of no significance to him, as he professes:

> ... the Woman is the Bargain, like the Mansion-House in the Sale of Estate, is thrown in, and what that is, whether good or bad, is not at all consider'd.
>
> (III, i).

True to his character he refuses Lucinda's hand when it becomes clear that half of Sealand's wealth will now go to Indiana. Cimberton is the favourite of Mrs. Sealand whose views in respect of matrimony are totally different from those of her husband. Being a woman of quality and high pretensions, she is more concerned with the status of her family and geneology. Her whole approach is based on her veneration for the aristocratic blood, specially of her stock. For this reason only she considers her cousin, Cimberton, who belongs to an ancient rich family, as the most suitable match for her daughter. She hates trading class and wants to marry her daughter above her present class, into an honourable family in order "to keep the Blood as pure, and as regularly descended as may be" (III, i). Steele has shown his disapproval of such views by frustrating the designs of both Mrs. Sealand and Cimberton. He endorsed Sealand's views and attitude and, to some extent, Sir Bevil's because they appear sensible and realistic to him. Accordingly, he sees to it that the endeavours and expectations of the two fond fathers are not discredited since they are governed by their understandable parental concern for the real and lasting happiness of their children. To Steele it is an exhibition of a rational approach if worldly considerations too are taken into account by the two alliance – seeking like-minded virtuous characters. Bevil Junior's approach is not blinded by love, nor is it a complete surrender to the authority of the guardians; it is strictly based on reason. He is full of sarcasm when he tries to explain the sordid motives of people whose approach to matrimony is totally mercenary. Speaking to his father, he says:

> A Woman that is espous'd for a Fortune, is yet a better Bargain, if she dies; for then a Man may still enjoy what he did marry, the Money; and is disencumber'd of what he did not marry, the Woman. (I, ii)

He considers love as the strongest foundation for marital bliss and fidelity. At the same time, he regards the blessings of the parents as equally necessary. Unlike the Restoration lovers, he does not want to marry clandestinely but wait patiently for his father's consent to marry Indiana.[22] He seems to be anxious to bridge the gap between the traditional and the modern values. Indiana too shares the virtuous thoughts of Bevil Junior and prefers death to a matrimonial alliance which is devoid of love or parental sanction. With regard to matrimony she gives preference to filial obligations than to love. On this point Lucinda also agrees with Indiana. She is in favour of a marriage which is based on love as well as on the consent of the parents. She tells Phillis, "(Myrtle) had my Parent's Leave to apply to me, and by that has won me, and my Affections" (III, i).

Besides these characters, the persons of lower strata also favour love-based marriage. Tom and Phillis are not hampered by upper class values and considerations and, therefore, are allowed to express their views on love and marriage without any inhibition. To them love is the only thing that matters but money too is not to be despised for it has its value. They are sensible enough to know that a happy married life needs both love and money. That's why both of them are trying to amass money; it would enable them to have a "pretty livelihood" after their marriage. This comes out when Phillis, mocking at marriage contracts among the people of quality, thus speaks to Lucinda:

> ... as we have no Parchments, or wax necessary in our Agreements, we squeeze with our Hands, and seal with our Lips, to ratifie [sic] vows and Promises.
> (III, i).

Tom has a touch of a romantic lover and, therefore, for him his beloved is a fortune by herself. He does not treat marriage as an economic bargain but, however, he does not totally reject the value of money. Besides. Indiana's recognition too as Sealand's daughter emphasises this point. Sir John Bevil, who had already been impressed by her mien and merit finds her as Sealand's rich daughter much more acceptable a match for his son.[23]

The false notions of prestige that led people to indulge in the fatal business of duelling is another aspect of the contemporary social scene that has been satirically noticed by Steele in the play under consideration. Duelling is one of the evils that he had repeatedly denounced in his writings. In the preface to this play he claimed that 'the whole was writ for the sake of the scene of the Fourth Act, wherein Mr. Bevil evades the Quarrel with his Friend.'[24] The scene contains very forceful arguments against duelling which only a man of reason and courage like Bevil Junior could utter. Speaking to Myrtle, he makes the following significant statement, "I abhorr'd the Daring to offend the Author of life, and rushing into His Presence" (IV, i). Myrtle too realises the evils of duelling. When his temper cools down and reason dawns on him, he says, "What had become of one of us, or perhaps both, had you been as weak as I was, and as incapable of Reason?" He adds, "There is nothing manly, but what is conducted by Reason, and agreeable to the practice of Virtue and Justice" (IV, i). He expresses his strong disapproval of "the Decisions a Tyrant Custom has introduc'd, to the Breach of all Laws, both Divine and Human" (IV, i). The reaction of this scene on the contemporary audience is described by Steele's friend, Benjamin Victor thus:

> With what sensible Pleasure I observ'd the chief part of the Audience receive your Hero's Behaviour...[25]

The expansion of international trade and the erosion of class barriers resulted in the rise of the enterprising merchant class. The 'cits' of the Restoration comedy were no more laughed at by the end of the Seventeenth century and the early eighteenth century presents them as respectable people well established financially and socially.[26] Sealand, the representative of this class, upholds the dignity of the same. Through his character Steele has shown how even the landed gentry is obliged to respect them and readily accepts marriage proposals from them. Mrs. Sealand, who belongs to an ancient family, is married into a merchant's family and Sir John Bevil, though sensitive to class distinctions, is quite happy to have Lucinda as his daughter-in-law. Steele also had very strong views (not dissimilar to Pope's)[27] regarding the way one's wealth is to be used. He consistently stressed that money is necessary but it is to be used prudently, neither to be hoarded nor to be thrown away. A God's blessing, it should not be turned into a curse by being spent on gaming, gambling and voluptuous pursuits that bring poverty and detested diseases. Rather it should be used in acts of unostentatious charity, to help the needy and the distressed. Bevil Junior has his mother's fortune but has never spent it on vicious pursuits as the people of quality usually did. That money should be chiefly used in making things easier for other, is exemplified through him when he helps Indiana in her misery and acts as her benefactor selflessly for several years. He is generous to his servant also. Tom and Phillis' efforts and Sealand's thrift exhibit the same tendency.

Steele has denounced false pride in one's geneology too. Sir John Bevil and Mrs. Sealand can be proud of their respective geneology but it does not give them any superiority over Sealand who, though without an impressive family background, has been materially successful and is highly respected in their circles. He represents the rising middle class of the eighteenth century which was becoming as respectable, if not more, in the eyes of the people as the aristocracy or the landed gentry.

To sum up, Steele's masterpiece, *The Conscious Lovers* is the full blossoming of his genius. The plot structure of this play is different from the conventional structure of the plays of the preceding age. It has no gulling, no love chases, no assignations nor a familiar boy-gets-a-girl plot of the Restoration type. It hinges on the conflict between filial duty and conscious (sensible) love. Reason, virtue and constancy are rewarded and thus the demands of the poetic justice are also met. In his other plays it is a human being who acts as a manipulator; either it is a Campley, or a Trim or a Pounce or a Bookwit. But in *The Conscious Lovers* it is clearly the Providence which helps the unhappy lovers. It is here, more than anywhere else, that Steele is pre-eminently concerned with preaching good sense and morality. Even the distress of the virtuous characters shows their triumph over some vice or human frailty. And it is this triumph that earns them admiration. It also provides, to the audience, a special kind of pleasure which is much more sublime and satisfying than the purposeless laughter of the Restoration comedy. Moral considerations are foremost in *The Funeral*, and *The Lying Lover* as well, but their significance and gravity are somewhat subdued by the preponderance of ridicule. In *The Conscious Lovers*, with the exception of one or two comic situations, the tone of the play is in keeping with its high moral ends. David Hume was not indulging in rhetorics when he described *The Conscious Lovers* as "a revolutionary theatrical innovation... an ideal and an aspiration..."[28]

NOTES

1. Swift in a lampoon directed at Steele, summarises the plot of a play which can be none but that of *The Conscious Lovers*. This is a reliable evidence in this connection. Loftis, p. 185.
2. Steele's letter to his wife dated July 16, 1717 refers to this situation.
3. Steele had already created the characters of Tom and Phillis in *The Guardian* No. 87.
4. *Plays*, p. 278.
5. Steele's concept of a fine gentleman presented in *The Guardian* (April 20, 1713) and *The Spectator*, No. 65 will be discussed in detail in a later chapter.
6. In *The Tatler* (May 16, 1710) Steele praises true friendship and says, The most important assistance, the mere well wishes of a friend, gives a man constancy and courage against the most prevailing forces of his enemy.
7. *The Spectator*, No. 88 gives Steele's views on such servants.
8. Steele did not favour open rebellion on the part of children because it went against his concept of an ideal young man. He always preached "mutual confidence and right understanding—between father and son." (*The Spectator* No. 425).
9. Etherege's *The Man of Mode* which Steele has attacked in *The Spectator*, No. 65.

10. Steele was a whig and, therefore, favoured the merchant class.
11. In *The Spectator*, No. 263 Steele cites the example of Camillus and his son who have so well cemented their relationship that the father is a blessing for the son and the son would endeavour to be a worthy off-spring of such a father.
12. *Old Adam* in *As You Like It* is a model of sincerity. He has spent best of his years in the service of his master and when his master's younger son, Orlando, is faced with banishment he is ready to go to the Forest of Arden with him.
13. Unlike Myrtle, Dorimant, a Restoration hero, who is keen on marrying for money, tells his friend, Young Bellair, that

    "The wise will find a difference in our fate:
    You wed a woman, I a good estate." (IV, i).
14. See *The Spectator*, No. 65.
15. See, for example, *The Spectator*, Nos. 266, 342, 449 and *The Tatler*, Nos. 302 and 449.
16. Aurelia and Graciana (Etherege's *Love in a Tub*), Palmyra (Dryden's *Marriage a-la-Mode* and the Queen of Cicily in *The Secret Love)*. These plays are typical Restoration Comedies, but there is an infusion of some 'heroic' element too.
17. In the *Apology* Cibber says that in writing this play Steele had much assistance of which evidence has been given upon oath by our several Actors. (p. 275).
18. Such as Warner and Rose in Dryden's *Sir Martin Mar-All,* Maskall and Beatrix in *An Evening Love* and Waitwell and Foible in Congreve's *The Way of the World*.
19. Tom's speech is of course a ridicule of the irresponsible and immoral life led by the men of quality of Steele's time.
20. Jeremy Collier, like Steele, saw no harm in allowing this kind of laxity in speech and conduct to the characters representing inferior classes.
21. In *The Spectator* No. 149 Steele explicity expresses his views on matrimony and advises a woman correspondent that she should select a man who loves her but is not rich rather than have a rich man who does not love her for her own *sake* and worth. He says, "The happy Marriage is, where two persons meet and make choice of each other, without principally regarding or neglecting the circumstances of Fortune or Beauty.
22. Farquhar's heroes, Roebuck (*Love and a Bottle*), Sir Harry Wildair (Constant Couple), Plume (*The Recruiting Officer*), however gay and licentious, reflect a gradual shift in the approach to the question of matrimony for they marry their beloveds with the blessings of their elders.
23. These opinions reflect the views of the sober section of the contemporary society. The Augustans believed that marriages based on mutual sincere love, though commendable in themselves, will not be a success without money. In such matters too they emphasised the middle path, the path of reason.
24. *Plays*, p. 299.
25. *The Critical Heritage*, p. 173.
26. W.D. Howarth maintains that *The Conscious Lovers* is 'the first liberal bourgeois comedy in Europe' and avers that 'it was a play that presented the moral and

social ideals of England's merchant classes in an assertive and self-confident manner,' W.D. Howarth, *Comic Drama*, p. 148.

27. Pope condemns avarice as well as prodigality and in the Epistle III of the Moral Essays praises the right use of wealth:

    To Worth or Want well weighted, be Bounty given,
    And ease, or emulate, the care of Heaven,
    (Whose measure full overflows on human race)
    Mend Fortune's fault, and justify her grace.
    Wealth in the gross is death, but life diffused;
    As Poison heals, in just proportion used;
    In heaps, like Ambergris, a stink it lies,
    But well dispersed, is Incense to the Skies. (Pope: *Moral Essays*, p. 264)

28. R.D. Hume, *The Development of the late Seventeenth Century Drama*, p. 485.

SECTION III

THE PROBLEMS AND ISSUES

9
Social Reform

Eighteenth century was an age of pronounced social and moral reforms though movements for effecting such reforms had started years earlier. The first decade of the century saw enthusiastic reformers like Addison, Steele, Swift and Defoe. In *A Project for the Advancement of Religion and the Reformation of Manners* Swift suggested various steps a government could take to reform the manners of the people. He bemoaned that people did not care for virtue and decency and were addicted to vices like gaming and philandering. He suggested that the princes should be the models of virtue and exercise their authority to cultivate commendable qualities in their subjects. Piety and virtue should be encouraged while vice should be put down in all departments and in all parts of the kingdom. Defoe, in *Mercure Scandale or, Advice from the Scandalous Club*, attacked drunkenness, swearing, marital unfaithfulness, duelling and the licence of the theatre, etc., and suggested remedies in a vein similar to that of Swift.

Steele, being primarily a moralist, was naturally a strong critic of the prevailing evils of the society. His didactive bent in conjunction with his zeal for reforms led him to write essays and plays to inculcate values found lacking in the people. The pamphlet, *The Christian Hero* (1701) was his first attempt in this direction in which he cited examples of great men from history as well as from the scriptures as models of moral behaviour. He also exhorted his fellow soldiers to act upon the "firm Motives of Duty, Valour, and Constancy of Soul" and follow virtuous principles of truth and innocence which would help them in their everyday life as well. He advised people in general to have honest motives behind their every single action and repose full confidence in God. He lavished praise on Caesar for his munificence and on Cato for his frugality, integrity and austere and rigid conduct.

From the scriptures Steele picked out paragons of virtue. Christ and St. Paul instruct humanity through their own examples. Their lives suggest such principles of conduct as are in harmony with the statutes of a civil government and in accord with the demands of religion and morality. To rise above ambition and abuse of riches, Steele considers meekness, the characteristic of a true Christian, necessary as it makes a man see his own faults and others' virtue, and thus awakens in him a correct sense of things. Steele considered such good men as the true children of God. He believed that "Eternal God has brought humanity together in the natural society which kindles the noble feelings of charity, compassion, kindness, good-will and service."[1] Steele finds his moral philosophy in accord with the tenets of Christianity.

Steele presented his moral percepts and suggestions for the reform of manners through *The Tatler* (1709-1711) and *The Spectator* (1711-1712). In the essays published in these periodicals he dealt with the social evils prevailing in the contemporary society and pressed the moral home with the help of various anecdotes, character sketches and humorous observations. Jenny Distaff, Sir Roger de Caverley, Sir Andrew Freeport and his zealous correspondents are some of the immortal persons inhabiting the world of his periodicals. Steele was the sole entrepreneur of *The Tatler* papers, getting some help from Addison occasionally. The cause to which the paper was devoted was thus stated in *The Tatler* itself:

> The general purpose of the whole has been to recommend truth, innocence, honour and virtue, as the chief ornaments of life...[2]

The purpose of *The Spectator* was to provide elegant amusement and rational reforms as stated by Addison in its tenth issue:

> I shall endeavour to enliven Morality with wit, and to temper wit with morality.... till I have recovered (the readers) out of that desperate State of Vice and Folly into which the Age is fallen.

The social vices that Steele waged war against are those of duelling, gaming, profligacy and libertinism, vanity and affectation, class distinction and mercenary marriages. In a sweeping observation he ascribed these vices to the "abandoned writings of Men of Wit, and the awkward Imitation of the rest of Mankind."[3]

Affectation, one of the social vices and consequence of "awkward imitation" of the other countries, especially that of France, was in his opinion, the cause of "ill-habits of life" which was eating up good sense and religion of the people.[4] His writings contain several examples of men and women with affected behaviour and language – such as Madam de Epingle (*The Funeral*) and Mrs. Clerimont (*The Tender Husband*) – who are in love with French ways and manners and are presented as ridiculous characters inviting abhorrence rather than envy and admiration.

Another common evil which Steele considers as an expression of barbarism, is duelling which is denounced by him in his essays as well as in the plays. In *The Tatler* No. 25 he calls it a "tyrant Custom" which condemns the duellist in the eyes of law while approving of his behaviour. Dwelling on the same subject in *The Spectator*, No. 97 Steele narrates the episode of the legendary Eucrate, who, after killing his friend in a duel, beseeched the King to pass a law against duelling. Besides, to heighten the enormity of the evil, Steele adds a religious tinge to this issue in *The Guardian* of April 13, 1713 where he maintains that "he that dies in a Duel knowingly offends God and in that very Action rushes into His offended Presence." Steele has expressed similar views in his plays also. In *The Lying Lover*, Young Bookwit, after he is supposed to have killed his fast friend in a duel, feels the pangs of compunction and repents for his supposed crime. Again in *The Tender Husband* he has shown the typical aversion of the sensible merchant class for the false honour associated with duelling by making Mr. Tipkin ignore the challenge of Sir Harry Gubbin. According to Steele, one particular scene in the fourth Act of *The Conscious Lovers*, was written to emphasize the necessity of discarding the evil of duelling.[5] Bevil Junior (*The Conscious Lovers*) acts as Steele's mouthpiece when he condemns duelling as a "breach of all laws, both Divine and Human" (IV, i), and declines to go on with it.[6]

Other evils which draw Steele's attention are those of drinking, gaming and whoring. He was of the view that drinking should be banned on the Sabbath day and in the Church (*The Spectator*, No. 75). In the plays he never fails to point out the harmfulness of excessive drinking. It is this vice that gets Young Bookwit (*The Lying Lover)* arrested for rioting. The condemned prisoners as well as the gaoler in the same play are addicted to this vice.[7] Like Collier and other religious minded persons, Steele was deadly opposed to the fashionable vices of swearing and using coarse and vulgar language. He thinks that a real gentleman should be particularly careful in this respect. In *The Spectator*, No. 75, referring to the habit of swearing of Etherege's Dorimant, he says:

> When a Gentleman speaks Coarsely, he has dressed himself Clean to no purpose .... To betray in a Man's Talk a corrupted Imagination is a much greater offence against the Conversation of Gentlemen, than any Negligence of Dress.

Since Steele believed in the presentation of positive norms his plays hardly have any character that swears or curses. If one of them is presented as a prey to this vice, at some stage, he is made to realise his fault and to repent and reform to virtuous ways.

Steele strongly believed that honour and respectability are not the monopolies of any particular class. To him a merchant can be as respectable as a squire or a titled gentleman. The criterion of social respectability and prestige, according to him, is not title or money but an individual's character and conduct. Mr. Sealand (*The Conscious Lovers)* upholds the dignity of the virtuous merchants and is as proud of being a merchant as is a landed gentleman of his birth. The conversation between Mr. Tipkin, the merchant and Sir Harry Gubbin, the Country Squire (*The Tender Husband*) reveals Steele's firm belief that the worth of a man does not depend upon his class. Steele's reforming spirit, so prominently displayed in his plays, tried to make theatre more conjugal and hospitable to the merchant class than it had been ever before. Loftis refers to the peculiarity of Steele in the following manner:

> There is ... a meaningful association in Steele's work between his allegiance to the reformers and his respect for the merchants.[8]

Matrimony was a thing of paramount importance in Steele's scheme of reform. He was at one with Collier in condemning the irreverent treatment of this sacred institution and condonation of the acts of infidelity by the Restoration playwrights. In his writings he has attempted to dignify matrimony in order to compensate for their cynical contempt for it. Between love and lust, the two innate aspects of sex relationship, Steele has denounced the latter in no uncertain terms. Steele upholds love as a natural impulse, an affection over which no one has any control. But at the same time, he favours a kind of rationalised courtship by making "reason" more dominant than "passion" in his exemplary characters.[9] Occasionally he also tends to give a platonic colouring to love. In *The Funeral* Lord Hardy and Lady Sharlot's courtship belongs to a plane which is almost ethereal. The same is the case with Bevil Junior and Indiana in *The Conscious Lovers*. Lovers in Steele's plays follow, by and large, the rules of decorum and the dictates of reason. There are no immodest love intrigues, no sexual wit, no promiscuity, no assignations, no light-hearted coquetry or libertinism and no mockery of conjugal life. Rather, most of his characters have only one woman or one man in their minds. Lady Sharlot thinks of Lord Hardy only and Lord Hardy finds felicity only in her. Similarly, Lady Harriot's heart is fixed on Campley only and Indiana has pledged to live and die for Bevil Junior who, in turn, is interested in no woman other than her. Likewise, Myrtle's love stands the test when he expresses his willingness to accept his beloved without fortune. Steele eulogises the role of reason in controlling one's conduct in *The Tatler* No. 33, where he says:

> The conquest of passion gives ten times more happiness than we can reap from the gratification of it.

Steele firmly believed that the desired reform in the manners of the people could be effected by administering instructions to men and women in "piety, religion and reason." That a man should bring "reason to support his passion" (*The Spectator*, No. 479) was what he himself was trying to do. In a letter written to his wife on August 12, 1708 he says, "I shall govern my Actions... but by the rules of morality and Right reason."[10]

Post-marital status of women was a matter of supreme concern to Steele. Time and again he expressed his annoyance at marriages of convenience which meant, in most cases, hemming together of two individuals of incompatible temperaments. To Steele the word "wife" was "the most amiable Term in Human Life"[11] and in *The Tatler*, No. 95 he presents, for his readers' emulation and edification a wifely wife, Jenny Distaff, who is leading a life of perfect bliss with her husband due to their mutual concern for each other. Nevertheless, Steele, shared the eighteenth century sensibility in believing that a woman's world is contained within the duties of a daughter, a sister, a wife and a mother. Discussing this point in *The Spectator* No. 144, he says:

> A right Woman, in a laudable Sense ... should have gentle softness, tender Fear and all those parts of life which distinguished her from the other Sex, with some Subordination to it, but such an Inferiority that makes her still more lively.

He gives his views on a woman's status in *The Funeral* where Lady Sharlot makes the following statement:

> And Woman's happiness, for all her Scorn,
> Is Only by that Side Whence she was born.
>
> (II, iii)

He extols a woman's role as a companion to man in a letter written to Mrs. Steele saying that "it is the glory of woman to be her husband's friend and companion."[12] He no doubt accepted the concept of male superiority in the social spectrum, but he was very critical of the prevailing double standards of behaviour. He wanted to have one and the same code of conduct and fidelity for both the sexes. The cause of conjugal coolness between Osymyn and Elmira, mentioned in *The Tatler*, No. 53 he ascribed to the inconstancy of the husband, Mrs. Clerimont's "innocent freedoms" threatening a breach between her and Mr. Clerimont appear less shocking and objectionable when compared with her husband's licentious behaviopur. Expounding his views on the topic in *The Talter*, No. 58, he states that "Chastity is ...as much to be valued in Man as in Woman."

Marriages with mercenary motives, treatment of women as commodities and belief in the idea that greater the fortune the higher the bid – are severely attacked by him in *The Tender Husband*, *The Conscious Lovers* and elsewhere.[13] Decrying such mercenary marriages and settlements he says:

> Thus is Tenderness thrown out of the Question; and the great care is, what the couple shall do when they came to hate each other.
>
> (*The Tatler*, No. 199)

Lucinda overtly denounces mercenary marriage in which women's feelings are ignored and they are treated as a means of gaining fortunes or as machines for propagation. Thus Steele has endeavoured to rationalise and dignify sex both during the period of courtship and after the establishment of conjugal ties.

All these vices and acts of moral degradation Steele ascribes to the faulty education of boys and girls and to the lack of emphasis on moral values. In *The Spectator*, Nos. 168 and 330, he expresses his ideas regarding the prevalent system of education of the young which comprised a study of the classics followed by a grand tour of the continent. He describes how the sons of the nobility and landed gentry did nothing except indulging in rioting, drinking, gambling and duelling. He considered all the existing methods of dissemination of knowledge as futile since they did not aim at making the people live a virtuous and purposeful life. He advocated good breeding and inculcation of moral values rather than mere accumulation of knowledge. Moral education, he held, could be imparted formally in Sunday schools, at home and through literature and the stage. He considered the last of these, that is, the stage, the most useful platform for the propagation of moral reforms and Christian virtues.

In *The Spectator*, No. 65, he describes the extraordinary potentialities of the stage in respect of the dissemination of ideas, both virtuous and vicious. He asserts in the Preface to *The Lying Lover* that the playwrights should serve the society by stripping "Vice of the gay Habit in which it has too long appear'd, and cloathe [sic] it in its native Dress of Shame, Contempt, and Dishonour."[14] He stressed, in *The Spectator*, No. 75, that the playwrights should encourage virtue by portraying "good natural impulses, as are in the Audience" and by creating characters which are "virtuous and have, besides Wit, Humour, Mirth, Good Breeding, etc." In another issue of *The Spectator*, No. 51, Steele condemned Etherege's *She Wou'd if She Cou'd* and Mrs. Aphra Behn's *The Rover* for their unhealthy effect on the audience. In *The Spectator*, No. 65 he denounced Dorimant (*The Man of Mode*), the typical hero of the Restoration comedy, and suggested his substitution by the exemplary character of what he calls the fine gentleman. He considered Dorimant as "a perfect Contradiction to good manners, good sense, and common Honesty"[15] and presented his model – the fine gentleman, — as one who had faith in Christian values and possessed qualities of tenderness, compassion, benevolence, modesty and frankness.[16] His fine gentleman is affable without being impertinent, complascent without being servile, and cheerful and humorous without being noisy. In a word, dictates of reason and good sense control his actions and carriage, thereby making him a possessor of "honest actions and refined language."[17]

The sub-title of Steele's *The Christian Hero — No Principles but those of religion [are] sufficient to make a Great man* — shows Steele's staunch belief in the superiority of Christian values. Accordingly, all his 'good' characters are conceived as the embodiments of these virtues. Lord Hardy, Bevil Junior and Young Bookwit are all basically good persons worthy of being called Christians. Myrtle and Captain Clerimont are honest and upright as Christians are required to be. Similarly, his chief female characters are women of honour and integrity. Lady Sharlot is the spring of domestic felicity and Lucinda a female malcontent but virtuous in every respect. Likewise, Indiana is virtue itself with self-effacing platonic devotion to her benefactor and due regard for her reputation and conduct. Besides these living examples of virtue, Steele extols and eulogises the qualities of sincere friendship, filial duty and true love. In his plays, generous parents of understanding nature are revered and womanhood is given its due regard. Erring characters realise their faults and are made to repent and reform.[18] With the exception of Lady Brumpton there is hardly any thoroughly vicious character in his plays. In all his plays virtue gets its due reward and vice its punishment. This is so not only because of the law of poetic justice but also because of Steele's own commitment to the Christian values.

Steele sees these exemplary characters in their social perspective and makes their morality practical and useful in everyday life. Sanctity of home is of paramount importance to him. He is a great champion of women's cause. In this respect he was far ahead of his contemporaries. In his writings he has tried to highlight the quality of a woman's mind and character as well as her myriad roles in society. Steele, contrary to the Shakespearean maxim, "frailty thy name is woman", considers the fair sex as basically a rational being at par with her male counterparts. Controverting the view in respect of a woman's supposed inferiority and mental incompatibility with man, he says:

> What we call in men Wisdom, is in Women Prudence.
> It is a partiality to call one greater than the other.[19]

Through his writings Steele wants to inculcate a sense of self-respect and virtue, the notion of a "fine-lady" as against the "fair-one" of the Restoration time, and thus he attaches greater importance to her moral qualities than her physical charms. Steele appears to voice his own feelings through Young Bookwit who says, "a Woman, methinks, is a Being between us and Angles."[20] Holding men responsible for the conduct of women who transgress the rules of morality, Steele makes Clerimont Senior admit, "The Impertinent (his wife) was guilty of nothing but what my Indiscretion led her to."[21] He took a keen personal interest in the publication, in 1714, of *The Ladies Library*, a three volume compilation giving the rules of conduct of women. Modesty, according to him is a prerequisite of all other virtues as without it "simplicity and innocence appear rude; reading and good sense masculine; wit and humour lascivious" (*The Tatler*, No. 84). Steele has presented several good women in his essays and plays to exemplify his precepts as well as Christian virtues. Most of them are presented as tender-hearted showing kindness to the wretched and even to the guilty and with compassion for the sick and the unfortunate. Eve, in *The Christian Hero*, is "softened into sweetness" and "tempered into smiles", sharing the loneliness of her companion, Adam; while Eudosia has a "Nobility of Spirit and a commanding beauty." Fidelia is a self-effacing daughter and Eucretia is all kindness. In his plays, as mentioned earlier, Steele has virtuous heroines. Lady Sharlot and Indiana are ideals of womanhood; Harriot and Penelope are basically good and virtuous; Lucinda though a bit self-willed behaves sensibly and submits to her parents' will; Mrs. Clerimont, in spite of her fashionable follies and weakness remains faithful to her husband; and Biddy, even though she is a product of romances, is innocence itself. Steele was of the view that "the great Happiness and Misfortune of mankind depends upon the Manner of Educating and Treating that Sex."[22] In the case of the young boys, he found the education prescribed for them equally faulty as it laid greater stress on superficialities, *i.e.* on "deportment" and "ornamentation of their persons" than on their mental and moral qualities. He suggested such education and training for them as would furnish them with "reflections and sentiments proper for the companions of reasonable men."[23]

To Steele ethical considerations mattered more than anything else. It was his persistent endeavour to bring about moral reform through the theatre. Unlike Collier who thundered from the pulpit, Steele raised his voice against the immorality in the theatre as well as in the society from the stage itself. He considered the stage as a very useful platform for propagating Christian values and he made full and proper use of the patent granted to him for managing the Drury Lane Theatre. While applying for the patent he had deplored the fact that the contemporary stage was not showing "such representations of human life as may tend to the encouragement and honour of Religion and virtue and discountenancing [of] vice."[24] Steele's observation in the aforementioned petition that the theatre has "for many years been much perverted to the great scandal [sic] of Religion and Good Government" and his promise to "remedy so inveterate an evil"[25] are an evidence of his zeal for reform. The flimsy argument of the Restoration writers that the satirical representations of Vice and folly were to caution the spectators against copying what is presented on the stage was not acceptable to Steele. He denounced Etherege's comedies, especially *The Man of Mode*, for presenting libertinism in an attractive garb as he was convinced that these comedies had encouraged corruption of manners and morals. Referring to *The Conscious Lovers* in *The Theatre*, No. 19, he claims that the positive values presented in his exemplary characters like Bevil Junior will be of great service to the society at large. Steele gave particular importance to the Christian concept of repentance and reformation. Erring characters in his plays repent sincerely of their follies and vices and revert to positive norms. One feels that Steele introduced these characters only to find opportunities to highlight the theme of repentance. Since mere verbal denunciation of vice does not evoke positive response, Steele felt that the stage could inculcate Christian values more successfully through the living examples of the admirable characters in a play.

Steele, a moralist to the marrow of his bones, believed that ridicule and laughter are not quite suitable instruments for reform in moral comedies. Dwelling on this in the epilogue to *The Lying Lover*, he said, "laughter's a distorted Passion, born of Sudden self-Esteem, and Sudden scorn."[26] Elaborating this idea in the Preface to *The Conscious Lovers* he stated, "anything that has its foundation in happiness and success must be allowed to be the object of Comedy; and it must be an improvement of it to introduce a joy too exquisitic for laughter."[27] Thus he considered joy, and not mockery or laughter, as an essential feature of comedy. He repeatedly put his virtuous characters in pathetic situations to provide occasions for the demonstration of the qualities of patience, endurance, benevolence and humanity and thus to reveal the natural means of moral reformation and regeneration. Thus, both in his essays and plays, Steele persistently strove to "Chasten Wit, and Moralise the Stage"[28] in order to bring about a reformation of the society – an aim he had devoted his entire career to but which was only fitfully followed by the dramatists of the earlier eras and was almost totally abandoned by the Restoration dramatists.

NOTES

1. *Tracts and Pamphlets*, p. 55.
2. *The Tatler*, No. 271.
3. *The Spectator*, No. 6.
4. *Ibid.*
5. Preface to *The Conscious Lovers, Plays*, p. 299.
6. Much against his will Steele had to fight a duel in June 1700 with Captain H. Kelly after vainly trying to convince him of its futility. His remorse at having almost killed Kelly led him to denounce the evil practice throughout his career.
7. Steele himself was no exception. He lived an irregular life and one of the vices that he indulged in was that of drinking.
8. Loftis, *Comedy and Conscience*, p. 33.
9. For example, through Lord Hardy (*The Funeral*) Steele chides those who are attracted by the physical charms of women and talk triflingly about them.
10. Quoted by Aitken in *The Life*, I, p. 217. Steele, as contemporary reports reveal; could rarely translate such noble resolutions into action.
11. *The Tatler*, No. 33.
12. Aitken, *op. cit.*, p. 217.
13. For example, in *The Tatler*, Nos. 185 and 199.
14. *Plays*, p. 116.
15. *The Spectator*, No. 65.

16. *Ibid.*
17. *The Guardian*, April 20, 1713.
18. In the repentant and reformed rake, Steele was following Shaftesbury who believed in the essential goodness of human nature. To some extent Steele himself was a rake. He had seduced Elizabeth Tonson (Jacob Tonson's sister) and had a daughter by her. He brought the daughter up along with his other children and thus atoned for the sin. Nevertheless, he wrote *The Christian Hero* as a self-admonition, and later reformed himself and proved a faithful husband.
19. *The Tatler*, No. 172.
20. *The Lying Lover*, I, i.
21. Steele held men responsible for poor or vicious tastes of women as well. In *The Christian Hero* he expressed his views thus:

    > Indeed it is, among other Reasons, from want of wit and Invention in our Modern Gallants, that the beautiful Sex is absurdly and viciously entertained by 'em.

22. *The Tatler*, No. 141.
23. Steele, though quite a liberal thinker, reflects the eighteenth century attitude towards women when, admitting their mental capabilities and other superior accomplishments, he confines their activities to family life, making matrimony as the goal of their life.
24. Quoted by Loftis in *Steele at Drury Lane,* p. 212.
25. *Ibid.*, p. 44.
26. *Plays*, p. 189.
27. *Ibid*, p. 299.
28. *Ibid.*, p. 304.

10

Moral and Sentimental Strain

With the disapearance of the Restoration coterie culture the satiric comedy of manners manifested a decadence, which, in due course, allowed diverse kinds of incursions on to the contemporary stage. After 1688 moral pressure from the Royalty and the society became more pronounced. Patronage of the stage gradually shifted to the bourgeois class, which along with the thinkers, reformers and the audiences objected to its immorality. Referring to the middle class patronage of the stage Farquhar in *A Discourse upon Comedy* (1702) avers:

> "The rules of English comedy don't lie in the compass of Aristotle or his followers but in the pit, box and galleries."

The 18th century middle class thinking to a great extent, was influenced by Locke's Philosophy and was hammered home, time and again, by the practical moralists like the third Earl of Shaftesbury. Restoration Libertine Philosophy had almost shattered the worth of traditional values giving rise to cynicism, materialism and pessimism a result of Hobbes' Philosophy. But the eighteenth century thinkers tried to restore faith and optimism in human life by propounding Locke's Philosophy, *i.e.* man is endowed with good sense, and with virtues like charity, generosity, devotion, tolerance and piety etc. He believed that with reason and self-discipline man can be god-like. It was the third Earl of Shaftesbury who tried his best to popularise his philosophy among the rising middle classes. This new faith infused optimism among the people through its use of the words reason and sentiment. A man with reason and sensibility is capable of feeling tender and refined feelings can distinguish between right and wrong, and thus with the help of his innate good nature is capable of preferring the right. This image of man with emphasis on morality and good sense suited to the middle class taste.

To please the middle class sensibilities the new group of playwrights *viz.* Cibber, Vanbrugh, Farquhar, Steele, Mrs. Centilivre etc. tried their best in writing sentimental comedies for which they had their inspiration from the morality plays, domestic tragedies of Thomas Heywood and the comedies of Terence. Let us examine a few definitions of Sentimentalism. A.W. Ward (*A History of English Dramatic Literature to the Death of Queen Anne* 1975, III vols.) defines it as a comedy founded on pity whereas Ernest Bearnbaum (*The Drama of Sensibility*) considers it to be the presentation of "goodness of human nature", the slogan of the third Earl of Shaftesbury. Nicoll considers the presentation of a moral problem as the marked feature of sentimental drama. Unlike the malicious satiric comedy of manners sentimental comedy tries to display virtue triumphing over vice or weakness of human nature which is redeemable.

The end of sentimental comedy was primarily instruction *i.e.* moral reformation of the society. Hence, the playwrights, under the banner of sentimentalism, attempted two types of plot patterns. In consonance with the eighteenth century sensibilities and their own didacticism the playwrights produced the comedies of the reformed rakes, whose latent good nature is hidden under the guise of roguery which they threw off before the close of the fifth act. It is either their scruples and conscience or some external moral force *viz.* the influence of the trnascendent virtue or a sermon from a mentor that brings about their reformation. They, consequently, shed copious tears of compunction and pledge to revert to positive norms of behaviour, thus pleasing every palate among the audience.

Another plot pattern cashed in on the virtuous protagonists (the fine gentleman and the fine lady) beset with a moral problem. The conflict between vice and virtue ends in crowning virtue with triumph thus arousing sympathy for the virtue in distress. Modelled after Terence the comedy makes audience weep tears of joy when the examplary characters are rewarded with happiness.

This type of moral comedy setting a model of exemplary behaviour before the audience found a champion in Sir Richard Steele who was committed to eradicate social vices of manners and morals through positive examples, arousing a social conscience. He shared with his contemporary critic – playwright, John Dennis, the belief in the usefulness of the stage. The spirit which had inspired collier's invective against the stage inspired Steele to use stage as a forum of moral reform. His moral observations are found not only in the body of his plays (*The Funeral* 1701), *The Tender Husband* (1703), *The Lying Lover* (1705) and the *Conscious Lovers* (1722) but also in the prefaces, prologues, epilogues and his periodical essays in *The Tatler* and *The Spectator* which he wrote zealously to inculcate values found lacking in the people. Through various 'precepts' and 'examples' he aims at 'tempering wit with morality' and preaching Christian virtues. His intention to promote moral and social improvement through sentimental comedy is stated in the preface to *The Conscious Lovers* thus: For the greatest effect of a play in reading is to excite the reader to go to see it: and when he does so, it is then a play has the effect of "example" and "precept". It was his conviction that through exemplary action and language the stage could effectively be used to remove immorality and thus reform the society.

The practical moralist Steele expressed his aim explicitly in the Prologue to *The Conscious Lovers* thus: " 'Tis yours, with Breeding to refine the Age, To chasten wit, and Moralise the Stage." He aimed at realising this goal through "an innocent performance" cleansed of the smut and obscenity of the previous comedy as well as through examples of moral conduct. He reiterated the same objective in *The Tatler*, No. 8, when he recommended:

> The apt use of a theatre, as the most agreeable and easie method of making a polite and moral gentry, which would end in rendering the rest of the people regular in their Behaviour, and ambitious of laudable undertakings.

He reiterates the same conviction in The Theatre, No. 19, too. Bevil Jr. endowed with sterling virtues that he exhibits in his behaviour as well as language is rewarded with success and happiness. So is Lord Hardy in *The Funeral*. In Collier's vein Steele condemns Dorimant in *The Spectator* No. 65 and censures the Restoration playwrights for making libertine rakes their heroes and for rewarding them with wealth and beauty. Etherege's gay abandon in portraying the dissipated society was simply outrageous to him. Steele replaced the gay couple of the Restoration comedy with the exemplary one comprising a fine gentleman and a fine lady. Lord Hardy and lady Sharlot in *The Funeral* and Bevil Jr. and Indiana are created for admiration and emulation. Bevil Jr., a perfect specimen of good morals and manners, exemplifies Steele's concept of a fine gentleman which he enunciated in *The Guardian* (April 20, 1713) and *The Spectator*, No. 65. His good manners, good sense, reason, kind-heartedness, honesty and his sober temperament, filial devotion along with his "tender obligations" to his father condition his conduct and actions throughout the play. He has taken an oath, as he tells his faithful servant, Humphry, that he would never marry without his father's consent. His father would never allow him to marry Indiana, a woman of unknown parentage. In order to resolve the predicament he is in Bevil Jr. tells Lucinda, the woman he is supposed to marry, of his love for Indiana thus expecting a refusal from Lucinda. And providence helps him, for Indiana turns out to be the long-lost daughter of Sealand, Lucinda's father, a respectable merchant friend of Sir Bevil. Bevil Jr's actions are governed by reason and "conscious honour" and not by passion even when his friend and Lucinda's lover, Myrtle challenges him to a duel. Steele finds ample scope of sententious moralizing against the "tyrant custom" of duelling which he time and again had attacked in *The Taltler* and *The Spectator* essays and had landed young Bookwit (*The Lying Lover*) to Newgate for supposedly killing his friend, Lord Lovemore, in a duel. Thus Steele's exemplary hero is a dutiful son, sincere friend and virtuous and conscious lover unlike the Restoration libertine rakes given to swearing, whoring, drinking etc. Steele's moral commitment is overtly displayed in his exemplary heroes.

The fine women of Steele's comedies, though considered by Hazlit listless and dull in comparison to the mad-cap heroines of the Restoration period, are innocent, modest, virtuous but strong in their sentimental fold. Lady Sharlot is on the verge of being sold by lady Brumpton to be raped by Cabinet, a vicious character, yet she seldom loses her control over her conduct or emotions. Lady Harriot, her sister, somewhat gay and flippant, is corrected by her sober and virtuous lover Campley, finally emerging as a serious virtuous woman. Indiana, another virtuous exemplary heroine in *The Conscious Lovers* loves Bevil Jr. on a platonic plane. They are embodiments of Steele's own sober middle class sensibilities.

A great champion of women's cause Steele infused their

characters with the qualities of the head and the heart. Contrary to Shakespearean maxim, "frailty thy name is woman", or the treatment of women as objects of pleasure and propagation as pictured by the Restoration comedy, Steele considers her, like Locke, a rational being at par with her male companion. Controverting the view in respect of a woman's supposed inferiority and mental incompatibility with man Steele, in *The Talter* No. 172 says:

> What we call in men-wisdom, is in woman prudence,
> It is a partiality to call one greater than the other.

Indiana is so intelligent, educated, graceful and virtuous that she carries our hearts with her. Even Sir Bevil who objects to his son's amorous inclinations for her is charmed by her "uncommon air, noble modesty and dignified conduct." Her inherent sense of decorum and decency does not allow her to accuse her lover or show disrespect towards his father. The personification of Steele's concept of womanhood she is the source of "pure delight" and "guiltless joy" to her lover as well as to the audience. Young Bookwit too regards a woman with the eyes of a scholar and considers her "a being between us and Angels", a person who gives "awe and Invitation" (I, i). Through these women characters Steele endeavoured to correct the Restoration image of women and to reinstate them to an honourable and prestigious status in the society.

In consonance with his dramatic theory of exemplary heroes and heroines, Steele lifted the physical and carnal love to an elevated platonic plane. Love in his comedies is not an intellectual game played by the wild rakes and the gay heroines, nor a physical appetite to be satisfied, but an exalted emotion, an experience of the platonic nature. It is a perfect understanding and a conscious respect for each other. Consequently, the lovers courtship is also tempered with sobriety, gravity, understanding, multual adoration and similar noble sentiments. Lord Hardy cannot think lightly of lady Sharlot who worships him like a God and finds his name written in the scriptures. She dreams of a heavenly bliss in his companionship whereas Indiana has a perfect understanding and adoration for Bevil Jr. When her aunt Isabella learns about Bevil Jr.'s marriage with Lucinda and questions his constancy she asserts:

> But by his behaviour I am convinc'd he will offer it,

> the moment 'tis in his power, or consistent with his honour, to make such a promise. (II, ii)

With an exalted vision of womanhood matrimony naturally received paramount importance in Steele's moral comedy. He was at one with Collier in condemning the irreverent treatment of this sacred institution and condonation of the acts of infidelity by the Restoration playwrights. In his works Steele has attempted to dignify matrimony raising it from the cynically contemptuous level it has fallen to in the hands of the Restoration playwrights. It is no more a a licence for adultrous intrigues nor it is sheer lust which Steele denounces in his plays as well as essays in no uncertain terms. He upholds love as a natural impulse an affection to be the foundation of matrimonial alliance. At the same time, unlike the romantic love which he ridicules in Biddy Tipkin in *The Tender Husband*, he advocated the role of reason and decorum in courtship which he has illustrated in Lord Hardy, Lady Sharlot and Bevil Jr. and Indiana. He also tries to give a platonic colouring to love and courtship which has echoes of heroic drama. There are no immodest love intrigues, no near-seduction scenes, no assignations, no light-hearted cuckoldry and mockery of conjugal love.

Post-marital status of women and domestic felicity and marital fidelity were matters of supreme concern to Steele. Time and again he has decried marriage of convenience, which, to him meant, in most cases, hemming together of two individuals of incompatible temperaments. This he has done through the precepts and examples in Lucinda's matrimonial alliance with Cimberton a coxcomb who is after her wealth only and through Biddy Tipkin's arranged match with the country booby, Humphry Gubbin and again in young Bookwit's matrimonial match with Victoria. Mercenary marriages treating women as commodities are severely attacked by Lucinda for a woman's feelings are totally ignored, "She is to be bartered for, like the Beasts of the fields, and that in such an instance as coming together to an entire familiarity and union of soul and body. Oh, And this without being so much as well-wishers to each other but for increase of fortune" (III). Myrtle, her lover, a fire gentleman, loves her for her worth but he is denied her hand by her father. When he learns about the discovery of Sealand's another daughter in Indiana, which means a division of Lucinda's fortune he says, "no abatement of furtune shall lessen her value to me". Bevil Jr. had already decided to marry Indiana in spite of her being a poor, hapless woman. This juxtaposition of marriage deconvenience and marriage founded on love clearly shows Steele's denunciation of the former and approval of the latter. In Myrtle and Bevil Jr. we have no traces of Dorimant who tells his friend Bellair:

> The wife will find a difference in our fate, you wed a woman, I a good estate. (IV, i)

To Steele the word "wife" was the most amiable term in human life (*The Tatler*, No. 33). Jenny Distaff and her husband are the specimen of marital felicity and fidelity. He extols a woman's role as a companion to man. In a letter written to Mrs. Steele he said, "It is the glory of a woman to be her husband's friend and companion" Lord Hardy expects domestic felicity in lady Sharlot's friendship, her constancy, her piety, her household cares, her maternal tenderness etc.," which are echoes of Mirabell's vision of a happy marriage.

Steele no doubt accepted male superiority, but was very critical of the prevalent double standards of behaviour. He wanted to have one and the same code of conduct and fidelity for both the sexes. Mrs. Clerimont's "innocent freedoms" threatening a rift between the couple appear less shocking than her husband's licentious behaviour. He expressed his precepts on marital fidelity in *The Tatler*, No. 58 where he asserts: "Chastity is as much to be valued in Man as in woman". Mercenary marriages treating women as commodities and the prevailing belief that greater the fortune the higher the bid are severely denounced by Steele in all his works.

So far for the positive morality of Steele's plays, Steele supported the cautionary theory of comedy. In Collier's vein Steele advocated the ridiculous denunciation of vice for, like Collier, he believed that the end of comedy is to laugh out the vices and follies of society.

Hence, he included negative morality also in his plays. His didactic bent in conjunction with his zeal for reforms prompted him to attack the prevailing social vices through sentimental scenes and situations. Drinking, gaming, duelling, cursing and swearing, profligacy and libertinism are some evils that attracted his critical censure. Duelling is denounced as a "tyrant custom" for a person "that dies in a Duel Knowingly offend God and in that very action rushes into His offended Presence", Young Bookwit's supposedly killing his friend, Lord Lovemore in a duel and thus landing him in Newgate and repenting for his supposed crime shows the typical aversion of the sensible middle calss for the false honour associated with duelling. According to Steele, one particular scene in the IV Act of *The Conscious Lovers* was expressly written to decry the evil of dueling. Bevil Jr. acts as Steele's mouthpiece when he condemns duelling as a breach of all laws, both 'Divine and Human'. He refuses to fight a duel with Myrtle. Moreover, the whole situation is latent with sentimentalism and didacticism which Steele makes maximum use of through moral aphorism and sententious pronouncements. Besides these sentimental scenes arousing pity and commisseration Steele has provided several other sentimental strokes to express his morality. Among the scenes replete with emotional appeal ranges the scenes of emotional outpourings of love by Trusty for his master, Lord Hardy. His tears of joy and affection touch the cords of the audiences' hearts. Similarly, in *The Lying Lover* the sight of Young Bookwit in chains is something that kindhearted Old Bookwit cannot bear, and he swoons. This pathetic heart-touching scene was expressly designed to provide, on the one hand, the picture of an ideal loving and bevelolent guardian completely different from the unreasonably authoritative tyrannical guardians of the earlier drama, on the other hand, it was genuinely sentimental in tone and tenor. Its emotional appeal aroused sympathy for the good natured characters. So, is the family reunion scene in *The Conscious Lovers* presenting Sealand discovering his long-lost daughter in Indiana. These pathetic scenes, though seem too heavy for the comic spirit of the plays as most of Steele's critics felt that this merit of Steele's plays almost killed comed . Fielding, Goldsmith, Hazlitt, Sheridan and even the modern critics shared this opinion. Whatever be the critical opinion on Steele's sentimental strain, Steele was happy that he had accomplished success and realised his goal.

Besides advocating moral comedy, Steele approved of the cautionary theory of the Restoration playwrights, He, in *The Spectator* No. 270 lauded the scornful lady for satirising the heroine's vanity and in *The Tatler* No. 3 commended Whycherley's *Country Wife* for punishing vice as it ought to be. He stressed that virtue should always be rewarded and vice invariably exposed and punished. Lady Brumpton in *The Funeral* is proved a bigamist and exposed. In *The Conscious Lovers* Ciberton, the man with no morals and manners, is denied Lucinda's hand.

Steele always decried vice and tried to correct the redeemable persons. Cabinet in *The Funeral* admits his marriage with lady Brumpton and repents for his fraud, consequently, he is pardoned. Madam de Epingle in *The Funeral* and Mrs. Clerimont in *The Tender Husband* both aping foreign morals and manners are cured of their folly. So is Young Bookwit made to realise the consequences of lying, drinking and duelling. These fifth-act tearful reformation scenes, much popular since Cibber's *Love's Last Shift* are full of sentimental strain. Moreover, pardoning the repentant is the quintessence of Christian doctrine. Admiring poetic justice in Steele's plays Krutch says:

> The extension of poetic justice, was one of the cardinal doctrines of his creed which in fact is a distinguishing characteristic of sentimental comedy. (p. 78).

Since Steele was trying to crusade against the immorality of the plays he aimed at providing "innocent mirth" by cleansing comedy of its smut and promiscuity. Denouncing Dorimant in *The Spectator*, No. 65, as a "direct knave" he inducted decency and decorum in his dialogue. There are ample sententious pronouncements, decorus and inoffensive speeches, maxims etc. with no trace of vulgarity or impropriety.

Even his method, *i.e.*, laughter of the vicious characters is tinged with sympathy and benevolence. As Steele was strongly influenced by Shaftesbury's philosophy of good nature and good humour, he tried to introduce a milder form of comic laughter, laughter infused with the spirit of innocent mirth befitting a benevolent good humoured gentleman. There is no room for the malicious heartless railery of the Restoration sort which was hitherto considered essential for satirising vice. Explaining the rationale of a comedy free from this type of laughter he in the epilogue to *The Lying Lover* says :

> For laughter is a distorted passion born,
> Of sudden self-Esteem, and sudden Scorn,

> Which when its over, the Men in pleasure wise,
> Both him that moved it, and themselves despise.

In his plays as well as essays, Steele shows that he was not an enemy to the conventional comic method, langhter (wit and satire) but felt that malice should be replaced with genial humour. He himself tried to temper wit with good nature. In *The Spectator*, No. 422, he avers, that "to rally well, it is absolutely necessary that kindness must run through all you say." In *The Talter* No. 242, he reiterated that the expression of a good natured satirist, "bear a pleasantry in them, which shows there is no Malignity at heart and by consequence are attended by his readers because they are unprejudiced." According to him wit should be alloyed with good humour and laughter with pity. To laugh at unavoidable defects is an abuse of wit and comedy both. It is not proper for the stage to laugh at a natural folly. In place of malicious laughter as the spirit of comedy Steele favoured the use of pity to chastise Delight, a woeful scene, a pathetic situation too poignant for laughter, yet redolent with joy born of pity and benevolence. While applauding Terence's *Self-tormenter*, in *The Speetator*, No. 502, he says that in this play there are "several incidents which would draw tears from any man of sense and not one which would move his laughter." Talking of pity and joy as the basis of his comic laughter Steele says in the preface to *The Conscious Lovers*:

> Anything that has its foundation in happiness and success, must be allowed to be the object of comedy, and sure it must be an improvement of it to introduce a joy too exquisite for laughter, that can have no spring but in Delight.

Hence, Steele the moralist, tried to display the triumph of good natured virtuous characters, with sentimentalism as a means to this end which thus becomes a source of sublime kind of delight for thc andience. Even the vicious characters are subjected to good natured benevolent laughter instead of being hcartlessly lashed as it was the fashion with the Restoration playwrights.

The moral and sentimental strain in Steele's comedies earned him so much popularity that he had several editions of *The Conscious Lovers* sold. It was followed by many playwrights. Though Fielding, Goldsmith, and Sheridan laughed at Steele's woeful comedies and held him responsible for killing comedy but the audience applauded him for his moral concern and sententiousness.

The overt didacticism and sentimentalism was highly commended by the 18th century audiences and moralists, nevertheless, Steele's moral concern and sentimental strain evoked a lot of criticism from the contemporary as well as the modern critics.

It worst affected the exemplary hero: Dennis, Steele's contemporary in his essay, *Remarks on a Play Called The Conscious Lovers* declared that "the filial obedience of young Bevil is carried a great too far for a man of economic independence and understanding it is unjustified and imprudent to make such a promise to his father as not to marry without his consent or even for a father to urge him to do it for the sake of doubling his estate." Bevil Jr. has been attacked by Bavies in his recent study, *Restoration and Eighteenth Century Comedy* (Oxford 1986), for his lack for honesty toward his father, friend and beloved. He avers that had he been more honest towards them he would have been really an exemplary hero. But, Bavies too admits that there would have been then no comedy at all. Paul E Parnell, in *The Sentimental Mask*, alleges that Bevil Jr. with his sentimental thinking wears a sentimental mask to conceal his morally ambiguous actions and "raises himself to the presumptuous level of self-adoration and self-worship for his Christ-like behaviour".

Besides his exemplary characters Steele is attacked for his heavy doses of sentimental moralizing. He did attain his goal *i.e.* "To chasten wit, and moralise the stage" as he puts it in Prologue to *The Conscious Lovers* but at the cost of the comic spirit which as Goldsmith says in the Prologue to *She Stoops to Conquer* :

> Pray would you know the reason why I'm crying?
> The comic muse, long sick, is now a-dying.
> To her a mawkish drab of spurious breed,
> Who deal in sentimentals will succeed.

Decrying Steele's didacticism B. Dobree maintains that, "to load aesthetics with directly stated morals is to deprive it of its wings" (p. 229) and Hazlitt goes on to such an extent of critical denunciation of Steele's overt moral concern that he asseverates that "it is almost a misnomer to call them comedies"; they are rather "homilies in dialogue". How moral preachings can be detrimental to comedy is expressed by Krutch who feels that, "The self-conscious moral movement, and the simultaneous development of sentimentalism, practically killed comedy" (256). The blending of the pathetic and the comic is disparaged by Salgādo in *English Drama: A Critical Introduction* (1980) in a most condemning tone:

> "It substituted a thin-blooded mixture of tears and happy ending and an undeviating determination to be exemplary which is it undoing."

How incursion of tearful comedy proved fatal to the comic spirit and gaiety of the previous comedy is examined by Krutch thus:

> When comedy left the path of laughter to seek sentiment, it went down and down until it not only ceased to be funny but became maudlin. (248)

The critical opinion given hitherto establishes one point that though Steele was successful in moralizing the stage as he desired, his didacticism proved fatal to the comic spirit of the Restoration comedy. However, it was not Steele's moral pronouncements and sentimentalism alone that killed comedy, for with the changing milieu comedy of manners would have disappeared even otherwise.

11
Marriage and Comedy

Comedy of the Restoration seems to have championed the cause of women seeking equality and liberty. In the contemporary society their condition was far from being satisfactory. Under the influence of the changed political climate during Charles II's regime and the advent of the new scientific thinking, the comedy of the period started challenging the age-old notions and conventions regarding man-woman relationship. It tried to show the possibilities of gaining more equality and liberty than what was hitherto allowed to them. And in this respect Restoration Comedy seems to be ahead of its time. Even the immorality and adulterous propensities of women in the Comedy can be interpreted in the light of this idea: its espousal of women's cause – a revolt against the age-old dogmas and beliefs and quest for existence.

Before studying the comedy of the time, it is worthwhile to have the historical perspective of man-woman relationship. Conventionally, marriages were arranged by parents without taking into account inclinations of the people concerned. In the male dominated society there was no scope of a woman dissenting with the marriage alliance which was, by and large, prompted by the mercenary motives of the parents. The mercenary marriage of marriage-de-convenience totally neglected the protestant ideal of love; and thereby it generated unrest among the youth. An alternative to the evils of marriage-de-convenience was found in marrying clandestinely. Some of the churches *viz*. Convent Garden Church, St. Pancras, Duke's Place etc. were notorious for clandestine marriages. Comedy of the time frequently alludes to such churches and such marriages.

Once married, either of the spouse, specially a woman, had no release from the marriage bonds except in the case of child marriage, fraud, bigamy etc. A wife could get only some financial relief such as separate maintenance allowance in the case of bigamy. The Canon Law showed no clemency to a wife committing adultery. Adulterous women were punished by the ecclesiastical courts and sometimes were even burnt alive. The Civil Marriage Act of 1653 also gave no succour to an unhappily married woman. Although it transferred jurisdiction over marriage disputes from the religious courts to the Civil Courts, it did not allow women to seek justice. Women, therefore, started objecting to male dominance and double standard of behaviour allowed by the society. Restoration Comedy joins their banner.

A shift in the contemporary matrimonial laws also contributed to the changing attitude towards husband-wife relationship and thus it provided the playwrights with ample material for marital discord plots. The Civil Marriage Act by its transference of jurisdiction shattered religious sanctity of matrimony as an alliance made in heaven. The Act considered marriage as a man-made contract latent with the possibility of annulment which it had vested with the Parliament. For a divorce decree, the separation petition had to be filed in and granted by the ecclesiastical courts. However, obtaining a separate petition from the religious courts was a very long, expensive and scandalous venture which only men could undertake for; the Act was silent over a woman's right to testify against her husband. Nevertheless, the very idea of separation seems to have created climate congenial to remedying the ills of unhappy marriages.

The Duke of Norfolk, who had obtained separation by mutual consent in 1685 and had to fight a long legal battle before he could get a Parliamentary divorce in 1700 was the first instance of legally ending the miseries of an unhappy marriage. His was an exceptional case, for; money and personal influence played a significant role in getting him released from the marriage contract: the Duchess' gallant was the half-brother to King William. But the case left the Duke a common gossip in the society. Again in 1701 two persons, Sir John Dillon and a London grocer, Ralph Rox, could get their marriages dissolved after obtaining separation from the Doctors' Commons, the religious court of England. In short, by the end of the seventeenth century the history of matrimonial laws evinced proclivity in favour of separation and divorce as a possible release from unhappy marriage bonds.

The contemporary writers and philosophers also contributed to finding a remedy to the evils of marriage. Locke in *The Second Treatise* (2.82) describes marriage as voluntary contract that provides a wife, "the full and free possession of what by contract is her peculiar right." He further allows her liberty to separate from her husband "where natural rights, or their contract allows it". Milton too crusaded against the double standard of behaviour permitted by the contemporary matrimonial laws. In *The Doctrine and Discipline* of Divorce which he had tabled before the Parliament in 1643 – he avers:

> Marriage is a cov'nant the very being whereof consists, not in a forc'd cohabitation and counterfeit performance of duties, but in unfained love and peace.
>
> (p. 645)

He considers mismatched alliances unnatural and destructive. He maintains that "harmony of the homogenous and divorce of the unlike elements is the law of nature". The thrust of his argument is that "to part from an unjust man is happiness, and no injury to be lamented". (p. 669).

The social perspective and the views of the thinkers given hitherto can further a better understanding of the issue handled by the contemporary comedy. It questioned the double standard of behaviour and revolted against male dominance. Maria, the champion of equality, in Fletcher's *The Woman's Prize, or, The Tamer Tam'd* (1633) corroborates:

> Take two small drops of water, equal weigh'd
> Tel me which is the heaviest, and which ought
> First to descend in duty? (III, ii)

Woman is no longer supposed to have been created from man's ribs. Subjugation and subordination of women is decried in comedy. It ushered her into a new liberated world and endowed her with equal wit and qualities of the head and heart. The comedy also ridiculed marriage alliances contracted for mercenary gains only. Revolting against the restrictive authority of the parents, marrying clandestinely the person of one's choice and entertaining gallants and cuckolding also seem to be approved redress to the ills of marriage alliances contracted with an eye, not on love, but on wealth. This is decried by Lucinda in Sir Richard Steele's comedy, *The Conscious Lovers* (1722):

> What is the world come to? No shame left! To be bartered for like beasts of the fields, and that in such an instance as coming together to an entire familiarity and union of soul and body. Oh ! And this without being so much as well-wishers to each other but for increase of fortune. (iii)

Palamede, the young spokesman of young lovers, in Dryden's *Marriage a-la-Mode* (1671) disparages marriage-de-convenience when he presents his predicament before his friend:

> In few words, My old man has already marry'd me; for he has agreed with another old man, as rich and as covetous as himself, the Articles are drawn, and I have given my consent for fear of being disinherited; and yet know not what kind of woman I am to marry. (I, i)

What marriage means conventionally to a woman is lashed by Lucinda in *The Conscious Lovers*, thus:

> Mamma says the first time you see your husband should be at that instant he is made so, when your father with the help of the Minister gives you to him, then you are to observe and take notice of him, because then you are to obey him. (III)

Happolita in William Wycherley's *The Gentleman Dancing Master* (1672) denounces marriadge-de-convenience for she thinks:

> Fathers seldom choose well and I will no more take my father's choice in a husband than I would in a gown or a suit of knots.... (I, i)

She appears to be the spokesman of the younger generation that considers love as the only foundation of happy marriage. She avers:

> The match soon made is happy still,
> For only lover has there to do;
> Let no one marry against her will,
> But stand off, when her parents woo.
> (II, i)

Belinda in Vanbrugh's *The Provok'd Wife* (1697) prefers to marry for love even a poor younger brother. So is Leanthe in Farquhar's *Love and a Battle* (1698) determined to marry a poor extravagant rake. Nevertheless, most of the lovers in Restoration comedy try and test each other's constancy. Their love is neither self-annihilation of the platonic love of heroic drama, nor mere rovings of the libertines but is a quest for the right companionship. Once the lover's sincerity is established, the quest for the compatible companion is over, they welcome matrimonial bonds only after each agrees to the provisos the other has. Mirabel and Millamant in *The Way of the World* are examples of such a quest.

People who marry for reasons other than love are ridiculed in marital discord plots. Right from Etherege's Lady Cockwood in *She Wou'd if She Cou'd* (1667) to Mrs. Sullen in Farquhar's *The Beaux Stratagem* (1707) there are a host of unhappy women who show how fortune and status are acquired at the cost of domestic felicity. Lady Cockwood has earned a title but is married to a fool, and so are Lady Fidget and Lady Jasper in Wycherley's The *Country Wife* (1675). In the same play Margery Pinchwife is married to a foolish jealous husband. Laetitia, a young beautiful girl is married to a puritan old man, Fondlewife in Congreve's *The Old Bachelor* (1693). Similarly Elvira, a young beautiful daughter of the nobility is married to an old miserly tyrant, Don Diego in Dryden's *The Spanish Friar* (1680) etc. In *The Provok'd Wife* Lady Brute marries Lord Brute for money and in Farquhar's *The Beaux Stratagem* Mrs. Sullen marries for 'protection' and 'happiness' and both suffer miserably. The common thread among such mismatched couples is absence of love and marital bliss. Their marriages have badly failed. It is their example that makes Lucia in Shadwell's *Epsom Wells* (1672) say, "see, what matrimony comes to, or makes Millamant in *The Way of the World* apprehensive of:

> if Mirabel should not make a good husband, I am a lost thing; — for I find I love him violently. (IV)

No wonder women find marriage vows null and void under the present conventions and in the world of extreme libertinism and double standards of behaviour. Revolt is a natural consequence indeed. Doralice in Dryden's *Marriage a-la-Mode* rightly does argue the futility of cohabitation forced by old values and traditions. Her objection:

> Why should a foolish vow,
> which long ago was made,
> Oblige us to each other now,
> when passion is decay'd? (I, i)

though quite logical is not justifiable in her case since she is happily married to Rhodophil. No doubt, her attempt to seek complete liberty after the manner of Hobbesian state of Nature is rendered unsuccessful by the Muse. The play depicts that there should be only one code of conduct for both the spouses. Nevertheless, the play has potent for a revolt that many an unhappy wife resorts to.

Many of the victims of unhappy alliances and double standard of behaviour seem to justify seeking extra-marital bliss that appears quite in keeping with the moral code operative in Charles II's Court. Lady Fidget in *The Country Wife* questions her husband's tyranny thus:

> Why should our damn'd tyrants oblige us to live,
> On the pittance of Pleasures which they only give.
> (V, iv)

Lady Brute, dissatisfied with her married life is allowed to defend her case in political terms:

> But he has n't kept his words. Why then I'm absolv'd from mine. Aye, that seems clear to me. The Argument is good between the king and the people, why not between the Husband and Wife? (I, i)

Lady Wronglove in Cibber's *The Lady's Last Stake*; or *The Wife's Resentment* (1708) expresses her discontent thus:

> Sure men think that wives are stocks or stones, without all sense of injuries or only born and bound to bear them. (I, i)

Comedy of the period is an evidence that neither adultery, even as a revolt, nor keeping appearance and making pretensions to virtue and honour will assuage the surging dissatisfaction and miseries of unhappy marriages. Lady Cockwood, Lady Jasper, Lady

Plyant and Lady Foresight might try their best to keep appearances of loving wives, their actions belie their words and their discontent can be seen and felt through the veneer of their appearances.

Not all the women seeking release from unhappy marriage bonds or pleasure through gallants are presented triumphant. Elvira, a virtuous young girl of a respectable family is married to Gomez, the old tyrant in *The Spanish Fariar*. She tries to escape from her captivity but Dryden does not provide her any release whatsoever. Mrs. Fribble and Mrs. Bisket, the citizen wives in Shadwell's *Epsom Wells* are doomed to lead a most miserable life in spite of their attempts to revolt against their cruel husbands. Perhaps, Dryden and Shadwell dared not violate the middle class morality and annoy the emerging bourgeoise among their audience.

However, the unhappy wives seeking redress through adultery are made either to revert to positive norms or to seek separation through mutual consent. In the last decades of the seventeenth century the desire of the miserable wives to seek happiness extramarital way is thwarted by the playwrights. The adulterous inclinations of the unhappy wives are ascribed to their avowed motives of reclaiming their errant husbands by rousing their jealousy. The libertine husbands are made to realise the havoc they cause to their domestic life, and repent, though in the V Act conversion scene, and revert to positive norms. Amanda in Vanbrugh's *Relapse* (1968) makes Lord Loveless realise the worth of conjugal fidelity through her gallant, Worthy. Lady Brute in *The Provok'd Wife* also entertains gallants in order to reclaim Lord Brute but Vanbrugh like Dryden fails to provide succour to a miserable wife. Mrs. Sullen's efforts in *The Beaux Stratagem* to reclaim Lord Sullen fail badly. Nevertheless, Farquhar disburses justice to her by allowing her to separate with mutual consent.

Some of the aforesaid bold strokes of the playwrights present before the audience the possible direction of change; the socially acceptable remedy to unhappy wives. The comedies elucidate that in the absence of a flexible divorce procedure only mutual consent for separation could alleviate litigation hardships and miseries thereof. Mrs. Sullen in Miltonic strain defends divorce when she argues her point with her sister-in-law, Dorinda:

> O sister, casual violation is a transient injury, and may

> possibly be repair'd, but can radical hatred be ever reconcil'd? — No, no, sister, Nature is the first law giver, and when she has set tempers opposite, not all the golden links of wedlock, nor Iron Manacles of Law can keep 'em fast. (III, iii)

Lady Brute's marriage like that of Mrs. Sullen has also come to nothing. She too wants to seek divorce and discusses her predicament with her niece, Belinda:

> I know according to the strict statute law of Religion, I should do wrong; But if there were a Court of Chancery in Heaven, I'm sure I shou'd cast him. (I, i)

Lady Brute also tries in vain to rouse her husband's jealousy by planning love intrigues. Finally, she seeks separation. Vanbrugh's sympathy for the wronged wife is voiced in his defence of her intrigue in *The Short Vindication*. He supports her behaviour against the husband, for it is instructive. He says:

> though his ill usage of her does not justify her intrigues, her intriguing upon his ill-usage, may be a caution for some. (pp. 207-208).

Nevertheless, Vanbrugh does not grant her separation by mutual consent which seems an evidence of Vanbrugh's avoidance of annoyance to the moralists and the rising citizen class. On the other hand, Farquhar (himself the victim of a tricked marriage) advocates separation in *The Beaux Stratagem*. Mrs. Sullen and Squire Sullen agree on no other point but separation and Farquhar makes them consent mutually to separate. Their attempt is highly praised by her gallant, Archer:

> Both happy in their several states we find,
> Those parted by consent, and those conjoined.
> Consent, if mutual, saves the lawyer's fee —
> Consent is law enough to set you free. (V)

Shadwell too had resolved this problem in *Epsom Wells* long before Farquhar attempted it in *The Beaux Stratagem*. The gulf between the Sullens is caused by a clash of temperaments but in *Epsom Wells*, Mr. Woodly, like Sir John Brute, provokes his wife with his libertine ways and brutish behaviour. Mrs. Woodly is so miserable that she wishes him dead at the hands of her gallant:

> If he kills Bevil, I am reveng'd, if he kills him, he rids me of the worst Husband for my humour in Christendom. (IV, i)

In a most comic proviso scene they consent to separate and celebrate it like their wedding as Mr. Woodly puts it:

> To show you, that there was never yet so decent a divorce, I have fiddles to play at it as they used to do at weddings. (v, i)

Mr. Woodly lauds the new approach to matrimonial disputes:

> Marriage that does the hearts and will unite,
> Is the best state of pleasure and delight;
> But when man and wife no longer each other please,
> They may at least like us each other ease. (V, i)

Not all the playwrights, however, support separation by mutual consent, they have a different solution to this problem. Colley Cibber, in *Love's Last Shift* (1696) presents Amanda, a virtuous wife in distress. Her poignant tears fill the husband with remorse in the fifth-act reformation scene meant to warm the hearts of the moralists. Her virtue triumphs in awakening the latent good in him and he pledges conjugal fidelity which he extols in his final speech:

> And sure the nearest to the joys above,
> Is the chaste rapture of a virtuous love. (V, iii)

In another popular comedy, *The Careless Husband* (1704), Cibber again presents reconciliation as a remedy to unhappy spouses believing in the fact that man by nature is good and reclaimable. Lady Easy, a virtuous wife, is married to Sir Charles Easy, a Libertine rake. Instead of exposing him, she patiently awakens his conscience by putting her scarf over his head lest he should catch cold. Not many unhappy wives do introspect like Lady Easy:

> And duty, too, forbids me to insult Where I have vowed obedience, Perhaps the fault's in me, and nature has not formed Me with the thousand little requisites that warm the heart to love. (V, v)

She knows that continual jealousy and negative ways on her part will rather fix her husband's aversion; it is only virtue and patience that can redeem him. Filled with remorse and penitence he reverts to positive values.

In situations where both the spouses are responsible for unhappiness, Cibber provides a mentor who by gently counselling brings peace and harmony between them. Lady Wrong Love and Lord Wrong Love in *The Lady's Last Stake*, or, *The Wife's Resentment* (1708) are no better than the Woodlys but Sir Friendly Moral advises Lady Wrong Love to lure her husband with "soft affections" and asks Lord Wrong Love to think of the "long-watched, restless hours she has already endured" on account of his misdoings. Both realise their mistakes, repent and are reconciled.

The presentation of amicability, harmony and reconciliation in such sentimental comedies was in consonance with the predominant middle class sensibilities craving for the tenets of Christianity discernible in *The Tatler, The Spectator*, and the periodicals of Steele and Addison. In cases where only separation could resolve the marital disputes, mutual consent was supported.

Whatever be the situation, comedy of this era approached marital disputes from women's point of view since they were the weaker sex and required pioneers to fight for them. Marriage laws in England did not consider them equal to the other sex. Even Lord Harwicke's Act of 1754, seeking to restrict informal marriage ceremonies and annulment, was silent on the miseries of the unhappily married women. The credit goes to the Restoration Society and comedy for making women voice their dissatisfaction and fight for equality and liberty. The battle was won when in 1801, Mrs. Addison got a divorce decree against her husband. It was then that the voice of Lady Wrong Love was taken note of :

> For if the husband's violation of his marriage-vow is in itself so foul an injury, whence is it that the law is so sparing in its redress? ... If she offends, the crime is unpardonable, yet if injur'd, has no right to compensation, it may be usual this, but sure 'tis unnatural. (II)

NOTES

1. G.S. Alleman in Matrimonial Law and the Materials of Restoration Comedy

(1942) has listed clandestine marriages presented in the contemporary comedies (pp. 84-92).

2. J.H. Smith in *The Gay Couple in Restoration Comedy* (1971) has studied the gay heroes and the heroines seeking companionship in marriage.
3. A.H. Scouten (ed) in *Restoration and Eighteenth Century Drama*. Macmillan (1980) opines that the Restoration Comedy is open-ended, for the reformation of the rakish hero is not conclusive.
4. Visiak, E.H. (ed). *Milton : Complete Poetry and Selected Prose,* The Nonesuch Press.

12

The Status of Women

The ascendency of the Parliament in the Seventeenth century and the preponderance of the Scientific philosophy of Hobbes and Locke expounding the contract theory shattered the age old institutions, *viz*. the state, the church, the family, etc. Consequently, marriage no longer remained a sacrament; husband-wife relationship also evidenced a change. Seventeenth century society and comedy started questioning the sanctity of their relationship presented in the genesis:

> God and Nature hath given the husband Authority to command, and the wife is bound to obey, however unnecessary or unfit she may think it to be...And thy desire shall be to thy Husband, and he shall rule over thee.

The Protestant ideal of marriage as spiritual companionship exhorted by Katharine in *The Taming of the Shrew* that

> The Husband is thy Lord, thy life, thy keeper,
> Thy head, thy Sovereign.
>
> . . . .
>
> Such duty as the subject owes the prince,
> Even such a woman oweth to her husband.

was turned a sceptical eye to and the absolute authority of the husband got further weakened after the Civil Marriage Act of 1653 that accepted marriage as a civil contract between the two spouses. Nevertheless, this Act as well as the two contract theories bowed to male superiority and required abject obedience from the wife. Whether the puritan family or the one founded on marriage contract, married women were mere cogs in the domestic machinery run by the superior male. If the husband erred or proved unfaithful to his wife the prevalent law seldom punished him but any revolt from the wife was treated as petit treason.[1] Women were burnt alive for killing their cruel husbands as is evidenced in the cases of Elizabeth Ridgeway in 1684 and Mary Hobry in 1688.

With the scientific thinking gaining popularity the status of women as equals to their male companions was raised and revolt against the absolute authority of the husband was justified specially in the light of the double standard of behaviour which allowed libertine ways to husbands and expected virtue from wives. Restoration playwrights, therefore, tried to present wives fighting for their freedom from domestic bondage and sometimes, by way of revolt, indulging in extra-marital relationship rendering the husbands the butt of the comic muse. Absence of any legal protection to abused wives perhaps deterred the comedy writers of the late seventeenth century from upholding the adulterous ways of the revolting wives and crowning their efforts with success. On the other hand, they were allowed to cuckold their foolish or tyrannical husbands, on the other, they were made to make pretences of honour, reputation, and domestic sanctity..

Satirical comedies with marital discord plots pivoting on the clash of temperaments or on mercenary marriages with no consideration of the age, intelligence, like and dislikes of the married couple, had ample scope for providing a glimpse into the abuses of marriage, a problematic institution; with, by and large, abused wives either resorting to adulterous ways or suffering endlessly or striving to reclaim their libertine husbands. The former was the convention of the comedy of manners whereas reformation of the libertine rakes by the virtuous wives was the staple comic device at the hands of the sentimentalists who dominated the stage in the last decade of the seventeenth century and thereafter. Laetitia Fondlewife (*The Old Bachelor*), Margery Pinchwife (*The Country Wife*), Elvira (*The Spanish Friar*: or *The Double Discovery*) etc. try to revolt against the absolute authority of their husbands and seek pleasure in extra-marital relationship. Their husbands – generally presented as rakes or foolish lords – indulging in whoring, drinking, and gambling are jealous as well as cruel. Laetitia in an assignation with Bellmour askes him to come disguised as a parson; Margery makes her husband an agent to promoting her love intrigue with Horner; and Elvira, the victim of Gomez' tyranny seeks escape through Dominic, the pimp, and opens negotiations with her 'lover' Lorenzo. In all these cases the beautiful young wives are captives of the cruel husbands and, therefore, they rebel and seek freedom and happiness in or outside the house. In most of the comedies, domestic piety is at stake, nevertheless, it is saved or supposed to have been saved by the timely arrival of the husbands or by the turn of the events against the intriguing wives. Fondlewife returns unexpectedly and thwarts his wife's intrigue,[2] and Elvira is discovered in the attempt of running away with Lorenzo and meets a worse fate at the hands of her husband. Husbands like Pinchwife, Fondlewife, and Gomez in the audience are warned of the inevitable threat to their marital felicity if the wives are abused.

During the Restoration William Wycherley, one of the foremost playwrights, focused his attention on the plight of the miserable wives. With the predominant cuckolding theme he, in *The Country Wife*, presented a satirical character, Mr. Pinchwife, a perfect whoremaster, who forbids his innocent country wife, Margery, all the town pleasures, such as going to friends or visiting plays, enjoying music, dance, etc. lest she should attract some gallants and cuckold him. Pinchwife does not realise that by denying all the town pleasures to her he sets her longing for them. She grudges that her husband goes, "everyday fluttering about abroad, whilst [she] must stay at home like a poor, lonely sullen bird in a cage" (III, i). Consequently, she is determined to disobey and deceive him. Thus it is Pinchwife's restrictive authority bordering on cruelty that opens the path of adultery for his wife and earns him horns. Wycherley, through Margery Pinchwife, teaches the audience a lesson that it is the husband who is responsible for the moral downfall of the unhappy wife. Even Margery Pinchwife's pretence to 'virtue' and 'honour', the only possible comic resolution to the problem of abused wives in the Restoration sexually liberated society still following the double standard of behaviour, is an evidence of the playwright's limitations as well as sympathy for the miserable wives

Dryden also followed the conventions of the satiric comedy and presented the plight of the unhappy wife in Elvira (*The Spanish Friar*), the beautiful, young, virtuous daughter of nobility married to Gomez, a covetous old man who is "the very quintessence of jealousy" and who allows no "male creature in his house; and from abroad he lets no man come near her" (I, ii). Elvira justly expresses her discontent before Dominic thus:

> You know my husband is a man in year; but he's my husband and therefore I shall be silent, but his humours are more intolerable than his age: he's grown so forward, so covetous, and so jealous, that he has turned my heart quite from him, and I durst confess it, has forced me to cast my affections on another man
> (II, iii)

When offered an opportunity to escape from captivity, Elvira does not welcome her gallant; rather wants to be satisfied with a proof of his true love for her. Her plight is aptly presented by her when she stands helpless "panting, like a bird that has often beaten her wings in vain against her cage, and at last dares hardly venture, out, though she sees it open" (IV, i). Dryden does not allow the married women in his comedies to violate the marriage vows though he allows them to question their sanctity as Doralice did in *Marriage-a-La-Mode* when she asks:

> Why should a foolish Marriage vow,
> Which long ago was made,
> Oblige us to each other now,
> When Passion is decay'd? (I, i)

Dryden too, like his contemporaries, bowed before the prevalent marriage laws and, therefore, refrained from allowing the abused wives seek either divorce or separate maintenance.

Restoration marital discord plots highly tainted with libertine philosophy, cuckolding scenes or near-seduction situations and characters keeping appearances of honour and virtue seldom reformed the erring husbands. But with the emergence of bourgeoise morality after 1688 the stage preferred presenting both erring spouses with an eye to reclaim them through some sentimental force whether it be external or inward awakening. The introduction of moral reform required tearful melodramatic situations imbued with remorse as well as penitence and the triumph of virtue over vice. In the case of the abusing husbands, virtue and fidelity of the abused wife aroused the latent good in him leading him to reformation. Some of the abused wives in the comedies of the period follow the negative norms of behaviour to reclaim their erring husbands. Both negative and positive norms of behaviour are followed by the abused wives to reclaim their erring husbands. Resentment is one such corrective measure adopted by the abused wives. No wonder, in the male dominated society, the resentment of the wife is no welcome, rather, it fixes the husband more in promiscuity and cruelty. The living example of such an effort on the part of the abused wife is presented by Colley Cibber in *The Lady's Last Stake,* or; *The Wife's Resentment*. The clash of Lady and Lord Wronglove's temperaments widens the gap between them to an extent that is irreparable. Lady Wronglove resents justly that

> not a day passes without some fresh discovery of his perfidiousness...This usage is beyond patience...Sure men think that wives are stocks or stones, without all sense of injuries, or only born and bound to bear them.
> (I, i)

The more she resents, the deeper he plunges into libertinism which further embitters their relationship. Eventually, She finds that the "bond of wife or husband no longer lies in force against [them]" (IV, i) and agrees to part from her husband. However, the timely arrival of Sir Friendly Moral and his exhortation of conjugal fidelity, an inartistic device necessitated only by the demand of morality, averts the imminent separation. The play ends teaching the audience that:

> the man that violates himself the sacred honours of his wife's chaste bed... ought at least to fear, as she is the frailer sex, the same from her; the injury to her strikes deeper than the head, often to the heart.
> (V)

and the wives are advised "to lure [their husbands] home with soft affection" (V). Both the spouses realise their faults and repent; and peace and amity is restored in the family.

But many an abused wife does not get a mentor like Sir Friendly Moral. Therefore, the problem of moral reformation of the promiscuous or cruel husband requires another device. The abused wives, realising that resentment and adultery on their part can at best revenge but seldom cure the evil, rouse the husband's jealousy so that the erring husbands react immediately and realise the worth of conjugal fidelity. This is closely presented in sir John Vanbrugh's *Relapse* and *The Provok'd Wife*. Vanbrugh, a severe critic of Cibber's fifth-act reformation of the rakish husband presented in *Love's Last Shift,* produced the *Relapse* as a sequel to Cihber's play. The *Relapse* has a virtuous wife, Amanda, who is abused by her husband, Lord Loveless, in spite of his avowed assurances of conjugal fidelity. Vanbrugh, a keen observer of human frailty, wants to show through Lord Loveless, that vice corrupts men in no time. Lord Loveless, the reformed rake, becomes an easy prey to lustful Berinthia, and has amorous intrigues with her in the true Restoration spirit. The innocent wife knows it well and suffers endlessly. She exposes the infidelity of her rakish husband to none, instead groans thus: "a base ungrateful man, after what I have done for him, too use me thus" (V, iv). No matter how virtuous, she feels like revolting and, therefore, puts her case strongly when she says:

> But let him know,
> My quiver's not entirely emptied yet,
> I still have darts, and I can shoot 'em too;
> ...
> or through another's heart
> I yet could find the way to make his smart (V, iv).

Nevertheless, when her gallant, Worthy, compels her to yield, her transcient virtue saves her as well as reclaims her gallant who repents and almost worships her. It is amazing that Vanbrugh, instead of employing the fifth-act reformation scene for the rakish, morally depraved husband has made use of this dramatic device to reform the gallant. Perhaps his thesis that man is frail would have been disproved had he reformed Loveless. The very purpose of writing the play would have been belied. Nevertheless, his sympathies rest with the virtuous, miserable wives. In Amanda, Vanbrugh has certainly raised a woman to a higher plane in the eyes of the audience and the other characters in the play, but he has left her more miserable.

Vanbrugh tried a similar attempt in *The Provok'd Wife,* a forceful comment on repurcussions of marriage-de-convenience. His realistic and down to earth approach toward marriage did not allow him to idealise marriage and create platonic characters like Cibber's Amanda, but flesh and blood beings like Lady Brute (*The Provok'd Wife*) who rouses the husband to reclaim him. Her husband, Sir John Brute, a boorish squire with cynical attitude towards marriage typical of the Restoration rakes renders her life unbearable. Stinking with wine, and covered with dirt and blood, the morally degraded 'beast' is scorned by one and all in the play and is a loathsome thing even to the audience. When he finds his wife resenting his vices he forces her, in a most wild manner, to accept his wooing, which is nothing short of a torture to her. Her intrigue with her 'lover', Constant, to rouse her husband, and her waveringly adulterous gestures during her most vulnerable moments can all be ascribed to the brutality of her husband. This is aptly discussed by Heartfree and Constant:

> This proceeding of his is the only thing on earth can make you fortunate. If anything can prevail with her to accept a gallant, 'tis his usage of her (II, i)

Lady Brute is so discontented with her married life that she is ready to plead her case even in the court of heaven, as she avers:

> I know, according to the strict statue-law of religion, I should do wrong; but if there were a Court of Chancery in heaven, I'm sure I should cast him (i, ii)

Her resentment that, "he has us'd me so barbarously of late, that I could almost resolve to play the downright wife – and cuckold him" (i, i) is born of discontent for she is unable to justify her wrong-way means to reform her rakish husband. "But can his faults release my duty?" reveals a dutiful wife in her. Vanbrugh rightly defends her in the *Short Vindication* when he comments on Sir John Brute's character thus:

> The ill consequence of his brutality appears in the miscarriage of his wife: for tho' his ill usage of her does not justify her intrigue, her intriguing upon his ill usage, may be a caution for some.[3]

Vanbrugh neither reclaims the brutish husband nor allows Lady Brute seek either adulterous ways or separate maintenence or divorce, which the logical development of the situation required. With Paul Mueschke one can maintain that in *The Provok'd Wife* "Vanbrugh has deliberately created, through the brutish caricature of the husband and the intelligent resentment of the wife; a situation which exposes from a rational and sympathetic, not a sentimental, nor a wholly comic, point of view, the cause of marital incompatibility and infidelity."[4] What Vanbrugh wants to say perhaps is clear in the back drop of the sub-plot; Belinda-Heartfree love intrigue which ends in matrimony based on mutual love and not on money like that of the Brutes.

Resentment on the part of the abused wife may rather fix the husband to aversion causing further damage to marital felicity; rousing jealousy may or may not lure the erring husband back to his wronged wife but may sometimes be disastrous to wife herself; but how patience, understanding and virtue may cause inner awakening, remorse and repentance leading to reformation is the staple of sentimental comedies. The triumph of virtue over vice through sentimental situations can best be seen in Colley Cibber's *Love's Last Shift and The Careless Husband. Love's Last Shift*, the first sentimental comedy of the time, presents Loveless, a rakish husband, drawn after the extravagant rakes of the Comedy of Manners. Loveless like Dryden's Rhodophil (*Marriage-a-La-Mode*) has a cynical approach toward matrimony, and has forsaken his virtuous wife, Amanda, for the "staleness of her love" and the quest for variety. To Amanda "the rules of virtue have never been ever sacred" and she longs for her husband's love. Young Worthy, her husband's friend, aptly describes her case as:

> Poor Amanda, thou well deservest a better husband; thou wert never wanting in thy endeavours to reclaim him. (iii, i)

She had tried her best to "lure this falcon back to love and virtue" but in vain. Hence she is advised to follow the apparently wrong means to gain her end, *i.e.* an intrigue in which she should act as her husband's mistress. Young Worthy justifies this intrigue for "it is less criminal to let him love you as a mistress than to let him hate you as a wife" (III, i). After great scruples she agrees to act as Loveless's mistress and succeeds in luring him back. The whole exercise and the moral exhortations from Amanda fill him with remorse and penitence and he says:

> And yet your words are uttered with such a powerful accent that they have awakened my soul and strike my thought with horror and remorse. (V, ii)

The seasoned rake, by the end of the play, not only promises fidelity to his spouse but also preaches and practises virtuous ways. His penitence is in the true spirit of sentimentalism and must have brought forth tears of joy from the audience as it did from the other characters. Virtue is acclaimed and a confession is made:

> Oh, thou has roused me from my deep lethargy of Vice! For hitherto my soul has been enslaved to loose desires, to vain deluding follies, and shadows of substantial bliss, but now I wake with joy to find my rapture real. Thus let me kneel and pay my thanks to her whose conquering virtue has at last subdued me. Here will I fix, thus prostrate sigh my shame, and wash my crimes in never-ending tears of penitence.
> (V, ii)

Though at the price of "uncovincing improbability" which Vanbrugh accused Cibber of in *The Short Vindication* the virtuous love of the abused wife was rewarded in the restoration of her long lost marital bliss.

Amanda puts an end to her sufferings by reforming her husband through "immoral" ways where as Lady Easy, the abused wife in Cibber's *Careless Husband* wins her rakish husband through virtuous ways. Lady Easy, a paragon of patience and understanding, instead of finding faults with her husband introspects:

> And duty, too, forbids me to insult,
> Where I have vowed obedience, Perhaps the fault's
> in me, and nature has not formed
> Me with the thousand little requisites
> that warm the heart to love. (V, v)

Finding that "continual jealousy may tease him to a fixed aversion" she is determined to reclaim him by patience and virtue. Her wish, "If I can make him once think seriously, Time yet may be my friend" (I) is soon fulfilled. On finding Sir Charles Easy without his periwig sleeping by her maid, Edging, the abused wife, like her counterparts in Restoration comedy, for once feels like exposing him:

> I'll throw this vizor of my patience off
> Now wake him in his guilt,
> And barefaced front him with my wrongs. (V, v)

but duty and virtue refrain her; and, instead, she takes a steinkirk from her neck and places it gently over his head lest an unkind wind may harm him. On waking, the erring husband broods over his wife's forgiving gesture and is filled with remorse. His confession: 'the thought has made me despicable en'n to myself', and his realization that "she has been long acquainted with my follies, and yet with what amazing prudence has she borne the secret pangs of injured love and wore an everlasting smile to me" (V, v) make him reform himself. He puts an end to his love intrigues with lady Graveairs and Edging and kneels before his virtuous wife exclaiming:

> Let me be therefore pleased to tell you now, your wonderous conduct has waked me to a sense of your disquiet past, and resolution never to disturb it more.
>
> (V, v)

The hearts of the moralists and lovers of marital fidelity must have been warmed at their reunion.

There are plays that suggest that this sort of reconciliation is not possible in every situation. There are spouses who do not follow Lady Easy's thinking that "errors from want of thinking might be bore, at least when probably one moment's serious thought would end 'em" (V, v) and there is no scope of adjustment between the spouses. Therefore, separate maintenance or divorce as the last resort, is sought, although it appears too radical a step even for the promiscuous society of the Restoration. Moreover, it was not easy to get a divorce decree. Therefore, the playwrights tried to please the audience with reconciliation scenes, the demand of the changing ethos. Shadwell and Farquhar championed separation through mutual consent, permissible under the old Teutonic customs. Milton also had advocated divorce in his treatise, *Doctrine and Discipline of Divorce* (1644) against unworthy bondage; thus ushering modern thinking. Divorce in the modern sense was unknown before 1700 when the Duke of Norfolk was granted divorce by the Parliament. Till then the common way of release and succour from unhappy marriages was mutual consent to separation, requiring no legal procedure. Cromwell's Act of 1653 also did not refer to divorce except in case of minor's marriage through fraud or abduction. Lord Roos case in 1671 is a major landmark in the history of marriage laws for it supported a woman's right to divorce a husband. Even the Hardwicke Act of 1753 hardly provided for divorce in the modern sense. It was only in 1801 when

Mrs. Addison got a divorce decree against her husband that abused women won their cause.

The prevalent legal code with regard to husband-wife relationship deterred the playwrights from presenting the logical solution to unhappy marriages. Credit goes to Shadwell who came to the rescue of the abused wives by providing Mrs. Woodly divorce by mutual consent in *Epsom Wells*. Farquhar followed the suit in *The Beaux Stratagem* and presented before the audience the most rational attitude toward matrimonial abuses, when he allowed Mrs. and Mr. Sullen to seek release from the marriage bonds by mutual consent. Both the plays, significant as they are in the history of comedy, need a detailed study.

Epsom Wells, much applauded by Charles II, presents Mr. Woodly, a libertine rake who has made his wife's life miserable. She complains:

> Thou inhumane Beast, to sit up anights late, and come home drunk and wake me, and lye like a statue by me all the rest of the night, flesh and blood can't bear it. (II, iv)

Her discontent expressed in the vein of a Lady Brute reveals Mr. Woodly being no better than Sir John Brute. He is not only a Sottish beast but also a libertine who is pursuing his own niece, Caroline. The double standard of behaviour on the part of the husband together with a deep scorn for him goads Mrs. Woodly seek happiness the immoral way. She not only plans assignations with the witty gay heroes, Bevil and Raines, in vain, but also wishes her husband's death as a good riddance. Her reaction to the news of a duel between the hero and her husband reveals her bitter scorn for her husband:

> If he kills Bevil, I am reveng'd if he kills him, he rids me of the worst Husband for my humour in Christendom
> (IV, i)

Indeed, she too is to blame, yet all her faults seem to originate from her husband's ill-treatment of her. The action of the play also shows Mr. Woodly's "lewd disorderly life" violating matrimonial vows. The abused wife has neither the satisfaction of cuckolding her husband – the practice which the eighteenth century sensibility denounced – nor like Amanda can she reclaim the incorrigible rakish husband. Therefore, by the end of the play, Woodlys, in a proviso scene, infused with the spirit of the comedy of manners, agree to part. The excerpts from the scene are worth quoting:

> Woodly: But let's execute our Divorce decently; for my part I'le celebrate it like a wedding.
>
> Mrs. W. To me it is a more joyful day.
>
> Woodly ... I do declare I will for ever separate from the company of Sarah my now wife.
>
> Mrs. W. Your lewd disorderly life made you separate before. The said Sarah having for this two years scarce seen you by daylight.
>
> Woodly And that I will never hereafter use her like a wife.
>
> Mrs. W. That is scurvily. Also all obligations of conjugal affections, shall from henceforth cease, be null, voide, and of none effect.
>
> Woodly Then, that I am to keep what mistress I please, and how I please, after the laudable custom of other Husbands.
>
> Mrs. W. ... But may enjoy all privileges of other separate ladies, without any lett, hindrance, molestation whatsoever.
>
> Woodly Is not this better than to live and quarrel and to keep a pother with one another. Faith take a kiss at parting for old acquaintance sake.
>
> Lucia See what matrimony comes to –
>
> Woodly To show you, that there was never yet so decent a divorce, I have fiddles to play at it as they used to do at weddings (V, i)

Mrs. Woodly gets her portion back with two thousand pounds as maintenance. The divorce is sealed gayly with a tone and tenor of the gay couple comedy. Nevertheless, as a foil to the gentry's bold stride towards divorce Shadwell has juxtaposed two citizen couples who dare not seek separation – a very expensive and difficult exercise – but bear the burden of unhappy marriages. Mrs. Fribble, the abused citizen wife is encouraged by her friend, Mrs. Bisket, to revolt, "You betray our cause, submit to a Husband, I'd see that Husband that I'd crouch to." But Mrs. Fribble's attempt to revolt against her husband results in her being beaten in public. The miserable wife kneels and apologises for disobeying her "lord and master" who cites law in his support:

> The law allows me to give my wife due correction. I know the law, Houswife, consider and tremble on.
> (IV, i)

In the backdrop of the citizen world and morality the bold conclusion of the play by the Woodlys heralded a new era in the following words:

> Marriage that does the hearts and will unite,
> Is the best state of pleasure and delight;
> But
> When man and wife no longer each other please,
> They may at least like us each other ease (V, i)

Another play bearing much resemblance with *Epsom Wells* is Farquhar's *The Beaux Stratagem* which allows the abused wife to seek divorce as a release from a loathsome wedded life. Mrs. Sullen, unlike Lady Brute, a victim of marriage-de-convenience, is married to Squire Sullen, "a Sottish drunkard who exasperates his wife by his brutish manners". He has married her only to "beget an heir to his estate" while she accepted him for "protection and happiness". Their hatred for each other springs forth from the fact that both had failed to get what they expected of each other. Like Lady Brute, Mrs. Sullen, in order to rouse her husband, connives with Squire Sullen's sister, Dorinda, to have an intrigue with a gallant. The lover intrigue first with the French Count and then with the spark, Archer, instead of bringing the Sullens closer confirms the adultery of the wife in the eyes of the husband who finally consents to divorce her.

The Sullens' plight much like the Brutes, is aptly described in a scene of altercation between them:

> Squire S: One flesh! rather two carcasses joined unnaturally together.
>
> Mrs. S. Or rather a living soul coupled to a dead body.

Mr. Sullen, in a Lockean vein, pleads her case with Dorinda:

> Casual violence is a transcient injury; and may be

> repaired; but can radical hatred be even reconciled? No, no, sister; Nature is the first Law giver; and when she has set tempers opposite, not all the golden links of wedlock nor iron manacles of Law, can keep 'em fast. (III, iii)

The play reveals them as "united contradictions, fire and fury" and that confirms their views. Nelson James in his detailed study of the play shows more sympathy with Lady Brute (*The Provok'd Wife*) than Mrs. Sullen and holds her responsible for her disastrous marriage as he avers:

> Mrs. Sullen is not altogether innocent in this matter, just as the provok'd wife, Lady Brute, is not altogether innocent in the failure of her marriage.[5]

Amplifying lack of virtue on the part of the abused wives Nelson James forgets that it is the brutality of the husbands combined with the urge to revolt against the double standard of morality, prescribing codes different for men and women, which virtually throws the abused wives into the arms of their gallants who they still spurn in favour of their virtue and honour. He reiterates:

> In a way, Mrs. Sullen, is more to blame than Lady Brute for the dissolution of her marriage, for Lady Brute has more provocation.[6]

To him Sir John Brute is a brute, according to the action of the play while Mr. Sullen is a brute only in the eyes of his wife. Indeed, there is a difference in the degree of their brutality. Sir Brute is too provokingly brutal and loathsome, whereas Squire Sullen is too freezingly sullen. Both of them forget nature of women which Mrs. Sullen describes thus:

> I own myself a woman, full of my sex; a gentle, generous soul, easy and yielding to soft desires, a spacious heart, where love and all his train might lodge. (IV, i)

It is love which is denied to them and which is the foundation of the citadel of domestic felicity as is illustrated in Belinda-Heartfree (*The Provok'd Wife*) and Dorinda-Aimwell (*The Beaux Stratagem*) matches which set off the unhappy married couples in the plays. Both the playwrights emphasise the significance of love in marriage alliance, the lack of which results in disastrous endings of Sullens' and Brutes' married life. It is beautifully summed up by Sir Charles Freeman (*The Beaux Stratagem*) in the hand imagery:

> Squire S: I always thought that we were naturally one.
>
> Sir Charles: Sir I know that my two Hands are naturally one, because they love one another, kiss one another help one another in all the Actions of life; but I could not say so much. If they were always at Cuffs (V, v).

The only logical solution to the problem then is to separate decently with mutual consent as Archer puts it in the last scene:

> Both happy in their Several states we find,
> Those parted by consent, and those conjoined.
> Consent, if mutual, saves the lawyer's fee —
> Consent is law enough to set you free.

Although the decision is logical still, "it would be hard to guess which of these parties is the better pleased, the couple joined, or the couple parted" (V, v). Nevertheless, it is better to end the experienced misery if the two hands (husband and wife) find their life unbearable. If mutual love does not join the hands together it is better to separate, is the message given by Shadwell as well as Farquhar. *Epsom Wells* and *The Beaux Stratagem* are the two plays which are perhaps far advanced for their time, that supported the abused wife in the male dominated society and have ushered a new era of thinking that finds full expression in the later centuries. It is not an exaggeration to agree with Paul Mueschke and Jeannette Fleisher:

> The Comedy of manners would have presented the revolted wife as either an incorrigibly lascivious strumpet, the "She Would if She Could" type of female, inoculated with the virus of licentious carnality, and ridiculed unmercifully by the male she pursues; or as the falsely ingenuous Country Wife of a jealous husband, who is more than willingly seduced by a resourceful Horner. The sentimental treatment would have idealised and romanticised the abused woman, would have converted the abusing husband, and would have

> ended in absurdly unconvincing reconciliation ... [But the] perception of social values in situations which had formerly been exploited solely for their comic possibilities resulted in a more human approach toward the social life of his time.'

NOTES

1. Thomas Heywood's *The Woman Killed with Kindness*, shows how the adulterous wife is punished barbarously.
2. Congreve was so engrossed with the gay couple comedy and the satirical sketch of the old bachelor, that the marital discord plot did not attract his microscopic attention.
3. Vanbrugh, John – *The Works of John Vanbrugh* ed. W.C. Ard, London: Lawrence & Bullen (1893), p. 207-208.
4. Paul Mueschke, "A Re-evaluation of Vanbrugh,", *PMLA*, Vol. 49 (1934), p. 888.
5. E.N. James, *The Development of Farquhar as a Comic Dramatist*, Mouton (1972), p. 270.
6. *Ibid*., p. 271.
7. Paul Mueschke, "A Re-evaluation of Vanbrugh", *PMLA*, Vol. 49 (1934), p. 889.

13

Conclusion

Early eighteenth century comedy underwent certain significant changes which had begun in the last decades of the previous century. The Restoration comedy which had reached its apex in the reign of Charles II saw its decadence after his death in 1685. The patronage of stage gradually began to shift to the bourgeois class which, along with the thinkers, reformers and female segment of the audience objected to its immorality and profanity. Thus tremendous moral pressure was exerted on the dramatists from various quarters against the apparent immorality of their plays. The most significant among these forces was Jeremy Collier who drew attention of the public to the abuses of the contemporary theatre.

As a result of these factors measures were taken to cultivate moral climate in the country. Writers and actors were prosecuted for writing and staging morally objectionable plays. The playwrights tried either to defend their plays or modified them to suit the new demands. Nevertheless, the basic features of the Restoration comedy continued for quite some time, though they were tempered by certain amount of morality. Colley Cibber, Sir John Vanbrugh and George Farquhar were some of the playwrights whose plays show this shift.

The shift is pai .icularly noticeable in the conception of the principal characters. The young heroes are seldom presented as swearing, cursing, drinking, whoring, graceless ruffians. They are, instead, portrayed as sensible beings with a sense of responsibility and decency. Thus they are more sober than their Restoration counterparts and even the rakes are infused with scruples and good sense. The licentious heroes, if any, give up their licentious ways and revert to positive norms of behaviour. They are accepted only when they show contrition over their past lapses and reform. Cibber is rightly credited for introducing this kind of reformation which usually occurs in the last act of a play for the specific purpose of moral edification. The errant characters, men as well as women, under the influence of transcendent virtue or an inner awakening or direct moralisings repent and pledge to revert to the paths of decency. The main thrust of the Restoration comedy was on the gay pursuits of the libertines but in the early eighteenth century comedy the emphasis is on their repentance and reformation. Poignant emotional sentimental scenes of remorse and joy are the marked features of these comedies, chiefly those written by Cibber. Triumph of inherent good sense and virtue over vice and evil is the central dramatic theme of most of these comedies.

Constructive efforts of these playwrights towards moral reform can be discerned in their direct association with the Drury Lane Theatre of which Steele was a governor for quite some time and whose patent he held jointly with Wilks, Doggett and Cibber. Because of his involvement in other activities, he could not devote all of his time to the task of remedying the theatrical abuses but still, he did his best to fight the immorality of the Restoration comedies. From 1709 to 1722, when Steele's comic muse remained silent, the moralist in him was actively crusading against the vices and follies of the stage through his essays in the periodicals, *viz.*, *The Tatler, The Spectator, The Guardian, The Town Talk, The Theatre,* and etc. The last two, published during his governorship of Drury Lane, were devoted entirely to the affairs of the stage. Since 1714 he had been preparing himself to write his masterpiece, *The Conscious Lovers*, his last complete play written wholly for the moral education of the audience. His moral observations are found not only in the body of his plays but also in the prefatory notes, prologues and epilogues. As his moral concern became stronger, the gaiety and naive charm and the satiric mode of the earlier comedies gave place to overt sermonizing. Yet a common urge, a common thread, runs through these plays which exhibit a gradually achieved synthesis of comedy and conscience.

Steele's interest in comedy was awakened during his college days but it became public only when he presented Christopher Rich, the manager of the Drury Lane Theatre, with his first comedy, *The Funeral* in 1701. His dramatic career, his governorship of Drury Lane, his active participation in the theatrical reforms and his comments on the immorality of the stage and the society in his essays bear ample testimony to his moral concern and his belief, like Collier's, in the urgent need of reforming the morals and the manners of the society. Steele's comedies were the products of the same moral concern that had prompted Collier to attack the Restoration comedy. He also shared with his contemporary critic-playwright, John Dennis, the belief in the usefulness of the stage for the society.[1] Etherege's gay abandon in portraying the dissipated society of the Restoration days was simply outrageous to Steele. He was also shocked by the Restoration concept of a man of honour which he tried to demolish by making virtue an essential concomitant of his hero. He made his "fine gentleman" a man of sterling qualities with profound regard for religion and morality. Steele believed in presenting characters which were meant to be not just satirically instructive but as objects worthy of emulation and capable of arousing good natural impulses latent in the people. Steele exemplified the 'fine gentleman' in Lord Hardy (*The Funeral*) and further, in a more developed form, in Bevil Junior (*The Conscious Lovers*). He also took pains to make his heroines equally virtuous. Lady Sharlot (*The Funeral*) and Indiana (*The Conscious Lovers*) are admirable young girls endowed with decorum, dignity and domestic virtues. The authorial intent behind *The Conscious Lovers* is expressed by Steele in his letter to Danniel Finch, the Earl of Nottingham, dated January 16, 1722 where he says:

> I have written a comedy, not only consonant to the rules of Religion and virtue, in general, but also in (words deleted) analogy even to the Christian religion.[2]

Cibber and Steele showed through their plays their belief in the inherent good nature of human beings. They were never tired of emphasising the possibilities of moral reform in the persons who for one reason or the other were contaminated by some vice. Almost all such characters in their plays are eventually cured of their follies and vices. In one respect, however, Steele is different from Cibber. His fifth act reformations look somewhat contrived whereas Steele's characters have an inner awakening, a realisation of their error which is often brought about by the influence or conduct of some considerable person. The repentance scenes, which are marked by genuine remorse, at times, remind one of the morality plays which were written solely to demonstrate the triumph of virtue over vice.

Nevertheless, eighteenth century comedy writers advocated satiric denunciation of vice and maintained that it ought to be presented in its "native dress", that is, made to look despicable, not adorable, as in the Restoration comedies. Steele's diatribe in *The Spectator*, No. 65 on Dorimant's Character is directly related to his concept of moral satire. According to him if Dorimant was really meant to be a satiric character he should have been thoroughly exposed and punished and if he was to be taken as a hero he should not have been presented as a "direct knave" but as a man of sterling qualities.

These comedies show their preference for good-humoured ridicule in place of the malicious laughter of the Restoration comedy which they considered as "a distorted passion" born of "self-esteem" and "sudden scorn".[3] In its place they favoured the use of "polite mirth" tinged with pity, like the one they found in Terence's *Self-Tormentor*. Hence the characters designed for ridicule, such as Humphry Gubbin, the country booby and Mr. Tipkin, the money-minded merchant in *The Tender Husband* are all portrayed sympathetically unlike in the Restoration comedy where these two classes are almost always laughed at. Steele's somewhat original comic creation Biddy Tipkin, in the same play is also sympathetically treated. His humane approach towards these stock satiric characters is an ample evidence of his belief in Shaftesbury's philosophy that everyman is good by nature and that goodness and greatness of character are not confined to rank or vocation. Even Pounce with all his professional roguery is not entirely an abandoned character. Steele's merchants, country gentlemen, aristocrats and soldiers – all have some commendable human qualities in them.

Eighteenth century satire was directed not at the comic type but at contemporary social evils. The Comedy tried to instruct and reform the society by exposing and denouncing those vices that had some bearing on public welfare. Denunciation of gambling, duelling and profligacy get its special attention. Fashionable follies, such as, affectation, hypocrisy and aping foreign manners are also lashed at. Another evil that is decried in these plays, as also in essays, was that of mercenary marriages which they considered unwise and immoral as they led to conjugal disharmony and, often, to acts of infidelity. Mercenary considerations had reduced the sacred institution of marriage to the status of a mere mercantile deal neglecting the 'union of minds' which constitutes the real foundation of domestic happiness. Their incessant effort was to restore matrimony to its original dignified position. Steele was perhaps the first playwright after the Restoration who gave to women an equal status with men and presented them as their friends and companions. He believed in rational courtship governed more by reason and understanding than passion.[4] Thus, through examples and precepts the playwrights tried to reform the image of women, love and matrimony in order to glorify man-woman relationship and to stabilize the family life which had received much harm at the irreverent hands of the Restoration wits.[5]

Eighteenth Century playwrights' sole task was the improvement of morals and manners of the society. Their comedies can be taken as a symptom of a social awakening that was gathering force in the early eighteenth century. Their ideas on some socio-economic issues signal modernity in the same way. Their preference for the prudent merchant class and its bourgeois values, though partly founded on the whig philosophy, was basically a product of a forward looking mind. Likewise, they had something new to offer in respect of the education and upbringing of boys and girls. Unlike the Restoration notion of an educated gentleman, who was a widely travelled though not much enlightened, university product given to pursuits of pleasures and who scorned business, they recommended liberal upbringing under the strict but benign supervision of the well-meaning guardians. They were equally in favour of such a plan of education which would be conducive to both physical and mental development. In respect of intellectual pursuits and refinements too they made no distinction between men and women.

Their crusade against the immorality of the Restoration comedy with its promiscuous wit led them to use reformed dialogue in their plays. They advocated clean comedy and, therefore, scrupulously avoided smut and double entendre. They maintained that "nobody writ bawdy except for the dearth of wit"[6] but, probably as a sop to the audience with Restoration palates, they did occasionally make their low characters use a kind of language which is not quite decent. But, on the whole, their comedies inculcate morality through clean dialogue and direct moralising. It is this abundance of sententiae that led Hazlitt to call Steele's comedies "homilies in dialogue".[7]

Their concern for morality is so strong and unflinching that at times they do not hesitate in sacrificing their dramatic art to it. It would not be wrong to say that occasionally the preponderance of morality over art proved fatal aesthetically. Talking of *The Conscious Lovers*, Gemini Salgādo refers to this fact and says that it is Steele's "undeviating determination to be exemplary which is its undoing."[8] The lack of vivacity in the exemplary characters and partial improbability of the plots in *The Funeral* and *The Conscious Lovers* are chiefly due to Steele's determination to make them morally instructive.

Assessing the worth of Steele's comedies Dobrée says:

> But if Steele's play have only a minor value in themselves, they are significant as a symbol, and were important as an influence. They are a part of the movement which culminated in the Comedie Larmoyante.[9]

This is illustrated in the history of English drama. Lillo, Fielding, Sheridan, Goldsmith, Hugh Kelly and Cumberland are some of the playwrights who were, in one way or the other, influenced by Steele's comedies. Lillo's bourgeois comedy and tragedy, and Goldsmith's and Sheridan's good natured characters owe a great deal to Steele, as do the 'sentimental' contents of the plays of Kelly and Cumberland. But his success in deflecting the course of comedy is best discerned in his influence on the continent.[10]

To sum up, the early eighteenth century comedy was primarily committed solely to art for the sake of morality and the playwrights endeavoured to reform the society, including the stage. The abuses that had crept into comedy, *viz.*, immorality and profanity, had distressed them much. They crusaded against the immorality of characterisation, situations, dialogue and the scandalously disrespectful treatment of women, love, matrimony and such other sacred matters also. Their comedies and the contemporary periodicals and epistles, reveal them waging a war against the vices and follies that infected the stage and got disseminated into the society. They continued to present models of good conduct, propagated due regard for morals, humanity, decorum and sobriety of manners with great spirit and courage even at the cost of the genre itself. Their efforts in bringing about healthy changes in society and in the theatre have been appreciated by their audience, readers and the critics as well.

NOTES

1. See Dennis' *The Usefulness of the Stage* (1698) and *The Stage Defended* (1726) printed in Hooker, *op. cit*, Vol. I and II respectively.
2. A.H. Scouten ed., *Revels History*, Vol. V, p. 233.
3. Epilogue, *The Lying Lover*.
4. This is illustrated in Bevil Junior and Indiana relationship and also in *The Spectator*, No. 479.
5. Rae Blanchard makes the following observations on Steele's female characters:

   'whether Steele writes of the "fine lady", the coquettish women or the "witty female" his reforming intention is unmistakable.'

   (*Studies in Philology*-xxvi-1929)
6. *The Spectator*, No. 51.
7. Hazlitt, *op. cit.*, p. 132.
8. Salgādo, *op. cit.*, p. 165.
9. Dobrée, *English Literature in the Early Eighteenth Century* p. 236.
10. For Steele's influence on the Continent see *Dobrée Restoration Comedy*, p. 236 and Howarth, *Comic Drama: The European Heritage*.

APPENDICES

14

Life and Career of Richard Steele

Sir Richard Steele was born in Dublin on March 12, 1672. He was orphaned in his early childhood but was brought up by his uncle, Henry Gascoigne, Secretary to the Duke of Ormond. Young Steele had his education at Charter House where he found a sincere friend in Joseph Addison. He often spent his holidays in Addison's house and received boundless love and affection from his father, Lancelot Addison, which further cemented their friendship. Later he joined Christ Church College on December 21, 1690 and matriculated the next year. He could not get elected as a senior student of the college which he was very keen for certain reasons. Instead he entered Merton College as a postmaster.[1] He esteemed and honoured the college so much that later in 1712 he presented the college library with a copy of the *Tatler* and the college had reason to feel proud of its student. Steele left Merton on January 12, 1693 to join the army as a private soldier under the Duke of Ormond. He was commissioned in 1697 and was later promoted as Captain in 1699.

During this period he led a life much exposed to irregularities. He got addicted to drinking and this led him to some other vices. His sallies of youth, combined with drinking, resulted in the seduction of Elizabeth Tonson for which he repented from his heart. His conscience, even awake, made him to look after the daughter born of Elizabeth Tonson as tenderly as his other children. It was after this incident that he wrote *The Christian Hero* (1701), a moral treatise to admonish himself for deviating from the path of piety. This incident gnawed at his heart so much that he came to hold men's gallantries and pruriency as being solely responsible for the moral downfall of women. He, thereafter, became an advocate of one and the same code of conduct for men as well as women against the double standards of behaviour common with the contemporary society. His moral resurgence is reflected in his comedies which highlights the reformation of his errant characters.

Another episode that affected Steele's mind was his participation in an alchemical fiasco. Steele joined hands with half a dozen persons to produce the philosopher's stone. He staked all his ready money but got nothing in return except despair.

There was yet another incident that left an indelible mark on Steele's mind. This was his duel with Captain Kelly. In this episode Steele acted as his character Bevil Junior is shown to act in *The Conscious Lovers*. He used reason and all the means of persuasion to convince Kelly about his innocence and, more than that, of the inhumanity of the custom based on false sense of honour. Captain Kelly, who is supposed to have been killed, survived the duel but the incident made a lasting impression on Steele.

He wrote three comedies in quick succession; *The Funeral* in 1701, *The Lying Lover* in 1703 and *The Tender Husband* in 1705. However, Steele's unprecedented interest in the stage was curbed in 1705 when he was appointed Gazetteer and also Gentleman waiter to Queen Anne's husband, Prince George of Denmark.

Steele resigned from the army in the first half of 1705, when his Whig Commander, Lord Robert Lucas, left his regiment. He liked both the government posts for they gave him preferment he had always aspired for and money that he was always in need of. The same year he married a rich widow, Margaret Stretch who died the next year leaving him all her property. Soon after he married Mary Scurlock, a friend of his first wife. It was a love match between two people who understood each other, the sort of match he has extolled in his comedy. He had a happy family life and had one son and three daughters from his second wife besides his illegitimate daughter Elizabeth Ousley. Mary Scurlock proved a kind and loving mother even to Elizabeth Ousley. Likewise, Steele proved a faithful and devoted husband, the evidence of which is found in letters that he wrote to her. Domestic happiness was of paramount importance to him and he got it in abundance from his second wife.

As a Gazetteer Steele found the going quite tough under the dominance of the Tory ministers. Nevertheless, he tried his best to pull on in the most trying circumstances. His hopes rose high and he felt almost sure of getting a more lucrative post when Addison was promoted as Chief Secretary to the Earl of Wharton and later as the Keeper of Records in Ireland. However, his expectations came to nothing and he even lost his position as Gentleman Waiter when Prince George died in 1708.

At this stage Steele needed some job that may solve his financial problems as well as provide him with opportunities of securing recognition. Accordingly, he started *The Tatler*, in 1709, under the name of Issac Bickerstaff. Besides writing on different subjects Steele expressed his views on politics and attacked prominent politicians including the Tory Minister, Robert Harley, the first Earl of Oxford. Addison who had returned to London in 1710 also joined Steele. The publication of the journal had to be discontinued probably because of its political slant after about twenty months. As a consequence of his political antagonism to Harley, Steele lost in 1710, his Gazetteership. This turned out to be a blessing in disguise. A few months after his removal from the office he along with Addison brought out *The Spectator*.

The year 1713 lured Steele back to political life. It was his genuine patriotism that led him to take more active interest in the political happenings of his time. Like Addison, he was a whig by conviction and, therefore, exerted himself, as he had done during *The Tatler* days, in supporting its policies and programmes through his writings as well as through active participation. He was elected to the Parliament on August 25, 1713 and soon became one of the chief spokesmen of the party in the House. But before seeking election on the Whig ticket he, a principled man as he was, resigned the post of the Commissioner of Stamps and also gave up the pension that he was still getting as an ex-Gentleman Waiter. Independent of political constraints, he unceasingly opposed Tories in the Commons as well as in his political pamphlets. *The Guardian* (March 12 – October 1, 1713), *The English Man* (Oct. 6, 1713 – Feb. 11, 1714) and *The Town Talk* (1715-1716), *The Plebeian* (1719) and *The Crisis* (1720) are some of his pamphlets in which he dauntlessly expressed his political views. Soon he was expelled from the Parliament in 1714 for 'libel' and 'sedition'.[2] He published his political writings in 1715 and dedicated them to his patron, The Duke of Newcastle. Steele was appointed the Governor of Drury Lane soon after the accession of George I vide the patent granted on January 19, 1715 which empowered him and other managers (Barton, Booth, Robert Wills, Thomas Dogget and Colley Cibber) to perform plays as they would deem proper and share the profits thereof. The patent entitled Steele to have his share of profits for his life time and three years after his death. With Newcastle's support Steele got himself re-elected to the Parliament in 1715 and also received a knighthood. Steele continued to enjoy both the honours, the membership of the Parliament and the Governorship of Drury Lane till his death, except for a short period in 1720 when he was suspended as the Governor of Drury Lane, probably because of opposing the Whig sponsored Peerage Bill. It was only after Walpole came into power that Steele got restored to the Governorship of Drury Lane (May 2, 1721).

Steele was at logger heads with the government for quite some time. His wife's death in 1718 had been a terrible blow to him.[3] Failures and personal disputes further soured his temper. Nevertheless, he offered to the Drury Lane his 'final blaze', *The Conscious Lovers* (1722) which he had been preparing since almost 1717. He started writing two more comedies, *The School of Action* and *The Gentleman* but both of them remained incomplete. Towards the close of his life he retired to his late wife's estate in Wales in 1724 where he suffered a paralytic stroke in 1726 and passed away on September 1, 1729.

Fortune had seldom smiled on Steele. Since his childhood he had to depend on others, such as Duke of Ormond, for financial support. He was never free from want of money and he had to borrow it frequently from wherever he could. Thus his debts involved him in law-suits with several creditors including Christopher Rich. He lost the suits every time but never learnt a lesson from them. Throughout his life he was harried by the baillifs, creditors and money-lenders and sometimes faced arrests also. So much so, that even after he had retired to Wales he still had to settle scores of issues of this nature.

However, he left his imprints on the history of the Parliament, political pamphleteering, periodical essays and of Drury Lane. Politicians, especially the Whigs, had a propagandist in Steele who through his political pamphlets fought the battle for them. His famous political pamphlets include *The Importance of Dunkirk Considered* (1713) in which he opposed the Tory viewpoint in respect of the war of Spanish Succession and *The Crisis* (1714) on Hanoverian succession, *The Plebeian* (1714) opposing the King's prerogative to create new peers and *The Crisis of Property* (1714) and its sequel *A Nation Family* on the South Sea Bubble (1720). All his political pamphlets are marked by his integrity, his belief in democracy and pure Whig convictions undiluted by unethical considerations.

Steele, because of these characteristics, had antagonised many people. Jonathan Swift was foremost among them. Steele and Swift belonged to two different parties. Swift was a Whig by birth and was loyal to the Established Church of England. Like Steele, Swift was a gifted writer and keen on preferment. Harley, a keen observer and a clever politician, had succeeded in winning Swift over to Tory party in 1713 with a promise of Queen Anne's bounty. Soon after Swift took over the Tory journal, *The Examiner*, and got engaged in a paper war with Steele. Swift was fully conversant with Steele's vulnerable points, his personal weaknesses – and often alluded to them. Steele launched *The Guardian* to counter Swift's attacks and arguments. They resorted to general accusations, which gradually became more specific and personal, finally ending in open attack on each other. Swift even stooped to writing lampoons on Steele who in turn mocked him in *The Guardian*. Their differences culminated in complete breach which formed the theme of an anonymous mock-heroic prose satire, *The Battle of Authors lately Fought in Covent Garden* (1720).

Almost at the same time Steele had a dispute with another great friend of his. Addison, as the Chief Secretary to the Earl of Sunderland, had to please his boss when he introduced the Peerage Bill. Steele, following personal convictions, opposed the bill in *The Plebeian* every time it was introduced in the House of Commons (1719). Defending the bill, Addison expressed in the two numbers of *The Old Whig* his annoyance with Steele. References to personal life and arguments led to a deep fissure between the two friends which, due to Addison's death in June 1719, could never be removed.

The third dispute, the most damaging to Steele's career at Drury Lane, was one with his former patron, the Duke of Newcastle, who became Lord Chamberlain in April 1717. The vigorous Lord wanted to exercise his power and, therefore, asked the actor-managers to resign their patent and accept a new licence. For some time Steele and the other managers did not pay any heed to Newcastle's orders. Initially the differences between Newcastle and Steele were related to the question of the patent only, but after 1719 politics widened the breach between the two. Steele had opposed the Peerage Bill while Newcastle had favoured it. The political disputes brought the stage dispute to such a crisis that the theatrical battle started at Drury Lane was fought politically in the House of Commons, ending in Steele's suspension from the governorship. After 1720 the actor-managers refused to pay Steele any share of the profit as Steele had virtually ceased taking active interest in Drury Lane affairs. But Steele fought for his right persistently and in 1725 had the satisfaction of getting it restored.

In 1719 Steele antagonised John Dennis, the well-known critic-writer and purist of his time. This time the battle was of a literary nature. Dennis attacked Steele in three pamphlets *The Character and Conduct of Sir John Edgar* (1720), *A Defence of Sir Fopling Flutter* (1722) and *Remarks on a Play, Call'd The Conscious Lovers, a Comedy* (1723). Nevertheless, all these controversies, instead of doing any harm to Steele's fame made him still more popular and brought throngs of people to the Drury Land theatre to applaud his masterpiece, *The Conscious Lovers.*

If Steele's life was a tale of strife and struggle, it was marked by great achievements as well. His essays in *The Tatler, The Spectator, The Guardian* and *The Theatre* bear enough testimony to it. He wrote about the people; denounced the fashionable London with its follies and foibles, introduced new ideas but always upheld the tenets of Christianity.[4] These periodicals are of great significance to the students of early eighteenth century literary history.

Another great achievement of Steele was the establishment of an academy under the name, The Censorium, which was based on the pattern of the Continental academies. Housed in York Building, it was planned during *The Spectator* days when Steele had got acquainted with Thomas Clayton, a great musician of his time. In *The Town Talk*, No. 4 Steele defined the purpose of the Censorium as to improve public taste through music, eloquence, poetry, lectures, etc. Music concerts were held from time to time but during his governorship of Drury Lane he tried to give it the shape of a little theatre complementing Drury Lane. On May 28, 1715 *The Censorium* celebrated the King's birthday with the recital of poems, prologues and epilogue, sung with musical background. In spite of his persistent efforts Steele did not succeed in his great expectations because of lack of finances, Government support and desertion of great artists like Clayton.

Besides his essays Steele has several verses to his credit. As early as 1694 he wrote a valentine poem, entitled "upon having Mrs. Selwyn, by Lot, my Valentine." Inspired by his love and regard for the recently departed Queen Mary, Steele wrote his famous elegy *The Procession* (1695), on the occasion of her funeral. The poem is marked by an undercurrent of pathos which later became a prominent feature of his comedies. His verses written to a nameless wood-nymph during 1698 have echoes of the gaiety and ardour of the songs found in his own plays. The "Prue" of his love poems is no one else but Mary Scurlock whom he married in 1695. *An Imitation of the Sixth Ode of Horace* shows his esteem for the great classicist. Besides these verses he wrote several prologues. The prologue to *The Way of the World*, to Vanbrugh's *The Mistake* (1705), to *The University of Oxford* (1706) and to Ambrose Phillip's *The Distressed Mother* (1712) are well known. These prologues embody his well-known views on the stage abuses and the one on Oxford shows his regard for the famous house of learning.

Steele's first[5] comedy *The Funeral* exhibits the same reforming spirit that dominates *The Christian Hero*. Steele had promised a comedy to Christopher Rich, but could not keep his word.[6] Instead, he offered him *The Lying Lover* and then *The Tender Husband*. His busy political life and his periodicals occupied his time until 1722 when he presented his last complete play *The Conscious Lovers*. This does not mean that he had lost interest in writing plays. Since 1705 he had been looking for a play best suited to his theory and convictions. He started writing *The Conscious Lovers* somewhere in 1713 and by 1717 he had written part of it under the title, *Sir Edgar*, later changed to *The Fine Gentleman*. Steele borrowed the plots and characters of his plays from Molière,

Corneille and others yet his approach to the source material is typical of his own moral fibre. An urge for reform of morals and manners of the people is the common thread that binds all his comedies and also gives them a distinct mark of originality.

NOTES

1. Students with intellectual promise were often given this honour at Merton.
2. Steele has refuted the 'charges' in *The Apology for himself and his Writings* occasioned by his expulsion from the Parliament.
3. Steele's wife died of child-birth.
4. These points are elaborated in the previous chapters.
5. Steele had written a comedy during his college days but destroyed it as it was found unsatisfactory (Aitken, I, p. 37).
6. Steele had decided to write a comedy *The Election of Gothem*, but due to some unknown reasons dropped the idea.

15

Steele's Contribution to Drama

When Collier tried to reform the stage from a religious platform he earned resentment and indignation from various quarters but when Steele tried to moralise comedy and reform the stage he won a general applause. The secret of his success was that he spoke from the stage itself, gauged his audience and drew upon the dramatic traditions of the previous era which his comedy was a strong reaction to. He is decidedly one of the most important dramatists of the early eighteenth century judged on the basis of the quality of his play and by the extent of impact on the contemporary and succeeding dramatists.

The most striking thing in Steele's career as a dramatist is that he devoted himself to the task of reforming the stage right from the days of *The Christian Hero* and stuck to it till his very end. His dramatic essays are but an enunciation of the theory that he had followed as a playwright. All the plays of Steele from *The Funeral* to his masterpiece, *The Conscious Lovers* and even the unfinished one, *The School of Action* reveal him as a dramatist well versed in the techniques and functions of drama. His output as a dramatist was decidedly meagre but, still, it earned him an enduring fame. Likewise, his influence was felt both by his contemporaries and the later writers. The edifice of his fame rests on his contribution to the reformation of the stage and, through it, of the society. This he did chiefly through his comedies which provide models of human virtues and conduct.

Steele sincerely believed that the stage could be an effective agent of moral reform since the theatre-goers, chiefly of younger age group, love to imitate what is presented on the stage. Referring to the character of Bevil Junior in *The Theatre* No. 19, he said:

> This example would have been of great service; for since we see young men are hardly able to forbear imitation of fopperies on the stage, from a desire of praise, how warmly would they pursue true gallantries

> when accompanied with the beauties with which a poet represents them, when he has a mind to make them amiable ![1]

He, therefore, advocated presentation of moral comedy as it provides exemplary characters imbued with Christian virtues. In the preface to *The Conscious Lovers* he expressed his view that by exciting the "Readers to go (to) see it; and when he does so, it is then a play has the Effect of Example and Precept".[2] This does not mean that he totally ruled out the cautionary theory of the Restoration comedy. He praised Fletcher's *The Scornful Lady*[3] in *The Spectator*, No. 270 for satirising the heroine's vanity and Wycherley's *The Country Wife* in *The Tatler*, No. 3 for punishing vice as it ought to be. He stressed that virtue should always be rewarded and vice invariably exposed and punished. Commenting on this recurring feature of Steele's comedies, Krutch says:

> The extension of poetic justice was one of the cardinal doctrines of his creed which in fact is a distinguishing characteristic of sentimental comedy.[4]

Another point that gives Steele a unique position in the history of English comic drama is his belief in an attempt to introduce the milder forms of comic expressions, *e.g.*, sympathetic kind laughter and innocent mirth. As Steele was strongly influenced by Shaftesbury's philosophy of good nature and good humour he tried to infuse his comedy with the spirit of subdued kindly laughter befitting a benevolent good humoured gentleman. There is no scope for the malacious laughter and raillery of the Restoration sort which was hitherto considered essential for ridiculing vice. Explaining the rationale of comedy free from this cheap kind of laughter, in the epilogue to *The Lying Lover*, he says:

> For laughter's a distorted passion, born
> Of sudden self Esteem, and sudden Scorn;
> Which when 'tis o'er, the Men in Pleasure wise,
> Both him that mov'd it, and themselves despise.

In plays as well as in his essays, Steele shows that it was not his intention to attack the conventional comic methods, *i.e.*, malicious wit and satire, but only their abuse. He himself tried to temper wit with good nature. He held that "to rally well, it is absolutely necessary that kindness must run through all you say."[5] He was also of the view that the representations of a good natured satirist "bear a pleasantry in them, which shows there is no malignity at heart and by consequence are attended by his readers because they are unprejudiced."[6] According to him wit should be allied with good humour and laughter with pity. To laugh at unavoidable defects is an abuse of wit and comedy both. Further, it is not proper for the stage to laugh at a natural folly. The stammering of the lawyer in *The Conscious Lovers* is explained by Bevil Junior (II, i) as originating from his impertinence and, therefore, it was made to occasion laughter. In Keeping with his views Steele's satire, in general, is mild, good humoured, good natured, compassionate and purposive.

In place of malicious laughter Steele favoured use of "Pity to Chastise Delight", a painted "woe", tender scenes of forgiveness and reconciliation. He introduced pathetic situations in his plays to highlight Christian virtues in his good natured characters. These situations are too deep and poignant for laughter, yet, they are redolent with joy born of pity and benevolence. While applauding Terence's *Self-tormentor*, in *The Spectator*, No. 502, he says that in this play there are "several incidents which would draw tears from any man of sense and not one which would move his laughter". In another issue, talking of the readers' response to the pathetic elements in Ambrose Phillips' *The Distressed Mother* he says:

> It was a most exquisite pleasure to me to observe real Tears drop from the Eyes of those who had long made it their Profession to dissemble Affliction; and the Player who read, frequently threw down the Book, till he had given vent to the Humanity which rose in him at some irresistible Touches of imagined sorrow.[7]

Steele defends his comedies which contain pathetic situations in the preface to *The Conscious Lovers*, saying that :

> ... anything that has its Foundation in Happiness and Success, must be allow'd to be the Object of Comedy, and sure it must be an Improvement of it, to introduce a joy too exquisite for Laughter, that can have no Spring but in Delight.

Steele introduced pathos (woe) in his comedies as it provided him with opportunities to demonstrate bevevolence, pity and other "reverened offices" of life through his characters' exemplary conduct. Bevil Junior's conduct in *The Conscious Lovers* is to be seen only in this light. His benevolent attitude towards Indiana and his sympathetic understanding of Myrtle's jealousy show his humane nature and add lustre to his character. Similarly Indiana's efforts to maintain her "conscious innocence" in spite of her distress raise her in the eyes of the audience. The distress of the virtuous characters allows no scope to ridicule and laughter as it can only evoke pity for them. Nevertheless, the moral courage of the exemplary characters revealed in the pathetic situations does become a source of sublime kind of delight for the audience.

Steele's greatest contribution to the early eighteenth century drama is to be found in his delineation of examplary characters. He criticised the Restoration playwrights for making libertines their heroes and for rewarding them with wealth and beautiful women. He denounced Dorimant as "a direct knave" in his designs and a "clown in his language" *(The Sepectator,* No. 65). Early eighteenth century comic conventions had changed with the growing dominance of the middle class and so had the concept of a comic hero, who now had to be a good natured gentleman not an immoral fop. Lord Hardy and Bevil Junior are two such fine gentlemanly heroes sketched both for admiration and emulation. Lord Hardy embodies good nature which reaches its highest point in Bevil Junior. These two characters do not appear as dynamic and flamboyant as Dorimant and Mirabel simply because they are men of principle and conscience.

Like Collier, Steele admired modesty and virtue in women. In his plays the witty gay heroines of the Restoration comedy indulging in flirtation and amorous intrigues are replaced by innocent modest women like Lady Sharlot and Indiana who are created more to be acted upon than to act. Lady Sharlot and Indiana may appear dramatically dull and listless (as they do to Hazlitt)[8] but are animated and strong within their sentimental fold and have proved didactically effective.

Steele was a playwright who wrote good humoured comedy. He was adept in transforming a serious and grave theme into comic. This is shown by his handling of such a grave topic as that of a funeral. Save the inherently serious title, it is not a real funeral and the comic effect is produced by taking the audience into the secret. A study of his early comedies reveals that he was at his best when writing comic plots, but the moralist in him was always asserting himself. This blending of the serious and the comic is expertly done in all the plays but more particularly in *The Funeral* where the melodramatic main plot and the comic love plot are perfectly integrated. Similarly, plots concerning Myrtle and Lucinda, Tom and Phillis, Latine and Lettice, Captain Clerimont and Biddy are lighter in tone and texture and are designed to modify the pathos of the more serious thread of the respective stories. The characters in the comic plots, from didactic point of view, belong to a lower plane but dramatically they are quite lively and vigorous. Like the conventional comic characters they have some weakness or folly which they are cured of. Campley, Harriot, Bookwit, Penelope, Myrtle, Mrs. Clerimont, etc. belong to this class of characters. They are more human and more given to mirth than the exemplary characters. Their light-hearted humour at time appears to acquire Restoration traits but it never degenerates into malicious laughter. These characters make use of disguise, indulge in horse play and thus provide the basic stuff of comedy.

Besides this blending of the comic and the pathetic, Steele distinguished himself from the earlier dramatists through his treatment of certain character types which were presented as contemptible and ridiculous by the Restoration dramatists. The country squires, the enterprising merchants and the rough hewn country boobies receive a sympathetic treatment at his hands. Dull, insipid cantankerous fathers (and guardians) of the previous comedy are now infused with humane qualities and given an understanding and accommodating nature. Similarly, the country squires are no more entirely governed by impulses, nor are the merchants the embodiment of greed and the boobies of ignorance and stupidity. Old Bookwit and Sir John Bevil are kind, considerate, and far less assertive than their forbears. Sealand is a respectable merchant who is neither ridiculed nor caricatured as a 'cit'.[9] Respect for the country gentry that is shown by Steele is symptomatic of the change in the society. His country booby, Humphry Gubbin, is not a foolish dolt bereft of wit and intelligence but a man with certain qualities which are likely to develop further.[10] He is definitely more well-mannered than Sir Wilful Witwoud *(The Way of the World)*. That his dullheadedness is not ingrained becomes apparent when he gets a chance to speak and act as an independent being responsible only to himself. Not only this, he shows himself as a clever person when he starts manipulating the affairs of others. At the same time he continues to please us by his plain dealing and simple country manners. The earlier bumpkins like Shadwell's Young Heartford *(Lanchashire Witches 1681)* could have hardly equalled his ingenious mischievousness. It would not be wrong to say that he has the qualities that earn him the goodwill of the audience instead of their ridicule. Biddy Tipkin is another character sketched by Steele that can be considered as original. She has been drawn as a rare specimen. Her humour to transfer romance into life and her soul of a *preciéuse* are presented with ample dramatic exaggeration in order to serve Steele's satirical purpose.[11] English comedy is indeed indebted to Steele for such creations.

Steele was not an original dramatist so far as themes and dramatic conventions are concerned. There is no doubt that he drew upon the heroic drama for the function of comedy as well as for creating exemplary characters. Similarly, he took sentimental elements from the tragedy.[12] He owed much to the great masters of the past in respect of the technique of plot construction. But the device of making the main plots uniformly serious in tone is Steele's own. So is his habit of subordinating the comic spirit to the moral bent of the plays, which is done by restricting the former to the sub-plots only.

So far as the plot construction is concerned, Steele proved no great craftsman. *The Funeral,* a comedy with sentimental elements and ideal characters, is a loosely woven fabric. Some of the characters introduced as objects of ridicule[13] are not fully integrated to the plot and, therefore, do not materially contribute to its development. Nevertheless, they do prove useful as through them Steele manages to voice his views on social and moral issues. The undertaker's staff is hardly essential to the plot, but besides creating mirth, it does help Steele to expose a particular kind of social convention. Steele contrived to link it to the title of the play and thus forcibly connected it to the main plot. Similarly, the recruits' scene and the one showing the widows visiting and condoling Lady Brumpton are also not quite necessary for the plot as they do not affect the action. Such scenes owe their existence to Steele, the moral and social satirist and not to Steele the dramatist. The recruits' scene, presenting a satirical commentary on the contemporary state of the army, does not blend well with Lord Hardy's patriotism and determined stand to fight against the enemies of his country. The burlesque nature of the scene does not harmonize with the sobriety of the hero's sentimental militancy.[14] *The Lying Lover*, written somewhat on the Restoration pattern is also full of dramatic inconsistencies. The characters though well drawn are not quite plausible. Young Bookwit, dramatically more dynamic than Lord Hardy and less sober than Campley, is inconsistency itself. The dramatist's theory of repentance and reformation is sound enough morally but it does not leave Bookwit exactly the same as what he is in the beginning of the play. This potentially comic character by Steele's contrivance and moral concern, becomes almost totally sentimental. Young Bookwit's transformation from an unthinking adventurer to a sober gentleman and his docile acceptance of Victoria do not seem plausible in the context of his earlier behaviour. Similarly, Latine's transformation from a comic side kick to a heroic friend of a higher plane, Lovemore's from a foolishly jealous lover to a man of noble stature, Penelope's giving up of her coquettishness all so suddenly and becoming a 'genteel' heroine, also have not been very convincingly managed. It seems obvious that Steele was not so much interested in maintaining the integrity of their character as to make them answer the demands of his didactic muse.

Steele's dramatic art at times suffers at the hands of Steele, the moralist. The denouement of the plays are all conditioned by his moral bias. Steele's strong belief in the triumph of virtue over vice leads him to conclude his plays in a way which does not always appear very natural or logical. This tendency is best illustrated in *The Conscious Lovers*. The denouement of the play has to present a happy ending in which the hero is to be duly rewarded. In the plot itself there is no signal for manipulation in this direction. Steele introduced a totally external element to solve the dramatic and moral problem posed in the play and bring into a happy close. This is done through Indiana's bracelet which is dropped purposely so that Sealand may notice it. The incident brings Indiana's trials to an end as the recognition of the bracelet leads to her union with her rich father. This type of crude manipulations inherent in comedies of this type has been duly noticed by Joseph Wood Krutch who says:

> Sentimental comedy failed because of an error in its method, *i.e.*, virtue be given material success and the honourable young man should infallibly marry an heiress.[15]

Krutch attributes the death of comedy to the "self-conscious moral involvement and the simultaneous development of sentimentalism"[16] in the first half of eighteenth century. This sounds as too severe an indictment of Steele's moral comedy but the fact is unquestionable. Steele's unsuccessful attempts to harmonise moral idealism with realism proved fatal to his comic muse as well as to the genre.

Steele's best comedy from the point of view of dramatic technique is *The Tender Husband*. The blank verse denouement of *The Funeral* and *The Lying Lover* are all contrived morally with musical entertainment and a maxim as a parting gift. The moralist dominates the comic muse in all the comedies except *The Tender Husband.* The characters in the play are well integrated to its two closely related plots. This technical feature is based on the pattern of the Restoration comedy and the treatment is also comic as well as satiric.

It is chiefly as a censor of the morals and manners of the time that Steele the dramatist is to be remembered and appreciated. He attempted to cleanse comedy of all its smut and bawdy. His disapproval of theatrical immorality and profanity of language is illustrated in his well-known denunciation of characters like Dorimant.[17] True to his didactic bent Steele emphasises the need of refined language and avoidance not only of bawdry but even of frankness. He was of the view that "no one ever writ Bawdry for any other reason but for Dearth of Invention" which, he felt, is an "Expedient, to supply the Deficiencies of Wit" *(The Spectator*, No. 51). He believed that only the writers of least learning and skill make use of salacious language. His dislike for smutty dialogue and luscious expressions would make him revise his own play to remove suspicious expressions.[18]

Besides, the style of his dialogue varies within a play; that of the serious scenes being distinct from that of the lighter ones. It is always in perfect harmony with the respective characters and situations. The serious parts of the play have, as they should, graver tone of dialogue than the comic ones. The former lack the comic gaiety which marks the latter. Instead, they are replete with sententiousness, aphorisms and maxims while the latter contain genial humour, quips, satirical strokes and verbal horse-play. The good-natured "model" characters of the serious scenes hardly ever utter the brilliant witty dialogue of the Restoration comedy. The sheen of the similitude and *double entendre* is not to be found there. Instead, a graceful humour pervades the dialogue and the moral tenor is reinforced by the concluding couplet tags. With morality always controlling their wit, the exemplary characters talk without subtle verbal refinements. The speeches of Lord Hardy, Bevil Junior and Indiana provide some such examples. On the other hand, witty and humorous dialogue pervades the comic sections of the plays. The lively lovers, the witty servants and the ridiculous characters speak humorously producing ripples of genial laughter. But here too, there is no malice or obscenity in their witticisms.

Steele's deftness in dialogue writing is further revealed by his ability to discriminate one character from the other through it.[19] This is amply illustrated in the interesting verbal exchanges between Sir Harry Gubbin and Mr. Tipkin. Their contrary humours and considerations are expertly conveyed through their dialogue.[2] The dialogue between the sparkish characters are equally but not similarly witty. The same is true about the sober sets of characters. Campley, Lady Harriot, Young Bookwit, Victoria and Penelope speak refined language in their own individual style. The dialogue of the servant class has moved away from the smutty dialogue of their counterparts in the Restoration comedy. The fresh breeze of the country can be felt in the plain talk of Daniel, Indiana's servant and in that of Humphry Gubbin. Biddy Tipkin's speeches are very amusing for the quality of their wit which reveals the peculiar aspect of her humorous character. Sometimes Steele makes the dialogue pleasurable by stressing its incongruity with the situation or event. For example, Lord Hardy's calling the roll of his ragged recruits produces laughter in *The Funeral* as do Lettice's simultaneous weeping and expression of eagerness to be wooed.

Besides sententious pronouncements and light-hearted humour, the plays are replete with emotional outbursts which sometimes impede the action. Trusty's emotional speeches before his young master and Indiana's narration of her tale of distress were meant to move the audience with pity and commisseration. On the whole, Steele's dialogue and speeches are apt, natural and reveal personality and character of the speakers and are cleansed of all the immorality found in the dialogue of the Restoration comedy. But writing inoffensive speeches was not the only or the main objective of Steele.

This is what Kenny meant when he said, "several playwrights consciously cleaned up their bawdry, but only Steele actively campaigned for a new kind of drama."[21]

Steele was not averse to the use of the traditional devices. In fact he was conscious of their popularity, usefulness and need, and, therefore, employed them to develop the plot and delineate the characters. The stock comic devices of disguise and mistaken identity are often used to create complications and interesting situations. Campley disguises as a woman, Myrtle as a solicitor and then as Cimberton's uncle, Latine as a servant, Captain Clerimont as a painter and Lucy Fainlove as a spark. The closet scene in *The Tender Husband* is infused with the Restoration comic spirit.

Steele made ample use of songs and dances in his plays. This he did probably to take full advantage of the musical talents of Purcell and other singers associated with the Drury Lane Theatre. In the early eighteenth century Italian Operas and pantomimes were growing popular, thus giving a blow to the native talents. Steele, along with the other writers of the time satirised this invasion of the foreign music and tried to encourage and popularize the English artists.[22] His ridicule of the foreign singers (as in *The Funeral*) was a patriotic move to pave the way for the acceptance of indigenous entertainments. But with the exception of Young Bookwit's remorseful song in *The Lying Lover*[23] and the one sung before Penelope in the same play,[24] the other songs do not perfectly fit into the framework of his plots. The Introduction of these songs into the body of the plays shows Steele's tendency to be carried away by extra artistic considerations.

Steele appeared on the horizon at English drama at the right moment. The Restoration comedy was on its way out and the stage was threatened with the loss of its popularity on account of the attacks of the purists and invasion of the foreign entertainments. It was Steele who along with Cibber tried to save the English comedy, vindicated its stand and entrenched it once again (though only temporarily) in the native soil. He had set out to demonstrate that the stage could provide pleasure without resorting to vulgarity and obscenity. More than that, he exhibited almost a missionary zeal in transforming the stage into a platform for preaching and effecting social and moral reforms as well as a healthy change in the tastes and interests of the theatre-going people. The success of his plays, which with the solitary exception of *The Lying Lover*, had more than the normal run and were often revived, shows that his efforts in the said directions were not in vain. His position and reputation as an outstanding comic dramatist with a laudable purpose and artistic vision are secure for all time.

NOTES

1. Loftis, *Steele at Drury Lane*, pp. 202-3.
2. *Plays*, p. 299.
3. Steele was referring to its recent performance, on Dec. 10, 1702.
4. Krutch, *op. cit.*, p. 78.
5. *The Spectator*, No. 422.
6. *The Tatler*, No. 242.
7. *The Spectator*, No. 290.
8. Hazlitt, *English Comic Writers*, p. 132.
9. Referring to the absence of contempt in the presentation of the merchants Loftis says:

   > That he did so is attributable as much to his sympathy for the dramatic reform movement as to his convictions about social relationship (*Comedy and Conscience*, p. 63).

   Loftis has overlooked the reflection of Steele's whiggism in his attitude towards this class.
10. Goldsmith's Tony Lumpkin *(She Stoops to Conquer)* owes a lot to Humphry Gubbin.
11. Sheridan's Lydia Languish *(The Rivals)*; Mrs. C. Lennox's Arabella (*The Female Quixote*) and George Coleman's Polly *(Polly Honeycombe)* are some characters that were probably drawn after Biddy.
12. Cibber had already tried sentimental heroines and pathetic situations in his comedies.
13. Even here the moral concern is visible. Only a few comical characters of the sub-plots have been sketched solely for exciting laughter. Most of them are to be cured of their folly.
14. This scene would go well with Plume's military manoeuvres in Farquhar's *The Recruiting Officer*.
15. J.W. Krutch, *op. cit.*, p. 239.
16. *Ibid.*, p. 256.
17. Quoted on p. 222.
18. He did this with *The Funeral*.
19. This quality is rarely found in the Restoration dramatists. Their love for verbal fire-works often made them overlook this aspect. Hence Pope had to pose the question: "Tell me if Congreve's fools be fools indeed?"

20. See, for example, their encounters in Act I, Scene ii and in Act V, Scene ii.
21. S. Kenny, "Steele and the Pattern of Genteel Comedy", *Modern Philology*, Vol. 70, (1972), pp. 22-37.
22. Evidence of Steele's zealous concern for safeguarding and promoting indigenous music is present in his founding of *The Censorium*.
23. Act IV, Scene 2 and Act V, Scene 4.
24. Act II, Scene 1.

SELECT BIBLIOGRAPHY

Primary Sources

Texts, Periodical Essays and Letters

Addison, Joseph. *The Works of Right Honourable Joseph Addison*. 6 Vols. ed. Richard Hurd. London: George Bell & Sons, 1891.

Scouten, A.H. *The London Stage, 1660-1800*. 6 Vols. Illinois: Illinois, Univ. Press, 1965.

Bracher, Frederick (ed.). *Letters of Sir George Etherege*, Berkeley: Univ. of California Press, 1974.

Cibber, Colley. *The Dramatic Works of Colley Cibber*, 5 Vols. New York: A.M.S. Press, 1966.

——. *An Apology for the Life of Mr. Colley Cibber*. ed. Robert W. Lowe, London: Dent, 1898.

——. *The Careless Husband* (Regent Restoration Drama Series), ed. William W. Appleton, London: Edward Arnold, 1967.

Collier, Jermey. *A Short View of the Immorality and Profaneness of the English Stage*, New York: A.M.S. Press, 1974.

Congreve, William. *The Complete Plays of William Congreve*. ed. Herbert Davies. Chicago: Univ. of Chicago, 1969.

Dryden, John. *The Dramatic Works of John Dryden*. 6 Vols. ed. Montague Summers, London: The Nonesuch Press, 1931.

Etherege, Sir George. *The Plays*. ed. Cordner Michael. Cambridge: Cambridge Univ. Press, 1982.

Farquhar, George. *The Works of George Farquhar*. ed. Charles Stonehill. 2 Vols. London: The Nonesuch Press, 1930.

Goldsmith, Oliver. *Collected Works of Oliver Goldsmith*. ed. Arthur Friedman. 5 Vols. Oxford: The Clarendon Press. 1966.

Hodges, John (ed.). *Congreve; Letters and documents*. London: Macmillan, 1964.

Lilo, George. *The London Merchant* (Regent Restoration Drama Series), William H.Mc. Burney. London: Edward Arnold Press, 1965.

Molière, J.P.P. *The Plays of Molière*. In French with English Translation) by A.R. Waller), 8 Vols. Edinburgh: John Grant, 1926.

Shadwell, Thomas. *The Complete Works*. 5 Vols. ed. Montague Summers. London: The Fortune Press, 1927.

Steele, Sir Richard. *The Plays of Sir Richard Steele*. ed. Shirley Strum Kenny. Oxford: The Clarendon Press, 1971.

———. *The Complete Plays of Richard Steele*. ed. G.A. Aitken. The Mermaid Series. London: T. Fisher Unwin, 1903.

———. *The Pelican Book of English Prose*. Vol. III, Eighteenth Century Prose (1700-1780) ed. D.W. Jefferson. London: Penguin8 Books, 1956.

———. *A Collection of English Prose (1660-1800)*. ed. Henry Petit. New York: Harper & Co. (1962).

———. *The Tatler, Guardian and Freeholder*. With an introduction by John Habberton. New York: Penguin Books, 1889.

———. *The Occasional Verse of Richard Steele*. ed. Rae Blanchard. Oxford: The Clarendon Press, 1952.

———. *The Spectator* (Everman's Series). ed. Donald, F. Bond. 5 Vols. London: Dent, 1979.

———. *The Tatler* (The British Essayists). ed. A. Chalmers. Vol. I to IV. London: Little Brown & Co., 1856.

———. *The Tracts and Pamphlets*. ed. Rae Blanchard. New York: Octagen Books. Inc., 1967.

Vanbrugh, John. *The Works of Sir John Vanbrugh*. ed. W.C. Ward. London: Lawrence & Bullen, 1893.

Wycherley, William. *The Plays of William Wycherley*. ed. Arthur Friedman. Oxford: The Clarendon Press, 1979.

Secondary Sources

I. *General*

Ashley, Maurice. *Charles II. The Man and the Statesman*. London: Weindenfeld & Nicholson, 1971.

———. *England in the Seventeenth Century* (The Pelican History of England). England: Cox & Wyman Ltd., 1967.

Brown, K.C. *Hobbes Studies*. Oxford: Basil Blackwell, 1965.

Carsten, F.L. (ed.). *The New Cambridge Modern History: The Ascendency of France 1648-1658*. Vol. V. Cambridge Univ. Press, 1946.

Clark, G.N. *The Later Stuarts*, 1660-1714 (The Oxford History of England). 2nd ed. Oxford: The Clarendon Press, 1980.

Clifford James (ed.) *Man* Versus *Society in Eighteenth Century*. London: Cambridge Univ. Press, 1968.

Cowie, L.W. *A Dictionary of British Social History*. London : G. Bill and Sons Ltd., 1973.

Davies, H.S. (ed.) *The English Mind*. Cambridge: Cambridge Univ. Press, 1964.

Edwards, Paul (ed.) *The Encyclopaedia of Philosophy*. Vol. I & II. New York.: Macmillan 1967.

Harris, R.W. *Reasons and Nautre in the Eighteenth Century*. London: Blandford Press, 1968.

———. *England in the Eighteenth Century, 1689-1793*. Indian reprint; Delhi. Surjeet Pub. 1978.

Huberman, Leo. *Man's Worldly Goods*. Bombay: People's Publishing House, 1948.

Marshall, Dorothy. *Eighteenth Century England*. 2nd edn. London: Longman, 1974.

Morrah, Patrick. *Restoration England*. London: Constable & Co., 1979.

Neal, T.A. *British History, 1660-1815: From Restoration to Regency*. London Nelson, 1968.

Ogg David, *England in The Reigns of James II and William III*. Oxford: The Clarendon Press, 1963.

Plumb, J.H. *England in the Eighteenth Century* (The Pelican History of England). Penguin Books Ltd., Harmondsworth, 1963.

Sabine, George H. *A History of Political Theory*. Indian rpt. Calcutta: Oxford & IBH Pub., 1968.

Trevelyan, G.M. *England Under Queen Anne*. London: Longmans, 1931.

———. *English Social History*, London: Longmans, 1978.

———. *England Under the Stuarts*. Indian rpt. Delhi: Surjeet Pub., 1977.

Whibley, J.H. *Wasley's England*. 4th edn. London: The P. Worth Pub., 1954.

Willey, Basil. *The English Moralists*. London: Chatto & Windus, 1964.

———. *The Seventeenth Century Background*. New York: Double Day Anchor Books, 1953.

———. *The Eighteenth Century Background*. London: Chatto and Windus, 1965.

II. *Critical and Literary Works*

Books

Aitken, G.A. *Life of Richard Steele*. 2 vols. London: Wn. Isbister Ltd., 1889.

Aitkins, J.W. *English Literary Criticism: Seventeenth and Eighteenth Centuries*: London: Methuen & Co., 1955.

Anselment, R.A., (ed.) *The Recruiting Officer and The Beaux' Stratagem* (A Case Book). London: Macmillan Press, 1977.

Axton, Marie, *English Drama: Forms and Development*. London: Cambridge Univ. Press., 1977.

Baugh, Albert C. *A Literary History of England*. 2nd edn. London: Routledge & Kegan Paul Ltd., 1967.

Bateson, F.W., *English Comic Drama, 1700-1750*. New York: Russell & Russell, 1963.

Bernbaum, Ernest. *The Drama of Sensibility: A Sketch of the History of Comedy, 1696-1780*. Massachusetts: Gloucester, 1958.

Beljame, A. *Men of Letters and the English Public in the Eighteenth Century 1660-1744*. London: Kengan Paul, 1948.

Birdsall, V. Ogden. *Wild Civility: The English Comic Spirit on the Restoration Stage*, Bloomington: Indiana Univ. Press, 1970.

Bloom, Edward (ed). *The Critical Heritage: Addison and Steele*. London: Routledge & Kegan Paul, 1980.

Boas, F.S. *An Introduction to Stuart Drama* Oxford: The Clarendon Press, 1958.

Bold, Alan (ed). *The Sexual Dimension in Literature.* New York: Barnes & Nobles, 1983.

Borgman, Albert S. *Thoman Shadwell: His Life and Comedies*. New York: N.Y. Univ. Press, 1928.'

Bruce, Donald. *Topics of Restoration Comedy*. London: Hutchinson Univ. Press, 1958.

Burton, K.M.P. *Restoration Literature*. London: Hutchinson Univ. Press, 1958.

Camden, Carroll. *Restoration of Eighteenth Century Literature*. Chicago: William Marsh Rice Univ., 1963.

Chadwick, W.R. *The Four Plays of William Wycherley*. The Hague: Mouten, 1975.

Connely, Willard, *Young George Farquhar: The Restoration Dramatist at Twilight*. London: Cassell & Co. Ltd., 1949.

———. *Brawny Wycherley*. London: Charles Scribner's Sons, 1930.

Craik, T.W. (ed). *The Revels History in Drama in English*. London: Methuen & Co. Ltd., 1976.

Daiches, David. *A Critical History of English Literature*. 2 Vols. London: Secker & Warburg, 1960.

Dickenson, H.T. (ed.) *Politics and Literature in the Eighteenth Century*. London: Dent, 1974.

Dobrée, B. *English Literature in the Early Eighteenth Century. 1700-1740*. Oxford: The Clarendon Press, 1959.

———. *Restoration Comedy, 1660-1720*. I edn. rpt. London: O.U.P., 1966.

Duff, J.W. and Duff, *A.M. A Literary History of Rome: Golden Age*. 3rd edn. London: Ernest Benn Ltd., 1953.

Fujimura, Thomas H. *The Restoration Comedy of Wit*. New York: Barnes & Nobles Inc., 1968.

Gibbons, Brain. *Jacobean City Comedy*. London: Methuen & Co., 1980.

Gill, Christopher. *Longman's Companion to English Literature*. London: Longmans, 1972.

Gosse, Edmund. *Life of William Congreve*. London: William Hienemann Ltd., 1924.

Hazlitt, W. *Lectures on English Comic Writers* (Everyman's Library Series). New York: Dutton, 1963.

Harbage, Alfred. *Cavalier Drama*, New York: Russell & Russell, 1964.

Hawkins, Harriett. *Likeness of Truth in Elizabethan and Restoration Drama*. Oxford: The Clarendon Press, 1972.

Hirst, David L. *Comedy of Manners* (Critical Idioms). London: Methuen & Co. Ltd., 1979.

Holland, Norman. *The First Modern Comedies*. Massachusetts. Harvard Univ. Press, 1959.

Hooker, Edward N. (ed.) *Critical Works of John Dennis*. 2 Vols. Baltimore: The Johns Hopkins Press, 1943.

Howarth, W.D. (ed.) *Comic Drama: The European Heritage*, London: Methuen & Co. Ltd., 1978.

Hughes, Leo. *The Drama's Patrons: A Study of the Eighteenth Century London Audience*. New York: Univ. of Texas, 1971.

Hume, R.D. *The Development of English Drama in the late Seventeenth Century*. Oxford: The Clarendon Press, 1976.

Humphreys, A.R. *The Augustun World: Life and Letters in the Eighteenth Century* England (Paperback) London: Methuen & Co., 1964.

James, E. Nelson. *The Developments of George Farquhar as a Comic Dramatist*. The Hauge: Mouten, 1972.

Jusserland, J.J. *A Literary History of English People 2nd edn.* London: T. Fisher Unwin Ltd., 1926.

Kauffmann, R.J. *Elizabethan Drama* (Essays in Criticism). New York: O.U.P., 1978.

Kenny, S.S. (ed.) *The Introduction to The Conscious Lovers* (Regent Restoration Drama Series). London: Edward Arnold Pub., 1966.

King, Bruce (ed.). *Macmillan History of Literature: Seventeenth Century English Literature*. London: Macmillan, 1982.

———. *Dryden's Major Plays: Biography and Criticism*. London: Oliver & Boyd, 1966.

King, John N. *Fnglish Reformation Literature: The Tudor Origins of the Protestant Tradition*. New Jersey: Princeton Univ. Press, 1982.

Knights, L.C. *Drama and Society in the Age of Jonson*. London: Chatto & Windus, 1951.

Knights, L.C. *Exploration* (Essays in Criticism). London: Chatto & Windus, 1951.

Knights, W. *Golden Labyrinth: A Study of British Drama*. London: Phoenix House, 1962.

Krutch, J. Wood. *Comedy and Conscience after Restoration*. New York: Russell & Russell, 1967.

Lamont, William and Oldfield Sybil. *Politics, Religion and Literature in the Seventeenth Century*. London: Dent, 1975.

Leech, Clifford. *The John Fletcher Plays*. London: Chatto & Windus, 1962.

———. *Man* Versus *Society in Eighteenth Century Britain: Six Points of View*. Cambridge Univ. Press, 1968.

Leech, C. (ed.) *Eighteenth Century English Literature* (Modern Essays in Criticism). London: O.U.P., 1977.

Loftis, J. *Comedy and Society from Congreve to Fielding*. California: Stanford, 1959.

———. *Politics of Drama in Augustan England*. London: The Clarendon Press, 1963.

Loftis, J. (ed.). *Restoration and Drama* (Modern Essays in Criticism). New York: O.U.P., 1972.

Love, Harold. *Restoration Literature*: *Critical Approaches*. London : Methuen & Co. Ltd., 1972.

———. *Congreve*. Oxford: Basil Blackwell, 1971.

Lynch, K.M. *The Social Mode of Restoration Comedy*. New York: Octagon Books, 1975.

Mair, G.H. et al. *Modern English Literature*. 1450-1959. 3rd edn. London: O.U.P., 1961.

Malekin, Peter. *Love and Liberty: English Literature and Society, 1640-1668*. London: Hutchinson & Co. Ltd., 1981.

Miles, Dudley Howe. *The Influence of Molière on Restoration Comedy*. New York: Columbia Univ. Press, 1910.

Miller, H. Knight. *The Augustan Milieu*. Oxford: The Clarendon Press, 1970.

Miner, Earl (ed.) *Restoration Dramatists: A Collection of Critical Essays*. New Jersey: Prentice Hall Inc., 1966.

———. Restoration Mode from Milton to Dryden. New Jersey: Princeton, 1978.

Mishra, J.E. *Dryden: Theory and Practice of Drama.* Delhi: Bahri Pub., 1978.

Moore, Frank Harper. *The Nobler Pleasure: Dryden's Comedy in Theory and Practice.* Chapel Hill: Univ. of North Carolina Press, 1963.

Morris Brian (ed). *William Congreve.* (Mermaid Critical Commentaries). London: Ernest Benn Ltd., 1972.

Muir, Kenneth. *The Comedy of Manners.* London: Hutchinson Univ. Library, 1970.

Nettleton, George H. & Arthur, E. Case (eds.) *Dramatists from Dryden to Sheridan*. London: George G. Harrap & Co. Ltd., 1939.

Nicholson, M.H. et al (eds.). The Introduction to *The Virtuoso (Regent Restoration Drama Series)*. London: Edward Arnold Pub., 1966.

Nicoll, Allardyce. *A History of English Drama 1660-1700* Cambridge: Cambridge Univ. Press, 1965.

———. *British Drama*. 5th edn. Delhi: Doaba House, 1973.

———. *A History of Early Eighteenth Century, Drama, 1700-1750.* Cambridge: Cambridge Univ. Press, 1966.

Novak, Maximillian E. *Eighteenth Century Literature.* Hongkong: The Macmillan Press Ltd., 1983.

Palmer, John. *The Comedy of Manners.* London: Russell & Russell, 1962.

Perry, Henery T.E. *The Comic Spirit in Restoration Drama.* New York: Russell & Russell, 1962.

Pettit, Henry (ed.). *A Collection of English Prose, 1660-1800.* New York: Harper & Co., 1962.

Potts. L.J. *Comedy*. London: Hutchinson Univ. Lib., 1957.

Rodway, Allan. *English Comedy: Its Role and Nature.* London: Chatto & Windus, 1975.

Rogers, Pat. *The Augustan Vision*. London: Methuen & Co. Ltd., 1974.

Saintsbury, G. *The Peace of Augustans.* London: O.U.P., 1948.

Salgādo, Gemini. *English Drama: A Critical Introduction.* London: Edward Arnold Pub. Ltd., 1980.

Scouten, A.H. (ed.). *Restoration and Eighteenth Century Drama*. London: Macmillan, 1980.

Senior, Dorothy. *Life and Times of Colley Cibber*. London: Constable & Co., 1928.

Sharma, R.C. *Themes and Conventions in the Comedy of Manners*. New Delhi: Asia Pub. House, 1965.

Singh, Sarup. *The Theory of Drama in the Restoration Period*. 2nd edn., New Delhi: Longmans, 1968.

———. *Family Relationship in Shakespeare and the Restoration Comedy of Manners*. Delhi: Oxford Pub., 1983.

Smith, J.H. *The Gay Couple in Restoration Comedy*: New York: Octagen Books, 1971.

Speck, W. A. *Society and Literature in England 1700-1760*. Dublin: Gill and Macmillan Humanities Press, 1983.

Spingarn, J.E. *Critical Essays of the Seventeenth Century*. 3 Vols. Inter-State Printers & Pub. Danvill, 1957.

Staves, Susan. *The Players' Scepters: Fictions of Authority in the Restoration*. Lincoln & London: Univ. of Nebraska Press, 1979.

Stephen, Leslie. *English Literature and Society in the Eighteenth Century* (Univ. Paper Back) London: Methuen & Co. Ltd., 1966.

Sullivan, Maureen (ed). *Introduction to Colley Cibber: Three Sentimental Comedies*. Connecticut: New Haven, 1973.

Sutherland, James. *English Literature of the late Seventeenth Century*. Oxford: The Clarendon Press, 1969.

Tave, Stuart M. *The Amiable Humourist,* Chicago, the Univ. of Chicago Press, 1960.

Taylor, D. Carne (ed.). *William Congreve*. London: Russell & Russell, 1963.

Thackery, W.M. *The English Humourists of the Eighteenth Century*. London: Gray Walls Press, 1949.

Thompson, Allan Reynolds. *The Anatomy of Drama*. Los Angles: Univ. of California Press, 1946.

Thorndike, A.H. *English Comedy: The Restoration 1660-1680*. New York: Macmillan, 1929.

———. *The Influence of Beaumont & Fletcher on Shakespeare*. New York: Ams. Press Inc., 1966.

Underwood, Dale. *Etherege and the Seventeenth Century Comedy of Manners*. New York: New Haven, 1957.

Voris. W.H. Van. *The Cultivated Stance: The Design of Congreve's Plays*. Pennsylvania: Dufour editions, 1967.

Wilson, J.C. (ed.). *The Augustan World*. New York: Harper & Row Pub. Inc., 1978.

Wilson, J.H. *Court Wits of the Restoration*. Princeton: Princeton Univ. Press, 1967.

———. *A Preface to Restoration Drama*. Massachusetts: Cambridge Univ. Press, 1965.

———. *The Influence of Beaumont and Fletcher on Restoration Drama*. Columbus: Ohio State Univ. Press, 1928.

Winton, Calhoun. *Captain Steele: The Early Career of Sir Richard Steele*. Baltimore: John Hopkins Press, 1964.

Journals

Berekeley, David S. "The Penitent Rake in Restoration Comedy", *Modern Philology*, XLIX (1952), 223-33.

Blanchard, Rae. "Steele and the Status of Women". *Studies in Philology*, XXVI (1929), 325-55.

Bond, Donald F. Book Review of Loftis "Steele at Drury Lane". *Modern Philology*, Vol. 50 (1952-53), 64-66.

Hume, R.D. "The Myth of the Rake in Restoration Comedy." *Studies in Literary Imagination*, Vol. 10 (Spring, 1970), 25-77.

———. "Theory of Comedy in the Restoration." *Modern Philology*, Vol. 70 (1973), 302-318.

———. "Marital Discord in English Comedy from Dryden to Fielding." *Modern Philology*, Vol. 74 (1977), 248-22.

Humphreys, A.R. "The Friend of Mankind (1700-60): An Aspect of Eighteenth Century Sensibility." *The Review of English Studies*, Vol. 24 (1948), 203-209.

Kenny, Shirley S. "Humane Comedy". *Modern Philology*, Vol. 75 (1977), 29-43.

———. "Richard Steele and the Pattern of Genteel Comedy". *Modern Philology*, Vol. 70 (1972) 22-37.

Lamb, G.F. "Short View of Jeremy Collier". *English (1948)*, 270-75.

Leech, C. "Restoration Comedy, The Earlier Phase." *Essays in Criticism*, I (1951), 165-84.

Madan Lal "Did the Church err in Condemning Galileo". *The Hindustan Times*, (Nov. 27, 1984), 17.

Mueschke, Paul & Fleisher, Jeannette. "A Re-Evaluation of Vanbrugh". *PMLA*, Vol. 49 (1934), 848-889.

Novak, Maximillian E. "Margery Pinchwife's London Disease: Restoration Comedy and Libertine Offensive of the 1670s." *Studies in the Literary Imagination*, Vol. 10-11 (1977-78) 1-23.

Parnell, Paul E. "The Art of Whining Love". *Studies in Philology*, Lii (1955) 478-496.

——. "Equivocation in Cibber's *Love Last Shift*". *Studies in Philology*, Lviii (1960), 519-534.

——. "The Sentimental Mask". *PMLA*, XXVIII (1963), 529-535.

Rothstein, Eric. "Farquhar's Twin-Rivals and the Reform of Comedy". *PMLA*, Lxxix (1964), 33-41.

Stanley, Mary Lyndon. "Marriage Contract and Social Contract in Seventeenth Century Political Thought". *Western Political Quarterly*, Vol. 32 (1979), 79-89.

Smith, J.H. "Shadwell, the Ladies and the Change in Comedy". *Modern Philology*, Vol. 46 (1949), 22-23.

——. "Tony Lumpkin and the Country-Booby in Antecedent English Comedy". *PMLA*. Vol. 58 (1943), 1038-1049.

Thomas, Keith. "The Double Standard". *The Journal of the History of Ideas*, XX No. 2 (1959) 195-216.

——. "The Changing Family". *T.L.S.* (Oct. 21, 1977), 1226.

Tuveson, Ernest. "The Importance of Shaftesbury". E.L.H. XX (1953) 267-279

Vernon, P.F. "Marriage of Convenience and the Moral Code of Restoration Comedy". *Essays in Criticism*, Vol. 12 (1962) 370-387.

Williams, Stanley T. "English Sentimental Drama from Steele to Cumberland". *The Sewanee Review*. Vol. 33 (1925) 405-426.

Wilson, J.H. "Rant, Cant and Tone of the Restoration Stage". *Studies in Philology*, Vol. 52 (1955), 592-599.

Wood, F. T. "The Beginnings and Significance of Sentimental Comedy". *Anglia*, LV (1931), 368-392.

———. "Sentimental Comedy in Eighteenth Century." I. *Neophilologus*, XVIII (Oct. 1932), 37-41.

———. "Sentimental Comedy in Eighteenth Century." II. *Neophilologus*, XVIII (July, 1933), 281-289.

INDEX

G

H

J

K

L

M

N

P

R

S